M

PLAYS TWO

Moira Buffini's plays include *Blavatsky's Tower* (Machine Room), *Gabriel* (Soho Theatre), *Silence* (Birmingham Rep), *Loveplay* (Royal Shakespeare Company), *Dinner* (National Theatre and West End), *Dying For It*, adapted from *The Suicide* by Nikolai Erdman (Almeida), *A Vampire Story* (NT Connections), *Marianne Dreams* (Almeida), *Welcome to Thebes* (National Theatre) and *Handbagged* (Tricycle Theatre).

MOIRA BUFFINI

Plays Two

Dinner

Dying For It

A Vampire Story

Welcome to Thebes

Handbagged

FABER & FABER

This collection first published in 2015
by Faber and Faber Ltd
74–77 Great Russell Street
London WC1B 3DA

Typeset by Country Setting, Kingsdown, Kent CT14 8ES
Printed in England by CPI Group (UK) Ltd, Croydon CR0 4YY

A CIP record for this book is available from the British Library

978-0-571-32490-3

2 4 6 8 10 9 7 5 3 1

Contents

DINNER

To my sisters
Fiona and Nuala

Dinner was first performed in the Loft at the National Theatre, London, on 18 October 2002. The cast, in order of speaking, was as follows:

Paige Harriet Walter
Lars Nicholas Farrell
Wynne Penny Downie
Hal Adrian Rawlins
Siân Catherine McCormack
Mike Paul Rattray
The Waiter Christopher Ettridge

Director Fiona Buffini
Designer Rachel Blues
Lighting Designer Pete Bull
Sound Designer Rich Walsh
Company Voice Work Kate Godfrey

This production was revived at Wydham's Theatre, London, on 9 December 2003, with the following cast changes: Adrian Lukis as Hal, Flora Montgomery as Siân, Paul Kaye as Mike, and Paul Sirr as the Waiter.

Characters

Paige

Lars

Wynne

Hal

Siân

Mike

The Waiter

Scene One

A table set for a lavish dinner, surrounded by darkness.
A Waiter stands on the edge of the light. He is formally
dressed and holds a chic floral arrangement.
  Paige enters, dramatically attired. She approaches the
Waiter.

Paige Everything you represent thrills me.
  May I?

  She kisses him. She puts a thickly stuffed envelope in
  his pocket.

Your fee
  It's all in advance as we arranged.
  There won't be any tip
  So I'm relying on you to serve with grace
  In silence.
  When the time comes

  She is interrupted.

Could you put that on the table, please?

  Lars enters, wearing a smartly casual suit. The Waiter
  places the floral arrangement on the table. Lars is
  examining his trousers.

Lars I've got something on here

Paige *(to the Waiter)* In the middle

Lars Some sort of / crusty stuff. These should have been
dry-cleaned

Paige The success of my evening depends upon you

7

Lars Why aren't they dry-cleaned?

Paige I hope your instructions are clear

The Waiter bows. He exits.

Lars I think it might be the cat

Paige Where?

Lars There, on the leg
It's made a stain

Paige Well, it doesn't show

Lars Maybe I should change them

Paige You always do this to me

Lars What?

Paige I am perfectly in control of the situation. You come in harassing me with your pathetic frets and I start to panic

Lars What about?

Paige The starter

Lars What's wrong with it?

Paige They might not understand its subtlety

Lars Your starters are always fantastic. And even if they hate it you can tell them that the main will be well worth the wait

Paige I want the main to confound them

Lars I'm sure it will

Paige It's already ruined by that friend of yours being a vegetarian

Lars Her name's Wynne

The Waiter enters with modish cruets. He places them on the table.

Paige It's ludicrous coming to dinner saying 'I can't eat anything that's been alive!' She should be eating granite because even the bunny food I'm serving up for her was once alive. It wasn't sentient; it didn't have a soul but it photosynthesised. Perhaps I'll point that out

Lars That would make her feel welcome, wouldn't it?

Paige (*to the Waiter*) We need drinks

The Waiter exits.

I know this meal's about your amazing brilliant success and everything, Lars, but it's my statement. It's my creation – like Frankenstein's monster.
    Food
    It takes on a character
    It looms
    I've had sleepless nights.
    Where *is* everyone? I said seven thirty!

Lars I expect they've got caught in the fog

Paige It's so *rude* to be late

Lars It's very foggy. I looked out of the window when I was dressing and I could hardly see the pool house

Paige It shows a distinct apathy about coming, a real reluctance, as if they'd rather be in a Little Chef. They're probably sick with dread. God, if I thought they were going to snub us, I'd kill myself

Lars What with?

Paige A gigantic pump-action shotgun

Lars What's wrong with pills?

The Waiter enters with drinks. He approaches Paige. She takes one. He approaches Lars. He takes the other.

Paige You
Are

Lars You're a tad overdressed, my love

The doorbell rings.

There. The fog has safely spewed up our guests

Lars is on his way to answer it.

Paige Let the waiter go

Lars I can get it

Paige It's his job

The Waiter exits.

Lars Did you get him from the usual place?

Paige No, I found him on the internet. He had his own website

Lars A waiter with a website?

Paige It was very well designed. I was intrigued by the wording

Lars What wording?

Paige It said let me hold your coat and snicker

Lars So you don't know him?

Paige His references were excellent. He's a man of experience

Wynne enters, taking off cycling paraphernalia. She hands it all to the Waiter. Underneath, she is dressed in bohemian style.

Wynne God, I'm so sorry; the fog is unbelievable! I had to cycle right down the middle of the road so I could see the white line

Lars Goodness

Wynne And I was really feeling watched, you know, as if there were eyes hidden in the mist, when this moron in a Saab zoomed by and sent me swerving right into one of those gryphon things on your gateposts

Lars You poor thing

Wynne Really knocked my knee

Lars Oh no

Lars hugs her. She kisses him on the lips.

Wynne It's so good to see you

Lars This is my wife, Paige

Wynne Paige, lovely to meet you

She kisses Paige on the cheek. The Waiter exits with Wynne's things.

Paige Lars said you were bringing your other half

Lars Bob

Paige I'm terribly excited

Wynne Don't be

Paige I adore politicians. The last one I met came to the door at election time. He was so persuasive I almost had his child

Wynne Um, he's in the pub

Paige I'm sorry?

Wynne Bob
I'm afraid he's not coming

Paige I'm devastated
   He was vitally important to my interesting mix of
guests

Wynne We've had a bit of a
   We've just parted company

Lars Wynne, are you OK?

   The Waiter enters.

Wynne He's been seeing someone behind my back

Lars Oh no

Wynne Her name's Pam

Lars That's *awful*

Wynne She's a temp with a crush. It's so tacky

Lars You poor thing

Wynne Don't be nice to me or I'll cry

Paige You didn't think of phoning me?

Wynne Pardon?

Paige To tell me that Bob had a new girlfriend and
wasn't going to come?

Lars Of course she didn't

Paige Only I have odd numbers now and a spare main,
which is a terrible waste. It'll probably rot in the fridge

Wynne I'm sorry but this has *just happened*. (*To Lars.*)
I found a letter. She called him Bobble
   She said he made her quiver like a jelly

Lars What a cliché

Wynne She had writing like a child and she signed
herself Cuddly Pam

Paige Were you rooting through his personal belongings?

Wynne Only his coat! He tried to tell me that Pam was
a harmless fantasy fulfilment and why was I getting so
het up? I said a harmless *what*? He said she was so
  Can I sit down somewhere?

Paige (*to the Waiter*) She needs a chair

Wynne So young

Lars I'll get one

Paige It's his job

  The Waiter arranges a chair for Wynne. Wynne sits.

Wynne Thank you
  It's in response
  He's never forgiven me for
  It was when I put my portrait of his genitals in my
exhibition
  I'd painted it from memory

Paige We need drinks

Wynne Vigorous
  And there was purple
  Perhaps I should have called the picture something
else but I thought why not call it Bob Patterson's Cock?
That's what it is

Paige (*to the Waiter*) I said drinks

  The Waiter exits.

Wynne He said how could you, it's nothing like mine
  I said it's impressionistic
  He said look at my balls; they're falling off
  I said that's a dreamlike quality
  A cartoon appeared in the Opposition newsletter
  The Member for Camberwell Green
  I meant it as a gesture!

*The Waiter enters with drinks on a tray. He
approaches Wynne. She takes one.*

He said I was trying to castrate him
   I said Bob
I'm not a feminist I'm an eroticist I'm free about
everything I don't hold back I did it to share why
shouldn't I share my feelings with the world?
   He said why shouldn't I share mine with Pam?
   He was triumphant
   I said no wonder she called you Bobble. Your cock's /
like a

Lars The man's a fool. (*As a toast.*) Here's to freedom

Wynne Freedom

Lars clinks glasses with Wynne.

Paige I'll drink to that

Wynne Lars, I love your book I really, really love it. It's
like everything I've always thought only I haven't known
I've thought it.
   Honestly, I read it and I just thought 'yes!' It was so
   I mean I know I've known you for ever but it's made
me feel
   Oh goodness
   Every time I think of it I know I'm strong

Lars Well, I

Wynne Paige, isn't it brilliant?

Paige I haven't read it

Wynne Pardon?

Paige I thought I'd wait till it came out in paperback.
Then I wouldn't worry if I dropped it in the bath

Lars She thinks of everything

Paige I'm just going to put that spare main away for the cat. (*To the Waiter.*) Would you come with me? I want to discuss the dessert

Paige exits, followed by the Waiter.

Wynne It's genius, Lars, honestly. I was blown away

Lars I'm glad he didn't come

Wynne The psychological apocalypse is such a brilliant concept
Putting a name like that to what so many of us feel
I mean it's obvious you've been through things
You know
Suffered

Lars Oh

Wynne You write with such insight

Lars Thank you

Wynne And your new morality thrilled me. It's so bold
You've said what we all think but daren't utter
Oh . . . To walk away from the choking weeds that failed us
To free oneself from liability, from blame –
I don't have to feel guilty for my elitism or the starving millions
Because that guilt is a false humility
Part of a dead moral code

Lars Be the Phoenix

Wynne I'm re-engendering myself right now. This stuff about Bob; it's just a negative influxion, isn't it?

Lars That's right

Wynne I can deflect it

Lars You certainly can

Wynne Overcome it even at the point of wound entry

Lars You look wonderful

Wynne No I don't. I'm all splodgy and cryey

Lars Think what the woman who'd read my book
would say

Wynne She'd say yes
  I look wonderful
  Thank you

Lars You're shining

Wynne Lars

Lars An embodiment
  Of everything alive

*They kiss; illicit, passionate and full of promise. The
doorbell rings. They separate as the Waiter enters. He
crosses the stage; exits. Paige enters with a drink.*

Paige Well this must be Hal and Siân. They're great fun.
  He's a scientist; works in the cutting-edge arena of
germs.
  He used to be married to my best friend Mags but he
left her
  And now he's married to Siân
  She's a sexpot

*Hal and Siân enter. The Waiter follows them. He takes
their coats.*

Paige Hello, newlyweds, lovely to see you

Lars Come in come in

Hal We have just had the worst journey. Thought we
weren't going to bloody get here. The fog is unbelievable

Wynne God yes, it's terrible

Hal Couldn't see your drive. Been going up and down that lane for about half an hour. Nearly knocked some mad witch off a bike and I don't know how we're going to get home. You might be stuck with us all night, Paige!

Paige What fun. (*To the Waiter.*) We need drinks

The Waiter exits.

Hal Do you know there was a moment when I thought this is getting really Stephen King, as if any minute Jack Nicholson was going to appear going – (*he laughs an insane laugh*) with a big blood-spattered axe and then the windscreen would shatter and – (*he throttles himself*) curtains. It's really spooky out there. More than spooky; überspooky.

Siân I expect he's busy playing golf

Hal Who?

Siân Jack Nicholson

Hal What?

Lars Hal, this is Wynne

Wynne Hello, super

Hal Great pleasure

Lars Siân, Wynne

Siân Hi

Wynne Nice to meet you

Lars Wynne and I go way back. We were actually at college together and we lost touch for years and years, then, just a short time ago, I decided to go to this life-drawing class and lo and behold, amazing coincidence, Wynne was teaching it

Wynne I couldn't believe it when he walked in. He was exactly the same. Except for the badges

Lars Do you want to know the truth?
I found out you were teaching it before I went

Wynne Did you?

Lars I'd been to your exhibition the week before

Wynne Why didn't you tell me?

Lars I thought it was brilliant

The Waiter enters with drinks. He serves them.

Hal So what do you exhibit?

Lars She's an artist

Paige Sadly undiscovered as yet

Hal Right

Wynne Probably because I'm figurative

Hal Oh, that's bowls of fruit and stuff, isn't it?

Lars It means she can paint. She doesn't just make crap out of crap and call it art

Paige Do you know anything about art, Siân?

Siân Yes

Wynne Great
So, what do you like?

Siân I don't like any of it

Wynne Oh you must like something

Siân I like the graffiti on the back of toilet doors. I saw some today that said 'Fuck Shit Up'. Is that art?

Paige It's literature

Wynne Do you know I've got a really funny feeling that I've met you somewhere before

Siân Right

Wynne I wasn't being funny or

Hal You've seen her on the goggle box

Wynne Are you an actress?

Siân I'm a journalist

Hal She's a newsbabe. Aren't you, love?

Wynne That's right!

Siân I decorate the rolling news

Hal Don't do yourself down

Wynne That is such a scary job. It must be awful when things go wrong

Hal Oh, she thrives on it. Sits there with a smile on her face and drops the other presenter in it

Wynne I'd be absolutely hopeless at it

Paige Yes

Wynne And gosh – it must cost you a fortune in suits

Siân I get an allowance
Can I smoke in here?

Paige You feel free. I'll spray around in the morning. (*To the Waiter.*) Ashtray

The Waiter exits.

Hal So
You've really done it with this book then

Lars I don't know

Hal Oh you have. You've really effing blinding done it. You're for sale on a special stand in John effing Menzies that's how much you've done it

Lars Well the reviews haven't all been good

Paige Have you read it, Hal?

Hal Yes
Yes
I read it

Lars And?

Hal Great
Loved it

Lars You don't have to lie

Hal No I did
Life changing
Really tip-top

The Waiter enters with an ashtray. He stands near Siân, holding it out for her use.

Siân He said it was as dry as old dog biscuits

Hal I did not

Siân But he was freaked / couldn't finish it

Hal That's not true
That's / not true

Siân He thought it was too nihilistic or something. I thought it was a smorgasbord of syllogisms that ultimately ate itself but that's only the opinion of a newsbabe, Lars, so I wouldn't take it to heart

Paige (*to the Waiter*) What are you doing with that? She doesn't want to stand there and flick ash on you

Siân I'll put it out

Paige No! Why don't you find something to stand it on?

The Waiter removes the ashtray just as Siân goes to stub her cigarette out. It falls to the floor.

Siân Sorry

She grinds it out with her foot.

Paige Waiter
Fuck shit up

The Waiter exits.

Well, here we all are. I'd just like to say welcome

Lars Absolutely

Paige Tremendous congratters for getting through the fog and sorry that we're odd numbers. Wynne's lover has just dumped her and can't attend

Hal Oh bad luck

Wynne 'S fine / 's nothing

Paige So that leaves just the four of us to toast Lars and his remarkable achievement in modern philosophy: for the third week running he's outsold Delia Smith's *Cooking for the Brain Dead*. To Lars

All Lars

Hal Well done, mate

Siân Tremendous congratters

Wynne To you

The Waiter enters with a dustpan and brush.

Lars Thank you all very much. It's actually quite humbling that my book, arguably syllogistic as I'm sure it is, should have tapped the twenty-first-century zeitgeist in / quite such a

Paige Well, our starter awaits, quivering in its prime

Lars Of course
My love
The food takes precedence

Paige Waiter, when you've dealt with that we'd like to sit

The Waiter nods. He sweeps up the ash.

Wynne He's very professional, isn't he?

Paige I hope so

Wynne Does he do the hoovering too?

Paige No

Lars Paige found him on the internet

Paige You can find anything you want on the internet, from plumbers and hired assassins right though to Siamese twin prostitutes who'll dance naked in front of your friends

Hal Is that what you've arranged for later?

Paige No

Hal Shame
Ha

The Waiter exits with the dustpan and brush

Wynne Lars has told me all about your dinners, Paige

Hal Oh they're famous

Lars She is indeed an artist of the Aga

Wynne I can't wait. I feel very honoured to be invited

Paige Well, it was Bob I really wanted to meet

Wynne Oh

Lars She's attempting a negative influxion

Wynne Ah, well then
  Deflected

Paige (*to Wynne*) Wynne, would you like to freshen up before we eat? I can lend you a clean pair of tights

Wynne (*looking down at her laddered tights, dismayed*) Oh

Paige And Siân, you probably want some mouthwash

Siân I'd like a piss actually

Paige Lovely
  Well we'll leave you boys to discuss the crisis in masculinity

  Paige, Wynne and Siân exit.

Hal Nice to see Paige on form

Lars Yes

Hal You still haven't have told her then?

Lars No

Hal Right. Tough business

Lars How did you do it with Mags?

Hal Sorry, mate; can't go there

  The Waiter enters with crockery for soup. He sets it at the table.

That's not what I thought, by the way. About your book. Siân can really put words / in my mouth

Lars Doesn't matter

Hal Well look. I'm going to admit

I didn't like the whole – I mean what? – psychological apocalypse thing. And the way it's being marketed like some kind of effing Bible when it's called
I mean I just don't think you can make a Bible out of lack of belief

Lars I'm not trying to

Hal Oh come on

Lars I'm not

Hal Look
I know that we're born for no reason and survive by accident
I know it every time I look down a microscope and see
Dumb organisms
Vacuously multiplying, gormlessly devouring, pointlessly expiring

Lars You need to get out of the lab, Hal

Hal Do you know
I think I hate it because you're probably right.
Anyway
Been feeling a bit mad lately and that sort of, you know –
Probably just jealous. I mean my book's been lying around covered in mildew in the section marked geeks for effing years

Lars We're alone in an uncaring universe, Hal

Hal Holy batcrap

Lars And the world is a mad cacophony of excess. Every living thing is either consuming or in a state of decay. You're right; we're no better than microbes

Hal I'm not saying that. Of course we're / better than effing

Lars All my book says is would you rather eat or have things eat you?

Hal The whole thing comes down to power for you, doesn't it. / Consume, consume

Lars Power sounds supremacist and my philosophy is not. I call it psyche-drive

Hal Yes / the psyche-drive

Lars With the psyche-drive of the will, you can decide to live and flourish or you can decide to rot. People let themselves putrefy! Look at Mags

Hal Could you just not go there?

Lars Well, look at Paige then

Hal Paige is the ultimate consumer

Lars Oh look harder; she's decomposing

Hal So anyone who professes to any pain or weakness is decomposing?

Lars It's their decision: do they indulge or deflect? I say you can leave pain behind

Hal Can you?
Because I can't believe that you can simply decide to walk away from life's pain and find yourself free

Lars (*to the Waiter*) Haven't you got anything to do?

The Waiter exits.

My friend
You're a deep-thinking man

Hal Yes

Lars For your own good
Abandon it

Hal You want me to abandon thought?

Lars This self-absorbed negativity. You're drowning in it

Hal So without all this um
Thought
What am I left with?

Lars Peace

Hal OK

Lars Freedom
Passion

Hal Uh-huh

Lars Hal, listen to the voice that says I Want. Abandon yourself to the sensual world

Hal I was hoping you wouldn't say that

Lars Why?

Hal I tried it
Doesn't fucking work

Scene Two

THE STARTER

The diners are seated at the table. The Waiter is serving with impeccable grace, ladling from a stylish tureen. Everyone but Paige is unnerved by the colour and texture of the soup. The Waiter finishes serving.

Paige We need drinks

> *The Waiter nods. He exits.*
> *The diners tentatively start to eat. The soup is disgusting. Only Paige manages to swallow it without extreme difficulty.*

I saw Mags the other day, Hal

Hal Great

Paige She's doing really well. They're allowing her into a halfway house. She might be home in a month or two

Hal Yes

Paige And she says the scars look so much better. She's going to have reconstructive surgery

Hal I know

Paige She was telling me how lovely and generous you've been. She really appreciated That Card

> *Hal involuntarily gags. The Waiter enters with drinks. He serves them.*

Paige (*referring to the empty chair*) The invisible guest. No dinner party is complete without one. When we were newlyweds, Lars and I used to have a joke at our

27

dinners: If a guest didn't arrive, we always called the empty seat Jesus' chair

Lars No we didn't

Paige Because I used to say what a great dinner guest Jesus would be. Lars said he didn't think he could bear entertaining someone who wore sandals but I thought he'd be witty and provocative and offer interesting carpentry tips. He'd also provide great entertainment raising the food from the dead and what-have-you

Hal Paige, Siân's a Christian

Siân No I'm not

Hal Yes you are

Siân I am not

Hal She's a Christian

Siân Christ

Paige I genuinely think Jesus would be a thrilling guest in all but one way

Siân And what's that?

Paige He'd hold us up to judgement. And who'd want that? We'd all get indigestion

Wynne Is there um
Any meat in this, Paige?

Paige Oh no. Lars told me you existed solely on vegetable matter and I absolutely respect that

Wynne There's um
A flavour I can't put my finger on

Paige Well I suppose there might be the odd zoo plankton in there – but they're pretty hard to eliminate in this dish. Would you object to eating zoo plankton?

Wynne I don't know

Paige They're single-cell animals so I suppose technically they're meat. I could have the waiter blast it in the microwave for you, then at least you'd know they were dead

Lars What is this, Paige?

Paige It's soup, my love. Lars loves traditional-type starters. He can't be doing with mimsy salads and little piles of swept-up drizzled-on chicken bits. He calls those kind of starters goat poo, don't you?

Lars No

Paige He likes something substantial and as this meal is entirely in his honour I'd thought I'd pull out all the stops

Wynne What's in it?

Paige It's an onion, celeriac and parsnip base, with algae

Wynne Algae?

Paige Simmered slowly at a very low temperature, in brine

Hal That would account for the salt then

Paige There's a bouquet garni in there and a dash of sulphur – which might be that indefinable flavour, Wynne. The only thing that's tricky is getting the temperature to stay low enough – and the cooking time

Siân Right

Paige Three weeks
    I was pulling my hair out thinking how can I cook this without Lars knowing? How can I keep it as a special surprise? And I came up with a genius solution.

I put the pan on the sunbed out in the summerhouse. That way, it's had not only heat, but light to photosynthesise. I've been out there to stir it every other day and about a week ago I added a sprinkling of yeast

Lars Well that's remarkable, Paige

Paige It's called Primordial Soup

Hal Great

Paige The living starter. Enjoy

The diners continue in their efforts to eat the soup.

This soup is actually in honour of you, Hal

Hal Is it?

Paige (*to Wynne*) Hal is a world expert on microbes

Wynne Oh

Paige He wrote a fascinating book a number of years ago called *The Microbe Within*. It was very informative; lovely diagrams – but it didn't quite get that Nobel Prize, did it, Hal?

Hal No, Paige, it didn't

Wynne What are you working on at the moment?

Hal It's not interesting

Wynne I'm sure it is. I'm mesmerised by science. Everyone's saying it's the new art

Hal Really

Wynne It would be so easy for you to make art out of your job and for me to make science out of mine

Hal Would it?

Wynne Oh yes. You could do an exhibition of microbes you know: project magnified images or paint representations of them breeding or eating other microbes or whatever microbes do. Because I'm sure – and I'll bet a lot of people don't think about this – that when you're close up to microbes, they're actually rather beautiful

Hal I've never thought about their aesthetic

Wynne And I could do the science of art with prisms and things. The boundaries between art and science are almost non-existent these days, don't you think, Hal?

Hal Sure

Wynne What exactly are you working on?

Hal It's really not interesting

Siân (*to Wynne*) He's studying the microbes in sheepshit

Hal That's not what I'm doing

Siân If it's not sheepshit it's pigshit or something

Hal That Is Not What I Am Doing

Wynne You know that's why I would never ever eat meat. We just don't know what's in it these days. Are you looking for mutantcy and hideous diseases?

Hal No

Wynne Because we pump them full of hormones and steroids and antibiotics, we feed them on bone slurry and keep them in cages where they develop muscular atrophy and drink each other's urine. Even seafood is caged now. Do you know, they're trying to breed clawless crabs so they don't go mad and kill each other in their overcrowded farming tanks and they're covered in vile moulds and sea lice and their eyes are all cataracted and –

Paige The main course is seafood

Wynne Oh

Paige So, a lot to look forward to

Hal My work has nothing to do with sheep or cows or any other farmyard animal, Wendy. That's just Siân's little joke

Wynne So what are you doing, Hal? Or do you just not want to talk about it?

Hal I'd love to talk about it, Wendy. But I can't

Wynne You don't have to be embarrassed

Hal I've signed the Official Secrets Act

Wynne Oh

Lars He works for the Government

Wynne Oh my God

Hal In a minor capacity

Wynne Biological warfare

Hal What on earth makes you say that?

Wynne Well I don't know
James Bond and things

Hal How could this country possibly be involved in something like that?

Wynne Well, I'm sure it's not, but

Hal But nothing. It isn't. And neither am I

Wynne I wasn't being serious. I mean I hope you don't think I'm some sort of you know, anti-whatnot person

Siân Hal's very touchy about his work

Hal As a matter of fact, Wendy, I work for the Ministry of Health

Siân Torturing lab rats

Hal Why are you
  I mean what is the

Siân What?

Hal Is this because I called you a newsbabe?

Siân No

Hal Because that was a joke. It was an effing joke OK?

Siân Sure, whatever

Hal Meet Siân, everybody. She's a *journalist*. She wants you all to know that her skill at reading an autocue has nothing to do with the way she looks

   Siân lights a cigarette.

Wynne Um, Hal, my name isn't Wendy

Hal What

Wynne You called me Wendy just then and my name's actually Wynne

Hal I'm so sorry. Wynne

   The doorbell rings.

Lars Are we expecting anyone else?

Paige No

Lars (*getting up*) No biblical figures or Siamese twins?

Paige Let the waiter go

Lars I can get it

Paige It's his job

The Waiter enters. He crosses the stage; exits.

Would anyone like any more? The great thing about this dish is that the leftovers breed, so you never completely run out. Hal, can I tempt you?

Hal I'm saving myself for the main

Paige The other extraordinary thing about this starter is that it creates its own oxygen. If you were to take it to Mars, lift the lid of the tureen and come back in a billion years or so, you'd find you were stepping into a new Eden. This soup is an irrepressible force of life. And that's why I wanted to share it with you all. When we're surrounded by so much excess I think it's wonderful to remember that we were once such persistent slime

Lars Bravo

Siân Slime is the agony of water

Hal What?

Siân Sartre

Hal What?

Mike is shown in by the Waiter. He's in his twenties, wearing nondescript clothes.

Lars Can we help you?

Mike Um, I asked him if I could borrow a phone. I've had an accident down on the lane and

He sees Siân.

Oh my God.
You're off the news
You were on this morning

Siân Yes

Mike That bit about cluster bombs

Siân Right

Mike They're fucking evil aren't they?

Siân Yes

Paige Who are you and what do you want?

Mike Just a phone. My van . . . It's gone into your gatepost. I just couldn't see. / I came out of the corner and

Wynne Oh you poor thing

Mike I'm really sorry to bother you but my mobile's dead. (*To Siân.*) I can't believe you're in here. I must be concussed

Wynne He's bleeding

Mike If you could just let me use a phone. I need to call out a tow-truck

Paige Waiter?
Show him the door

Lars Paige
The man only wants to make a phone call

Paige (*to the Waiter*) Show him out

Lars No. He can make his call and sit in the warmth while he waits for help

Paige I want him to leave

Mike I / don't want to cause

Lars It's no problem

Paige Show him out

Lars (*to Paige*) What's the matter with you? Waiter, take his coat

Mike It's OK, I'll go

Paige Please do

Lars Take his coat!

Paige (*to the Waiter*) Remember what you're here for and be very, very careful what you do

Lars Why don't you join us? / There's a spare place here. Take the weight off your feet and the waiter will bring you a phone in a minute

Paige / You've walked in on a very special party. You haven't been invited and I think you should leave

Lars He's not leaving this house until we've helped him!

Paige Show him out

Lars NO TAKE HIS COAT – NOW

Mike Really, I'm

Lars SIT DOWN

Pause.

Paige Waiter, would you take the gentleman's coat before my husband reaches apoplectic collapse

The Waiter removes Mike's coat.

Mike I only want to use a phone; I'll be

Paige   May we know your name?

Mike Mike

Paige We need drinks

The Waiter exits.

Mike
 I'm Paige

36

This is Lars, my husband, who hasn't lost his temper since 2005

And these are our guests: Wynne, she's an artist; Hal, a very famous microbiologist; and his wife Siân, who you know

Siân Hi

Mike Hi

Hal Bad luck about your van, mate

Wynne (*getting up*) Mike, you've got to let me look at that cut for you

Mike It's OK

Wynne Paige, have you got an Elastoplast?

Paige No. Tonight, Mike, we're having a little party; just a few close friends to celebrate the successful publication of my husband's book

Mike Right

Paige You might have heard of it. It's called *Beyond Belief*

Mike Is it a thriller?

Paige Lars, is it a thriller?

Lars No

Wynne It's a guide book, Mike, a guide book to life

Hal Modern philosophy, mate

Mike Oh I know. Like one o' them *Armchairs of the Gods* books

Lars I'm sorry?

Wynne is fussing over Mike's cut with her napkin.

Wynne Poor you

Paige Lars? What do you suppose Mike means by *Armchairs of the Gods*? Do you think he might be equating your insightful philosophical text with the 'aliens built the pyramids' genre?

Lars I'm sure Mike doesn't mean any offence

Paige What if he does?

Lars (*standing*) Paige
I have a request

Paige What's that my love?

Pause.

Lars (*to Mike*) Make yourself at home, mate
Excuse me

Lars exits. Wynne goes to follow him.

Paige (*to Wynne*) Where are you going?

Wynne Well . . . is he all right?

Paige He's in shock. Helping Mike is the first altruistic thing he's done since he adopted a penguin at London Zoo for my birthday. I expect he's gone to fetch you all our jewels and valuables

Mike What d'you mean?

Paige Well, that is why you're here, isn't it?

The Waiter enters with drinks. He serves them.

Mike I don't understand why you'd say that

Paige Why have you come here?

Mike I just want a phone. My van's / gone into

Paige That's the most stupid story I've ever heard

Mike You can go out and look

Paige And find the place ransacked when we get back?

Mike If I'd come to steal from you, why would I knock on the door? I'd go round the back, wouldn't I, and break in

Paige Would you now?

Mike I rang your bell; he let me in. If you didn't want strangers in here you should've told him

Paige No one blows in here off the street

Mike And if you tell him to bring me back my coat / I'll put it on and go

Paige What do you want?

Mike My name is Mike
My van's in a ditch
I asked for simple help.
Fuck, I should of known better asking from people like you
What a waste o' time

Paige What do you mean, 'people like us'?

Mike Rich cunts

Wynne Oh I can't bear that word

Hal No call for that, mate. You'd better steady on

Paige Less than one minute and he's held us up to judgement
He's worse than Jesus

The Waiter is offering Mike and Paige drinks.

Mike Could I have my coat back please?

Paige You don't really want to leave

39

Mike I want my coat

Paige Take a drink first

Mike Why?

Paige See how the rich cunts live

Hal Paige, give him his coat and let him go

Paige Pick one up
Sip it
It's like ambrosia
The gods themselves drink stuff like this
Sitting in their armchairs

Mike takes a drink.

Bravo

*Paige takes one. Mike downs his in one. He wipes his
mouth.*

Mike Babycham

Paige I'd like you to join us for dinner

Hal Oh come on

Paige Why have an empty seat in the pleasuredome
when we could extend a benevolent hand to a stranger?
It's what Lars wants. Mike, on his behalf, I'm inviting
you to join us

Mike No thank you

Paige Why not?

Mike I'd rather sit in my van

Paige It's no imposition

Mike I wouldn't care if it was

Paige That's why I'm inviting you

Mike I might pick your pockets

Paige This outfit doesn't have them
  You won't get a tow-truck for hours in all that fog.
You might as well stay

Siân Come on, sit down. The food's great

Hal What?

Paige There's even a place set for you.

Siân Jesus' chair

Paige Take it. We're all dying to know if you think we're redeemable

Wynne Mike, look. I'd be very happy for you to stay but I really object to that word that you just said

Mike Then I'm sorry for saying it

Paige Wynne hates anyone calling her rich

Mike I see

Paige So that's settled. You'll stay

Mike Well, I could try to grab my coat and make a dash for it but (*referring to the Waiter*) I don't think I'd get past him. You got me trapped, Paige

Paige Mike
  Welcome to dinner

Scene Three

THE MAIN

Mike is seated at the table with the other diners. The soup dishes have been cleared. The Waiter is laying out all the equipment needed for the consumption of lobsters.

Mike So when I came out of the army I didn't really know what to do with myself. All my friends were going into full-time alcoholism or the prison service but I knew that wasn't for me, so I started up this business doing removals, deliveries, property relocation, that kind of thing

Wynne That's amazing

Mike Not really

Wynne You're an entrepreneur

Mike More of a van driver

Hal So what's the most interesting thing you've ever had in the back of your van, Mike? Apart from your girlfriend, of course

Mike Well, Hal, this one guy I was helping was a reptile freak and he had a collection of snakes and lizards and this chameleon, which really did change colour. Its eyes swivelled round; it had feet like pincers and a tongue like a coiled spring

Hal Bit like Siân

Mike It was the most amazing living thing I've ever seen

Paige We need drinks

The Waiter exits.

Wynne Do you miss the army, Mike?

Mike I liked the travel, but in the end I was glad to leave. I think you reach a certain point when the idea of killing lots of people just loses its appeal. Anyway, Siân, what about you?

Siân What about me?

Mike I mean how did you end up doing what you do?

Siân They just chose me from a photograph

Mike Yeah right

Siân Obviously they had to check I could read. And they did a test to ensure that I didn't have any speech impediments

Mike OK

Siân I had to pronounce words like 'Shi'ite' and 'Taoiseach', then I had to screen test with the senior male presenter to satisfy them that we had the right chemistry

Mike Does it get to you?

Siân What?

The Waiter enters with drinks. He serves them.

Mike You're the first port of call for all the bad news in the world. All day digesting horror and violence and tragedy – I suppose it's no wonder you're detached.

Siân It's not all horror and tragedy. We always do a fun item at the end

Mike Yeah. Like the badger who crawled into someone's washing machine

Wynne Oh my

43

Siân People want the facts but they also want to be reassured

Mike Reassured what?

Siân That despite the headlines things are essentially OK. Which is why it's so important to end with people safe in the knowledge that the badger survived the rinse and spin

Wynne (*relieved*) Oh

Siân So it's my job to make events on this fucked-up planet more palatable; peppering the violence and tragedy with tales of plucky burrowing mammals

She lights a cigarette. The Waiter exits.

Mike You demolished that cluster-bomb guy. You made it sound like everything that came out of his mouth was a fucking lie – and it was. And when you tell us about the lucky badgers you always look like it's making you barf. So I think, despite everything you say, that you're on the side o' truth

Siân (*pause*) Thank you

Hal Mike, Siân's up for the Rear of the Year Award. Did you know?

Mike Congratulations

Siân Thanks

Mike If you win, you'll have to read that night's news with your arse

Siân (*bursts out laughing*) I'd love to

Paige (*to Mike, confidentially*) Did I just ask for drinks?

Mike Yes

Paige has already finished hers.

Hal So, Mike, what's in the back of your van today?

Mike Well, I'm just on my way from robbing the house next door, so quite a lot of antiques, couple o' paintings and some jewellery

Only Siân laughs.

No, seriously, when I say I do property removals that's usually without the owner's knowledge or consent

Paige Bravo

Hal You've just robbed next door?

Mike Yeah. Nice place

Lars enters, wearing different trousers. He coolly sits at the table.

Paige So?

Lars Just dived in the pool

Paige Was it pleasant?

Lars Very. Very calming

Paige Well, I'm glad. That's consolation for the fact that we've all been waiting for our main for half an hour now

Lars You should have started without me

Paige Well seeing as this dinner is in honour of you and your fabulous, brilliant success, I thought that would be a little rude. *Waiter!*

Lars Mike

Mike Hi

Lars Hi. Are they treating you OK?

Mike Very well, thank you

Lars Have you made your phone call?

Mike Yeah

Paige I've invited him to dine with us

Lars Cool

Mike I'm afraid you're stuck with me for a couple of hours. They can't get a tow-truck here any sooner

Lars No problem. Long as you like

The Waiter enters.

Paige We need drinks. Then we're ready for the main.

The Waiter nods. He exits.

Mike was just about to tell us how he's ripped off old Mrs Allingham next door

Lars Oh

Paige Apparently his van is full of swag

Lars That's cool, Mike, really cool

Paige We're all agog with shock

Wynne You haven't, have you?

Mike Haven't what?

Wynne Well, you wouldn't just sit there and tell us would you?

Mike Why not?

Wynne Oh Mike, you're having us on

Mike Why? I'm very proud of what I do

Siân Good

Hal Do you steal from the rich and give to the poor or something?

Mike No, I just flog it and keep the money like anyone else. But I'm proud of my skills

Wynne You're a bit of a tease, aren't you

Mike I don't think so

Hal So how did you get started then? What was your first big break in the tea-leaf trade?

Mike Well I got this perfect training see, courtesy of Her Majesty's Armed Forces, and when I left it seemed a terrible waste not to do something with it

Paige Quite right

Mike The obvious choice was crime. I mean I aim low – just private houses and that – and I don't do anything where I'd have to carry a weapon – even a knife – because I took a sanctity of life pledge. After the killing of two Serbs and a Liberian I'm not ever, *ever*

Wynne You killed a librarian?

Mike A Liberian. Someone from Liberia. It's next to Sierra Leone

Wynne Oh

Mike I witnessed their murder; I've never actually killed anyone myself

Lars Did you take her Klimt?

Mike What?

Lars She has a Klimt in her study – Mrs Allingham. Did you take it?

Mike A what?

Wynne Gustav Klimt. He's a painter, Mike

Mike Oh that painting

Wynne A provocative eroticist, like me

Mike I thought it was a print

Lars It's her most valuable piece

Mike Shit. I hate art. I never know what I'm looking at. I thought it was greeting-card crap. Do you think I should go back for it?

Hal Never revisit the scene of a crime

Mike It's OK, I disabled the alarm and I know she's out. I've been casing the joint all day

The Waiter enters with drinks. He serves them.

Lars Are you going to be doing our joint?

Mike Well, obviously not tonight. I think that'd be a bit ungrateful don't you?

Lars Yes I do, Mike

Mike But I tell you what, Lars, if you want to stroll over later and get that Klimt yourself, there's nothing to stop you

Lars Why her? There are far better houses on this road; ours for instance

Mike Well, I mean they're all something fucking else aren't they?
This is gothic-window plastic-pillar heaven
But after extensive research I discovered that next door it was just one old doll with a lot of nice gear. And it was going great. No hitches at all until the van went into your ditch
I thought, I don't believe it

I thought just walk away and forget the whole thing
But it was so thick with fog I couldn't see
I thought I could go round and round for hours in this
End up in Timbukfuckingtu
So I thought find a house, brazen it out, get a tow-
truck, get a tow, act the innocent and you'll get away
with all that stuff no fucking bother

The Waiter exits.

Hal Well you won't now, will you?

Mike Won't I?

Hal I mean you've just told us all about it, haven't you?

Mike Oh yes so I have

Hal We could make a citizen's arrest

Mike You're right

Wynne We could tie you to your chair

Mike I'm in big trouble

Pause.

Paige I'm sorry, are we gawping?

Mike Just a bit

Paige You'll have to excuse us. It's been years since any of us spoke to anyone working class

Lars That's a great story, Mike

Mike Thanks

Lars You'll have to tell us what you really do some time

Mike Well, I just get by, Lars, in a working-class kind of a way

Wynne Mike, my parents were working-class

Mike Right

Wynne I'm only middle-class because of my education

Mike Right

Paige You could say the same for Lars. He comes from a very deprived background.

Lars That's not true

Paige Oh it is. He never shuts up about how deprived he is

Lars There is nothing deprived about my background, Mike

Paige Sorry, I meant depraved

Lars My father was a small-town dentist and my mother was a self-educated chiropodist

Paige Wait for his funny joke about teeth and feet

Lars Paige went to the Cruella De Vil charm school

Paige Whereas Lars' parents sent him out to work when he was just a child. They forced him to do a paper round and he still bears the emotional scars

Hal Oh come on you two

Paige Come on what?

Hal You're like a couple of
 I don't know

Paige Newlyweds?

Mike Lars

Lars Mike

Mike Can I ask you a rude and personal question?

Lars Sure

Mike How did you make all your money?

Paige What makes you think it's his?

Lars Paige had a small trust fund when we married, which I invested for her. She's welcome to have it back at any time – with interest
  I used to trade in the city

Mike As simple as that?

Lars Making money's as simple as sneezing. You just have to want to do it. And for a while I did. But it began to bore me – just seemed like figures moving around on screens in the end – so a few years ago I retired and went back to my first love; the study of philosophy

Wynne You've achieved so much in your life, Lars. You put the rest of us to shame

Paige (*angrily*) Oh, where is our food?

  Paige takes her glass and goes into the kitchen.

Lars Well, I think the important thing about anyone's journey through life – whatever their background – is that they follow / the

Wynne / The positive dictates of the psyche-drive and pursue their aspirational fantasies

Mike Is that what it says in your book?

Lars In a word, yes

Siân It's a zingy read

Mike What's an aspirational fantasy?

Wynne You can make things happen. It's all down to the strength of the psyche-drive, Mike. It's such a liberating concept. I mean you can't deny that we're all at the epicentre of our own universe. What Lars says is don't be meek about it, don't be humble; you can be the god or the goddess of your own psyche. Action is the key

Mike OK

Paige returns with a full glass and sits.

Paige Everything is perfectly prepared. He's so diligent.

Wynne A lot us feel scared of action; afraid of instigating change. But *Beyond Belief* will revolutionise your life. All you have to do is say yes to the strength within you and release the spirit of self

Siân Because you're going to die anyway

Wynne Well yes, but surely you can handle the idea of your own death? I know I can. I've worked through all that fear to a place of
Inspired Resignation
And now I feel I can do anything

Mike Sounds great

Lars Here

Lars reaches into his inside pocket.

Have a copy, Mike

He holds out a small blue book. Mike takes it.

Mike Well, thank you, Lars. Nice-looking book

Lars (*winks*) Clever marketing

The Waiter enters with a raw savoy cabbage on a plate.

Paige Ah, the vegetarian dish

The Waiter puts the cabbage down in front of Wynne.

Wynne Goodness me
  What is it?

Paige It's a cabbage. (*To the Waiter.*) We need music

  The Waiter exits.

Wynne You are so clever
  You've made it look as if it hasn't been touched
  What have you stuffed it with – or is it a surprise?

Paige I haven't stuffed it with anything
  It's raw

Wynne Oh

Paige I thought it was particularly appropriate for you,
Wynne

Lars Why?

Paige It's the ultimate vegetable

Lars Paige, when my patience with your rudeness runs
out

Paige Yes?

  Lars is silent.

You were about to say something, my love.
Was it the beginning of a threat?

Lars I don't make threats

Paige No, action is your name

Lars You're treading a very fine line

Paige Wynne, was I rude?

Wynne I

Paige Of course not. I wanted something special for you,
knowing that you're an artist. If you'll notice I've had

this cabbage in the freezer to simulate the winter frost it naturally endures. It'll melt into diamonds of dew, which the leaves will cradle in their melancholy folds. It's a culinary poem. I felt that to cook it, indeed to prepare it in any way, would be to spoil it. So as an artist, enjoy

Wynne Well

Paige And now for the seafood

Wagner. The Waiter enters. He carries two plates. Each of them is holding a huge North Atlantic lobster. They are alive, their claws tied with satin ribbons, presented on a bed of salad. The Waiter serves the ladies.

Before you ask, this is another of my creations
Apocalypse of Lobster

The music ends. The Waiter exits. Wynne shrieks, backing away.

Wynne That one just moved. I saw its thing move!

Paige Of course it moved. It's looking for the North Atlantic

Wynne Are they living?

Paige I should hope so. I've been nurturing them in the bath all day

Wynne whimpers, distressed. The Waiter returns with three more lobsters. He serves the gentlemen.

Hal Are you expecting us to eat them alive?

Paige Well, you can if you'd like to, Hal

The Waiter exits, returning almost immediately with drinks. He serves them.

Lars What is the meaning of this?

Paige I think it's fitting that Lars, the philosopher whom we are honouring, should ask the meaning. Perhaps you can fathom it, my love

Lars I don't intend to try

Paige Then I'll share my gastronomic journey
　I haven't read my husband's book but I have read the jacket and all his reviews
　There was one – I think it was in the *Hairdresser's Journal* –
　That said Lars Janssen obviously thinks he's God

Lars Oh shut up

Paige So with this dish, I thought we could all imagine we were Lars and be God. There is the lobster, soft and naked beneath its defences, as helpless as mankind, awaiting its final fate

Lars This is pathetic

Paige So, there's a pot of boiling water in the kitchen and an ornamental pond out there on the patio, which I've had the waiter fill with brine. If you want your lobster to live, take it out and release it to its natural element. If you want to consume it, take it into the kitchen, put it face first into the boiling water, listen to it scream, and when it's cooked the waiter will bring it in for you. You can crack it open, remove its stomach sacs and intestines and eat it with the attractive salad. That way lies lobster apocalypse and that way lies salvation. The choice, ye Gods, is yours

　The music ends.

Mike Wow

　Siân scrapes her chair back. She picks up her lobster and walks determinedly towards the kitchen. Wynne stands.

MOIRA BUFFINI

Wynne No!
Don't kill it

Siân Why not?

Wynne It's horrible

Siân Damn right

She exits.

Paige (*to the Waiter*) Would you follow your instructions please?

The Waiter exits to the kitchen. Hal gets up, takes his lobster towards the patio.

Paige Hal, I'm moved by your compassion for these lowly crustaceans

Hal Eff off

He exits.

Paige Mike?

Mike I don't think I could eat this. No offence, Paige; but I generally like my food to look like food

Mike goes out to the patio. Siân returns. She lights a cigarette.

Siân They don't exactly scream; it's more a kind of wail

Wynne Paige this is
I'm having great difficulty coping with this

Hal and Mike return with empty plates.

Hal It's getting worse out there

Mike You can't see the pond at all

Hal Nearly effing fell in it

56

Wynne I'm a guest / in your house

Paige / This lobster reminds me of me. Which is why she has to go in the fiery pot

Paige takes her lobster towards the kitchen. Wynne gets up.

Wynne I'd like you to stop!

Paige If you want to stop me you'll have to use force
You're the goddess of your own psyche, Wynne

Wynne Please stop!

Lars There's no point speaking to her when she's like this

Paige Take it. Do something

Wynne I beg you to stop

Paige I despise begging

She exits. Lars gets out his mobile phone. He dials.

Lars (*into the phone*) Hi, I'd like to order some pizzas please. One vegetarian and a selection of others; five in total, ham and mushroom, yep, spicy chicken, something with spinach

Hal Pepperoni

Lars And one with pepperoni. No seafood. The White Lodge, Oak Avenue. Tell the guy there's a big tip if he gets here quickly. Yes, I know it is; just tell him to get here.

Lars puts his phone back in his jacket. Paige enters. She sits.

Siân How long do you think it takes them to die?

Paige Until the last synapse stops firing? A minute or two

Siân A long time

Paige An eternity, I should think
Which just leaves you, my love. What kismet for your lobster?

Lars Waiter?

The Waiter enters.

Would you take that away?

Paige Are you asking him to cook it for you? How godlike

Lars I don't give damn what he does with it. Take it away

The Waiter is about to remove the lobster.

Paige Don't touch it

Lars Take it away

Paige Don't touch it

Lars Waiter, would you please get rid of this?

Pause.

What fee have you offered him?

Paige Twenty-five thousand pounds

Lars Sure. I'll double whatever my wife has offered you, if you take this thing away. Let's make it a hundred quid

Pause.

Five hundred, cash

Mike I would definitely take that

Paige His motivation's far more complex than you think. He has charitable principles

Lars He's doing this for charity?

Paige The biblical sense of it. The sense that's often translated as love

Lars I see
  (*To the Waiter.*) One thousand pounds

Paige You can't bribe a man of integrity

Lars Very well, it can stay there. We can watch it slowly drown in air

Mike Not wanting to be crass or anything Lars, but if I took it away would you give me a thousand pounds?

  Wynne takes Lars' lobster out to the patio.

Paige Waiter, we need drinks. Thank you so much

  The Waiter exits.

Lars So he calls it love?

Paige He calls it service. I call it love

Lars That's very sad

Paige There's nothing sad about love, my darling

  Wynne enters. She sits.

Lars (*to Wynne*) Thank you

Wynne That's OK . . . It's in the pond, but what about your goldfish?

Paige We're having them tomorrow, with pasta

Wynne And I thought Lars was exaggerating when he warned me about you

Lars (*to Paige*) I warn everyone

  Pause.

Mike Paige, can I ask you a rude and personal question?

Paige Yes

Mike What do you do, you know, for a living? While Lars is writing his books and that?

Paige Mike, how sweet of you to think that I might do something.
I do nothing. I never have
My entire presence on this planet
Is a waste of time and space
It always has been
And I think everyone here would agree with that

Hal Oh . . . no

Paige Everyone except Hal

The Waiter enters with drinks. He serves them.

Hal Come on, Paige
All that personal grooming. I wouldn't call that nothing
And you organise things for charity

Lars Oh, call it love

Hal You're always making us buy those effing raffle tickets

Paige 'Flowers for the Homeless'

Hal And there's your genius in the kitchen

Lars She's always visiting the penguin pond at the zoo

Hal And Paige, half the vintners in Kensington would go out of business if it weren't for you

Paige You see, Mike, my life is chockful. And if ever I tire of these thrilling pursuits, there's always the Open University or psychotropic drugs

The Waiter exits.

Mike It's just that I think you'd be very good at what I do

Paige You mean
You think I'd make a good thief?

Mike Burglar, yeah

Paige (*moved*) Really?

Mike You've got the nerve; I can tell

Paige Mike, I'm thrilled

Lars Hah

Paige I'm unbelievably moved that you should think that

Mike I think you'd actually love it. Have you never considered crime as a career?

Paige Well, it wasn't one of the options at school and I hardly need the money, do I?

Mike You'd do it for the subversion

Paige Yes, yes

Mike It's such a thrill

Paige I'm sure

Mike And no one would suspect you in the way that they all instantly suspect me. As soon as I walked in here, you had me sussed, didn't you? Whereas you're

Paige Such a rich bitch

Mike You could get in anywhere; pilfer anything. You could do top jobs

The Waiter enters with two cooked lobsters. He places one in front of Siân and one in front of Paige.

Paige Oh look
Yum yum

Siân Could I have some HP Sauce please?

Hal sighs loudly.

Bring me some ketchup as well

*The Waiter exits. Siân cracks her lobster open. She
removes the intestines.*

Hal What about me, Mike? What are my chances in the
crime league, because between you and me I'm effing
sick of my job and I'd love a bit of stealth, bit of
ducking and diving, dodging and weaving, breaking and
entering, you know what I mean?

Mike Well actually Hal, don't take this the wrong way
but I wouldn't trust you

Hal Oh great

Mike Not that I think you'd try and / personally stab me
in the back or anything

Hal No, no, no that's great, Mike

Mike I just think you might lose your cool under
pressure and you know, do something stupid or violent

Hal Trigger-happy you mean

Mike Well

Hal Effing great. Psycho Hal, loose with a sawn-off
shotgun. Watch out Twickenham, here I come

*He aims and fires an imaginary machine gun at the
diners, letting off a long volley at Siân. She continues
to devour her lobster.*

Siân (*to Paige*) This is absolutely sensational

Wynne I once tried to shoplift some earrings from Laura Ashley – must be about fifteen years ago – and I was so tense that I almost had a nervous breakdown. I was sweating and shaking and I stuck them in my pocket and crept past the till having this awful panic attack – I could barely see; I was nearly sick – then I felt so guilty that I went back and paid for them and they were such a rip off and they turned out to be horrible anyway and I cried

Lars Poor you

The Waiter enters with condiments. Siân liberally helps herself.

Mike You would definitely be the worst burglar that ever lived

Wynne Oh well
Better stick to being the worst artist that ever lived

Lars Hey
That's a self-wounding influxion

Wynne You're so right.
Deflected

Siân I'd like to be a con artist

Mike Good choice

Siân I'd like to disguise myself as someone warm and caring and rip off the old, the vulnerable and the bereaved

Lars And what about me, Mike?

Paige You are a con artist, my love

Lars You're so funny. You are so hilarious. Look: my sides have split

Mike Well Lars, I'd actually put you right at the top of a huge crime ring. I'd say you wouldn't be so good on the ground but you've got the nous to hire a couple of heavies and a good accountant to do it all for you. You have the um –

Paige Sangfroid, the glacial, hyperborean stare

Mike The er –

Hal The cool

Mike I just don't think anyone would fuck with you

Hal He's effing perceptive this kid, isn't he? For a tea leaf

Mike Paige?

Paige Mike

Mike Could I use your toilet, please?

Paige Of course.

Mike I've been busting for a while but I didn't like to say

Paige Mike, I want you to feel that our home is yours. (*To the Waiter.*) Would you show our guest to the little boys' room?

Mike I'm not going to rip anything off; it's OK

Paige Oh, feel free. Take the cupid; it's French, seventeenth-century; Lars gave it to me on our anniversary. I use it as a loo-roll stand

Mike Are you sure?

Paige You could keep it in your van for emergencies

Mike You think of everything

Paige The sign of a good hostess

The Waiter shows Mike out. Lars gets out his mobile phone. He dials.

Siân Paige, I genuinely think this is the best dead thing
I ever ate

Paige That's great

Siân And do you know what's particularly satisfying
about it?

Paige You killed it yourself

Siân It's an honest meal

Lars Police, please

Paige (*leaping up*) Don't you dare. Don't you *dare*!

Lars Hello, yes, I'd like to report a burglary

Paige grapples with Lars for the phone.

Paige He's a guest in your house

Lars He's a parasite

Paige I want him to stay

Lars He's a two-bit thief

Paige And you're a ten-pound cunt

Wynne Uhh!

Lars (*struggling*) Get – off – you

Paige I will not have police in this house!

*The guests watch in silence as the struggle becomes
more vicious.*

Lars GET – OFF!

Lars shoves Paige away from him.

Yes, hello, this is Lars Janssen at The White Lodge, Oak
Avenue. I'd like to report a burglary. That's correct, yes

Paige knees Lars in the groin. He doubles up. She takes the phone.

Paige Hello, this is Paige Janssen, Oak Avenue
I'm so sorry my husband should never have called you

Hal Holy batcrap

Lars (*to Hal*) Get / me the phone

Hal hesitates. The Waiter enters. Paige motions him to stay where he is.

Paige He's on medication – this is terribly painful to say – for pre-senile dementia and he's having a persecution episode

Hal (*holding his hand out for the phone*) Come on, Paige. Be decent

Paige Well, he thinks there's a burglar in the house but I'm afraid to say that the poor man he's picked on is actually one of our dinner guests. No, it's a degenerative psychosis; really sad . . . No, that absolutely won't be necessary; I have his medication right here. Yes, yes. Thank you. You're most understanding

Paige ends the call. She hands the phone to the Waiter.

Would you throw that into the pond, please?

The Waiter exits. Paige sits. Lars sits.

Lars One day, Paige, you will get what you deserve

Paige Yes. I will

Hal That was really ugly, guys

Mike returns with a seventeenth-century cupid. There's a toilet roll on its arrow.

Mike Is this the thing you meant?

66

Paige Do you like it?

Mike Yeah, it's really nasty

Paige It's yours

Mike Are you sure?

Paige Only if you promise to keep it in your loo

Mike No fucking problem, Paige
Thanks very much

Lars I'm afraid it's not yours to give

Paige Do all the presents you've given me over the years still belong to you? What about Beaky?

Lars What?

Paige My penguin.
Is he still yours?

Mike Well, thanks a lot, Paige
You can keep your bog roll

He places the toilet roll in front of Lars, then sits, the cupid beside him. Siân belches loudly. The Waiter enters.

Paige We need drinks

The Waiter exits.

Do you know, I had a feeling that conversation might flag at this point in the evening; with everyone feeling so replete, so carried away on a tide of bonhomie. So in order to facilitate an easy flow of chat, I've arranged a little game. Under your side plates everybody, I've put an envelope. In the envelope there's a card with something written on it. You simply have to read the card and then stand up and speak for two minutes on whatever it inspires you to say. Now, who's first?

Hal I hate games

Paige Then get the ball rolling

Hal No thanks

Siân I will

Paige Splendid

Siân I like games

Siân stands and opens the envelope.

Mike Um, sorry Paige, but my envelope says Bob

Paige Yes, Bob is Wynne's ex-lover who couldn't attend – because his genitals are hanging in her gallery – but Mike, we're very fortunate to have you here in his place

The Waiter enters with drinks. He serves them.

Siân 'Murder Weapons'. What makes you think I'm qualified to speak about this?

Paige I should think everyone's qualified.

Siân 'Murder Weapons'?

Paige Just speak. First thing that comes into your head

Siân You mean what would I use if I were going to murder someone?

Paige Just in fun of course

Siân A lance

She mimes lancing Hal across the table.

A cudgel, a meat cleaver, a chainsaw, a saucepan over the head, the flex from a mobile phone charger, um, a cluster bomb, a bin-liner, rat poison, chloroform, an asp, a blunderbuss, a sawn-off pump-action shotgun

Paige That's certainly a favourite of mine

Siân A pit filled with tigers

Mike A pool filled with sharks

Siân A malmsey butt

Mike What?

Siân It's a tub of sherry; you can drown in it. A mallet, any kind of electrical appliance and a bath

Mike Death by hairdryer

Siân Kalashnikovs, hand-grenades, daggers, a flick knife, a penknife

Wynne Pliers

Siân Pliers?

Wynne I'm sure you could murder someone with pliers

Hal Really slowly

Mike Lead piping

Siân Yes, candlestick, revolver, hatpin, neutron bomb, boiling oil

Mike A scorpion

Siân Red-hot poker

Mike Any kind of poisonous frog or spider

Siân Blow dart

Wynne Tights

Mike Bow and arrow

Siân Tights?

Wynne mimes being hanged with a pair of tights.

69

Mike Liquidiser

Siân How?

Mike A big fuck-off one

Siân Razor blade, javelin

Hal An anthrax spore

Siân A concrete mixer, plastic explosives, killer ants

Wynne Can't you kill someone with noise? You know if it's subliminal enough it makes all your internal organs implode or something

Siân Noise, a peanut, a letter-opener, thin ice

Hal A ducking stool

Siân A bus. A sword, quicksand, mercury in the ear

Mike Wow

Siân A set of darts, bees

Mike Wasps

Wynne Cheese

Siân Pardon?

Wynne You could plug every orifice with cheese

Lars Cool

Siân A bull whip, a cruise missile, mustard gas, nerve gas

Mike Fart gas

Siân A truncheon, a baseball bat, a cat o' nine tails, um mud

Mike One of those things with spikes coming out of it on the end of a chain

Siân Yes, a

Mike What are they called?

Siân A gladiator thing

Mike One of those

Lars A flail

Siân A flail, thank you. A trident

Mike A trident missile

Siân A syringe full of air

Wynne A combine harvester

Siân OK

Hal Weaponised marburg

Wynne What's that?

Hal It's a filovirus. It chomps away at human body organs – including the skin – until they liquefy, so that victims die awash in their own blood and putrefaction

Siân Thank you, Hal; weaponised marburg

Wynne Um, one of those things that crush cars in scrapyards

Siân A hacksaw, an electricity pylon, a banana skin at the top of a cliff, a plastic bag

Mike Gaffer tape

Hal Botulism, ebola

Siân Any other fucking microbe, have we had bleach?

Wynne Don't think so

Siân Bleach, a silver bullet

Mike A voodoo curse

Siân holds up a lobster knife.

Siân And one of these. That must be two minutes

Paige Jolly good

She starts a round of applause. Siân sits.

Siân I had a lot of help

Paige You missed out my favourite

Lars A stake through the heart

Paige A traitor's kiss

Siân What about a lobster? Could you kill someone with a lobster?

Paige Only if you poisoned it

Hal And have you?

Paige No

Hal Shame

Siân What did you say?

Hal Nothing

Siân What did you fucking say, Hal?

Hal I was making a joke

Siân Well, I'm on the floor

Paige When it comes down to it, if you really wanted to kill someone it would have to be a knife, wouldn't it?
    They're so commonplace, so hard to trace
    And silent
    (*To the Waiter.*) What do you think?
    You don't have to answer that. Poor chap, I'm embarrassing him
    Now Hal, I'm sure you'd love to follow Siân

Hal No thanks

Paige Oh don't be a spoilsport. Come on

Hal No

Mike Shall I open Bob's?

Paige Good idea, Mike. We need drinks

The Waiter exits. Mike stands and opens his envelope.

Mike And the winner is . . .
'Telling the Truth'
Oh

Paige Bob's a politician, you see. I thought truth'd stump him

Mike Two minutes on the truth?
Fuck
Why is it that lies seem much more definite than truth? What do you think, Lars? Because as a great thinker I suppose you deal with truth all the time. Are we scared of it or are lies just better fun?

Lars I think you're shirking the issue, Mike

Mike And what issue is that?

Lars 'Telling the Truth'

Mike You want the truth, Lars?

Lars I think we should be on the level, Mike

The Waiter enters with drinks. He serves them.

Mike OK. On the level: I'm a van driver, freelance. At the moment I'm delivering for a company in King's Cross that mass-produces cakes

Lars Cakes?

Mike Yeah

Hal What, as in cakes?

Mike And pastries, yeah

Hal You deliver cakes?

Mike Throughout the Greater London and Home Counties area. They offered me the Midlands too but I said no

Hal You're not a burglar?

Mike No

Hal So everything you've told us has been a lot of pork pies?

Mike I was in the army and I did witness the deaths of three people but everything else, yes

Wynne Mike, you've told us lies

Mike Right the way down the line

Hal Effing typical

Wynne Why did you feel you had to lie to us?

Mike I didn't feel I had to. I just wanted to

Wynne Have we intimidated you somehow?

Mike No

Wynne Because I'm sure no one's meant to. Is it a class thing? Because like I said I'm very nearly the same class as you. And I'm Welsh

Lars He's lied because he's a nobody who does a shit-boring job

Mike That must be it

74

Wynne Oh Mike, did you think it would make you seem more interesting?

Mike Paige, I still think that if you ever decided to opt for a life of crime that you'd be fantastic at it and that if you ever need a driver or any kind of a sidekick, I'm your man

Paige Thank you

Mike Because just from lying about it I think I'm beginning to develop a bit of an aspirational fantasy in that direction

Paige Are you?

Mike Do aspirational fantasies generally start out as lies, Lars? Because just to come back to telling the truth for a minute – now that we're on the level – I'd like to ask you something

Lars Fire away

Mike Do you believe everything it says in your book?

Lars Absolutely

Mike Do you live by it?

Lars I follow the primary life-force instinct

Wynne The instinct of 'I Want'

Mike So: supposing that my true aspirational fantasy was to come here and join your party tonight? As a nobody with a shit-boring job, suppose I thought I could change my life by eating with you kind and shining people here? That if I was to sit with you at your table, I'd somehow leave a different man? What would your book tell me to do?

Lars It would tell you to be audacious

Mike Right

Lars It would tell you to do or die

Mike Right. And once I'd achieved my fantasy – been accepted at your table and treated like your home was mine – supposing I found that the shining people were actually hollow and empty? What if my aspirational fantasy turned out to be a lie? What would your book tell me then?

Pause.

Siân Put me right if I'm wrong here, Lars. When your fantasy loses it allure you move on
    I think the expression Lars uses is 'The Consumption of Experience'

Mike I'd be consuming experience?

Siân Yeah

Mike Like food?

Siân I think so

Mike But there's always a waste product with food, isn't there? What's the waste product with experience? I mean what do you do with it?

Wynne Listen, Mike
    It's through experience you find enlightenment and I don't think there's anything hollow or empty about that

Mike I just want to know what you do with your shit

Wynne *Beyond Belief* is the most life-enhancing book I've ever read.
    OK?

Mike I think my two minutes are up, Paige

He sits.

Paige Bravo, Mike

Mike Can I still keep this cupid even though I've lied?

Paige Of course; stick it in your loo

Mike Thank you

Paige You have got a loo, haven't you?

Mike I didn't lie about that

Paige I'm so glad. So that's one fact we know for sure; you're a man with a flush. And I think that answers your question about what to do with your metaphorical waste. Pull the chain – isn't that right, Lars? – and forget it exists. Now Hal, stop brooding and open your envelope

Hal No

Paige Why not?

Hal I don't like your game

Paige (*to Siân*) He's a terrible sulker, isn't he? Go on. It's all in the name of fun

Hal I bet

Paige And I'm dying to hear your remarks. You'll have so much to say

   Hal opens his envelope.

Hal I have nothing to say. Nothing to say on this subject at all

   Hal screws up his card and throws it on to the floor.

Paige Oh Hal, come on. Be a player

Lars What did you give him?

Paige I think it was 'The Euro'. Don't know why he's so upset

Hal It was 'Suicide Attempts'

Lars That's beneath even you

Hal I have not one word to say

Paige It was 'Suicide' actually. A suicide *attempt* is a failure to achieve it

Hal Well why don't you talk about it, Paige, seeing as you're the effing expert?

Paige I gave you the subject because you're the expert, Hal. How many times did Mags / attempt suicide?

Hal You gave me the subject because you hate me with a vengeance because you once drunkenly tried to shag me / and I said no

Paige You liar! I was crying on your shoulder / and you took advantage

Hal With your vodka-soaked tongue down my throat?

Paige You conceited *pig*

Hal That's the kind of friend / you were to Mags

Paige You tried to shag every one of her friends

Hal I had to peel you off

Paige Oh the / vanity

Hal Bat you away / like an effing *parasite*

Paige Do you honestly think I would touch you? I *know* you. Eughh!

Hal The 'eughh!' is entirely mutual

Paige I'm with the Ancient Greeks and the Japanese on the subject of suicide

Lars Shut up

Paige I think it's a noble and honourable way to die. To take control of one's death requires the kind of courage that few of us possess. To attempt and fail is a tragedy. One has to seek and embrace it with complete dedication

Lars WELL WHY DON'T YOU?

Pause.

Siân It was five times actually. Once in her teens, once when she lost her baby, once when she heard about me, once when she was diagnosed with cancer and once more on our wedding day. Poor old Mags. (*A hysterical giggle.*) Bit of a hobby really

Hal Jesus
    You have no idea, no idea what you're talking about

Siân Oh forgive me. Have I dared to speak of the precious Mags? I'm not worthy to mention her beloved name

Hal You wait until the wound is open and then
    Pounce
    Like a slavering hyena

Siân D'you know something, Hal
    You want to watch it

Hal Oh / do I?

Siân Because you're rapidly turning into one of the undead

Hal The what?

Siân Sucking youth and life out of the living
    Like a dried-up burnt-out stuck-on barnacle

Hal And you
    Are a praying mantis looking for a mate! /
    You want to fuck me

Siân Oh, stop this disgusting self-pity / and get on with your life

Hal Then pull my head off and devour it
  Just like you did to that lobster

Siân I didn't fuck the lobster
  You Stupid Sad Old Man

  Pause.

Wynne Um, shall we, you know, talk about something else? We're all getting a bit bogged down in
  You know
  Grimness
  And um

Hal Siân

Siân What?

Hal I am not undead

Siân And I am not a
  I'm your wife, you lucky cunt

Wynne Look, I'm sorry but please
  Cunt is an orchid, a moist purse
  It's the apex of eroticism, not an expletive

Hal Why do you undermine me in front of my friends?

Siân Because you don't shape up, Hal. You do not fucking shape up

Siân I don't even know what *job* you do
  Who the *fuck* are you, Hal?

Hal I've told you about my

  Siân exits.

Shit

Hal follows her out.

Paige We need drinks

The Waiter exits.

Wynne I know Siân's probably a post-feminist and everything and she thinks that in trying to reinvent the word cunt she's empowering herself – or something – but I don't think it gives her an excuse. She's abusing a beautiful thing

Mike Why don't you open your envelope, Wynne?

Paige Great idea

Lars (*standing*) I'll open it. I want to see what you've subjected her to

Lars takes Wynne's envelope and opens it. He reads.

'How Wynne met Lars'. Do you know, it would be a pleasure to speak about this

Wynne Oh, yes, go on please. It's a funny story. Let's have a funny story

Paige Ha

Lars This is more than twenty years ago
When we were

Wynne Gorgeously young

Lars Wynne came to my stall at the Freshes' Fair. She was in the first year and I was in the third, sole member of the Nietzsche for Now Soc. She was such a breath of fresh air. She was wearing this green skirt – a terrible thing, which it later transpired she'd made herself

Wynne Out of that pretend turf you get in greengrocers. I thought it was so Bowie

Lars Anyway, she asked who Nietzsche was and I tried to tell her about Zarathustra and the Will to Power and she made a joke

Wynne I said willy to power because it sounded like a lot of cock

Lars You remember

Wynne Yes

Lars And she smiled and these dimples came into her cheeks – look, still there – and I thought I'd never seen anyone so delightful in all my life. Anyway she went and joined the Wooden Earrings Society or something and I felt bereft. She wasn't interested

The Waiter enters with drinks. He serves them.

Wynne I was a feminist separatist then and I thought I was a lesbian but it was just a phase and anyway I was still a virgin so what did I know – although I still find women attractive

Lars Great. Anyway I found out she was studying Art with Drama so I started to hang out with the Artniks. When I heard she was in a production of *The House of Bernarda Alba* I put myself forward for one of the roles and got laughed out of the room

Wynne I was playing that girl whose breasts burst like pomegranates and that's when I began to think about eroticism as a means of personal growth. Of course I was reading a lot of Anaïs Nin at the time

Lars She'd died her hair black. Why?

Wynne And I started to look for a man who could, you know, take my cherry. It was becoming such a burden. I mean I'd slept with women but I just thought I wouldn't know myself until I'd had that penile experience. Nin spoke about being joyously impaled on a man's sensual mast and I thought crikey, that sounds fun. And there was Lars, hanging around with books of German philosophers under his arm and a badge saying 'Vote for the Antichrist'

Lars Wynne, I had no idea it was your cherry

Wynne Oh you must have known

Lars I hadn't a clue. I feel really honoured

Wynne I was just using you as a sex object

Lars Well, any time

Wynne giggles.

Wynne Why don't I open your envelope?

Lars Don't bother; it's / a stupid game

Wynne I want to. I really do

She opens Lars' envelope.

'Death'

Lars Oh don't touch it

Wynne I want to

Lars Don't even go near it

Wynne I can and I will. Willy to power

Paige We need drinks

Lars We've got fucking drinks, my love

The Waiter exits. Wynne prepares herself.

Wynne Death is the end of life
If I was to paint it, it would be hideous and yet
I don't think death is a hideous thing

It is physically hideous and that makes us afraid
But as I said earlier I've actually come to a calm place
about death
A place of resigned

Paige 'Inspired resignation' was the wonderful phrase

Wynne Yes. I don't know whether I should say
But yes
My mother died a year ago and
And actually one of the things that's helped me move
away from that place is Lars' book
As he says
Nothing enhances life more than death

The Waiter enters with drinks. He serves them.

Knowing that we face death,
We are forced to live
Or succumb to darkness.
Um, I used to think that –
I can only say it in the words of Keats –
'It would be sweet to die, to cease upon the midnight
with no pain'
That to hurl oneself at death would be somehow to
cheat it
That death was linked to desire
That if death was a figure he would be Byronic in a
dark suit
Death would wear Hugo Boss
But now I think that death is nothing
I can face it calmly and feel its power
It must be the biggest orgasm one ever has
That's all. The end

Lars Death is nothing. You're right

Wynne Bit waffly

84

Lars Well done

Lars holds up his glass. Wynne clinks it with hers.

Paige Waiter, could you clear? I think we've finished
with the main

The Waiter begins to clear.

Wynne Aren't you going to eat your lobster, Paige?
Having gone to the trouble of murdering it

Paige I'm going to have it preserved and made into a
telephone

Siân enters.

Siân Just chucked up

Wynne Oh no

Siân Really sprayed

Paige Where?

*Siân looks round as Hal enters. He's taken his jacket
and shirt off. He wears a white vest and Lars' trousers
from the opening scene.*

Hal Um, got a bit hot
Saw these down by the pool
Thought I'd try 'em for size

Lars They look cool, Hal
Really cool

Hal sits.

Siân Hal

Hal (*angrily*) What?

Siân Nothing

Lars Don't you have an envelope, my love?

Paige I thought it unfair to choose my own subject
So my love
You have an envelope for me

Lars Do I?

Paige It arrived from your lawyer aeons ago and you put it in your desk.
Why don't you go and fetch it?

Lars Whatever you wish
My love

Lars exits.

Siân Mike, while you were on the loo getting your cupid, Lars tried to call the police to tell them that you'd robbed next door. Paige grabbed the phone and stopped him. Just thought you might like to know

Mike Thanks. Fuck

Wynne I don't think he wanted to shop you, Mike. I just think he wanted the police to know that, you know, there may have been a burglary next door and everything because, you know, they like to know these things

Mike Right. And Paige stood up for me?

Siân She kneed him in the bollocks

Wynne Well, anyway it doesn't matter because you just deliver cakes and it would have been awfully embarrassing if the police had come and searched your van and just found profiteroles. I mean, you'd have looked silly and they'd have / been cross and

Mike (*rising*) I think it's time I went

Paige (*grabbing his hand*) No

Mike I better had

Paige Don't go
  Please

The moment is held. As Mike sits, Lars returns with an envelope. He hands it to Paige. She opens it. She takes out some documents and reads.

How Lars Dumped Paige.
  I'm sorry; it's just too boring.
  So my subject for tonight
  Is T. E. Lawrence

Lars God spare us

Paige Yes
  One Christmas
  My uncle who worked in the city threw a fabulous party
  We were all to arrive in fancy dress
  And there was to be champagne and magic and dancing till dawn
  I wanted to come as a gorilla but my mother forced me into a
  Grecian robe
  Athene, goddess of order and justice
  I'd put rubber pythons in my hair
  And when I was announced
  Raging at the shallow splendour of it all
  The first thing I saw was a
  Dazzling young man
  Dressed as T. E. Lawrence.
  He was just a graduate serving drinks
  But Uncle Moneybags liked him
  Liked the gleam of that pristine psyche-drive
  So he introduced me.
  Lars of Arabia
  We ended up
  We laughed at them

Laughed at their age and their lies
And then in the darkness we

Paige abruptly sits.

Siân (*to Hal*) I'm pregnant

Hal is dumbfounded.

Hal (*to Siân*) Are you?

Siân Yes

Hal starts to sob. Siân goes to him. They cling to one another.

Wynne What is it? Have I missed something?

Paige (*leafing through the papers*) I think she's up the spout

Wynne Oh gosh. That's super

Lars Well done, mate. Thrilled

Hal continues to sob. Siân comforts him.

Mike Have you got kids, Paige?

Paige No

Wynne Oh, couldn't you have them?

Mike I've got a daughter

Paige Oh?

Mike She's beautiful

Paige I don't doubt it

Mike Here

He shows Paige a photograph. She is moved.

She lives with her mum but I see her a lot

Paige She's very like you

Wynne I've got two grown-up sons;
Tower over me
Can hardly believe it sometimes

Paige Thank you

Paige hands the photograph back to Mike.

Wynne One's doing GCSEs and the other's
Well he's in rehab actually

Lars (*sympathetically*) Hey

Paige They're wonderful aren't they
Offspring
You can lose yourself in their laughter and simplicity
And in their joy and openness you can forget
For years and years
That life is completely

Pause.

Mike Can I get you anything, Paige?

Paige Where's the waiter?

Waiter I'm here

Paige Yes

Paige takes the Waiter's hand.

Let's do as we arranged

The Waiter bows. He exits.

Lars And what's that, Paige? What have you arranged?

Paige Desserts.
Just desserts

Scene Four

DESSERT

Hal and Siân are sitting together, the sobbing over. The Waiter is serving the diners with fancy frozen desserts. He finishes.

Paige (*to the Waiter*) We need drinks

Lars Yes, drinks, I'll have five

The Waiter exits.

Paige It seems that this is our last supper, darling
And the dessert I've created is more appropriate than I hoped. It's an indication of what your life will be like without me

Hal What is it?

Paige Frozen Waste
Tuck in

Paige begins to eat. Mike joins her.

Mike This looks like a baked bean

Paige Probably is. I just went through the contents of yesterday's bin and added sugar

Mike Right. It's really tasty

Paige It contains no slaughterhouse products, Wynne. I picked them all out

Mike I think that's a tea bag

Paige Fortnum and Mason's breakfast blend – only the best, Mike. And someone very lucky's got the furred tomato that I found at the back of the fridge

The Waiter enters with drinks. He serves them, giving five to Lars.

Mike Well it's great, Paige. Really nice

Paige Thank you

Mike Is there any more?

Paige I'm afraid not. But I could always rustle some up. Our bin's a cornucopia of delights

Siân involuntarily retches. Paige and Mike continue to eat.

Hal What happened to those pizzas, Lars? Got a woman eating for two here

Lars Shall I phone and bother them?

Hal Expect the delivery kid's got lost in the fog. They send them out on those rickety little scooters; poor sod's probably come a cropper

Wynne My eldest son delivered pizzas for a while. I couldn't believe the conditions; I told him he should start a union. But he didn't seem to mind. Scooted about every night, happy as Larry. Turned out he was using it as a cover for his dealing

Paige What pizzas are we talking about?

Lars The pizzas I ordered when it became obvious that your food was inedible

Paige Has my meal failed to please you, my dearest love?

Lars No, I'm just thrilled with everything that you've done tonight

Paige Thank you for saying so. I tried so hard

Lars Your meal confirms everything that I believe about you

Paige I thought you'd gone Beyond Belief, Lars

Lars You're a black hole

Paige Really dear?

Lars A centre of negativity, actively destructive of all that's around you

Paige That's nice

Lars The kindest thing I could say is that you're not responsible for the depth of your psychosis

Paige Thank you

Lars But I'm not kind, I'm truthful. You're a slow poison. And here in my house, surrounded by my friends I'm going to liberate myself. I wash my hands of you, Paige. You can creep to decrepitude alone

Paige Well
(*Standing.*) That brings me on to my joke for the evening
I think every hostess should have a joke up her sleeve. When her guests have drunken, sobbed and letched their way through her repast there's nothing quite like a funny joke to finish things off. It fills the air with joy and melts even the sternest of hearts. So There once was a woman who

Paige suddenly lets out a gasp of fear. She sits.

Mike I think I know this joke
There was once a woman who married a block of ice, thinking that it was a man

Lars What's the punch line, Mike?

Mike There isn't one. It's just a fucking joke

Lars I don't see anybody laughing

Mike Are you going to eat your Frozen Waste, Lars?

Lars No

92

Mike I think you ought

Lars Why?

Mike Because the dish was created in your honour

Lars I'm not hungry, Mike. Why don't you have it?

Mike Paige made it for you

Lars It's out of the bin

Mike That's not the point

Lars I don't want it, thank you

Mike Why not?

Lars Because the thought of it makes me want to spew

Mike Lars, I think you should eat up your Frozen Waste

Lars I'm sorry?

Mike You should eat your Frozen Waste before it melts

Lars Mike, are you fucking with me? Why are you
trying to fuck with me at my own table? I don't think it's
very polite

Wynne Mike, why have you taken a dislike to Lars?
  Only I think he's been nice to you
  He let you in here
  And I don't think he deserves it

Mike Do you know what I think, Wynne?

Wynne What?

Mike I think Lars is a cunt

  Pause.

Hal Well done, Paige. Must be nice to know you haven't
lost your touch

Lars Yes, she's still got it, hasn't she?

Hal Good old Paige; it's quite amazing. She could always pull at thirty paces

Lars And so subtly too

Hal She has them wrapped round her finger before they're even aware. Mike, old pal; you're being had

Mike I'm not old. And I'm not your pal, Hal. I think you're a sad fuckwit

Hal I'm not sad

Mike And Lars is a cunt

Hal Listen, mate, you're a cocky little git and if you try anything funny I'm on your effing case

Mike What sort of funny thing do you think I might try? Lighting my farts?

Hal I'm warning you. I used to box for effing Wiltshire

Mike Is that some kind of a speech impediment you've got, that you can't say fucking?

Hal Watch it, tosser

Siân Hal

Hal What?

Siân I beg you to grow up

Lars Why do you think I'm a cunt, Mike? I'm intrigued

Mike Well frankly, Lars, you've got it tattooed on your forehead in big black letters

Hal Bullshit. You don't like Lars because he's got more money than you'll ever dream of and it's so obvious it's almost sad

Mike Why are you so loyal to him?
  He couldn't give a toss whether you lived or died

Wynne That's so not true

Mike He couldn't give a toss whether *anyone* lived or died

Wynne You're so wrong, Mike. Lars has a huge soul

Mike Wynne, good luck
  'Cause if you're throwing yourself at him you're going to need it
  That man is Frozen Waste
  He is totally fucking sterile

Lars OK
  Party over, Mike.

  He stands.

Get out

Paige (*standing*) Before we've had the cheeseboard? Unthinkable

Mike Paige would like me to stay

  Lars approaches Mike.

Lars Out

  Mike eludes him, walking over to Paige.

Mike Thanks for a really great dinner, Paige

  They kiss a long, passionate kiss. Paige touches his face.

Paige Goodbye

Lars Out
  Scum

  Mike chucks Lars' book at him.

Mike I think this is yours

Lars Fuck Off

Mike I need my coat

Lars (*to the Waiter*) Get him his coat

The Waiter doesn't move.

I said get this scum his coat

Paige Are we ready for coffee, everyone?

Mike Maybe you should get me my coat, Lars, 'cause I can feel a big negative influxion coming your way

Lars Fuck Your Coat

Mike What about my cupid? Paige gave it to me and I'm taking it home to my bog.

Lars GET OUT OF MY HOUSE

Paige Waiter
I think it's time

The Waiter pulls out a knife, the movement almost invisible. Before Lars is aware, it is at his throat. Shock. Silence.

Now then
Siân

Siân Yes?

Paige Would you like a coffee?

Siân Don't think so, no

Paige Coffee, Hal?

Hal What?

Paige I said would you like a coffee?

Hal What?

Paige How about you, Lars? Coffee?

Lars There's a knife at my throat

Paige Yes

Lars Why's that, Paige?

Paige It's all part of the service
Wynne, you'll have a coffee, won't you?

Wynne No

Paige Mike?

Mike I don't think so

Paige I also have herbal teas for anyone who's keen

Wynne You can deflect this, Lars
Whatever it is
Just refuse wound entry

Lars WHAT DO YOU WANT?

Paige Well, seeing as everyone's passed on coffee, I'll move straight on to my joke. There was once a woman who heard that you could get anything you desired on the internet

Lars Let me GO

Paige But this woman had everything. And when she searched her heart she realised that all she wanted was a person's death

Lars PAIGE

Paige So she set about looking for a man who'd provide it

Lars No
No

Paige Days went by as she sat by her screen and just as she was on the point of giving up, she found what she was looking for: easefuldeath.com. The man used metaphors to describe what he could provide but to those truly seeking an executioner his meaning was clear

Lars Hal

Hal Yes

Paige He could bring death right into your home

Lars Do something
Just fucking

Hal Yes

Paige Now, there was only one person the woman knew who truly deserved such a top-drawer death

Hal exits.

This person yearned for peace, for freedom, for passion. And what greater passion do we ever face than the orgasm of our own mortality?

Lars So this is your man of integrity?

Paige Yes

Lars I don't believe you, not for a second

Paige Then you are true to your philosophy

Lars (*to Mike*) You – army man – what do we do?

Mike Stay cool, Lars

Lars How much have you paid him?

Paige I told you, twenty-five thousand pounds

Lars Cheap

Paige He's a charitable man

Lars You've got no idea
No idea what you're doing

Paige Oh, give me credit

Lars (*to the* *Waiter*) Put the weapon down
    Put it down keep the money and go

Hal enters.

Hal Can't get your phone to work

Paige I disconnected them

Hal Where's your mobile?

Siân In the pond

Hal I need a phone, Lars

Wynne There's one in my coat

Hal Where's your coat?

Wynne (*pointing to the* *Waiter*) He took it
    Oh my God oh my God

Hal Fucking Fuck

Lars (*to the* *Waiter*) I'll double it
    Fifty thousand, a hundred
    What do you *want*?

Paige is laughing.

Lars Is this your fucking joke?

Paige Oh Lars, don't disappoint me
    I was hoping for inspiration – because what does one
say at the moment of one's death?
    I've been trying to imagine it for weeks
    One could try and lamely wheedle out of it
    I suppose one could scream and run or stand and
sing – Bassey style
    Ending all on a piercing shrill

Paige gestures to the Waiter. He lowers the knife.

99

Or one could embrace the silence that's to come

Lars You
Are

Paige Cleave the dark –
Do it now –
And say nothing

> *The Waiter comes for Paige.*
> *She puts her arms around him.*
> *He stabs her.*
> *He helps her to the ground.*

Waiter Shhh . . . shhh . . .

> *As Paige dies, he puts his hand on her forehead with*
> *the compassion and authority of a priest.*
> *He closes her eyes.*
> *Lars drops to his knees.*
> *The Waiter stands. He pulls a handkerchief from*
> *his pocket and wipes the knife. He places it neatly on*
> *the table.*
> *The Waiter removes the envelope of money from*
> *his pocket.*

Lars Who are you?

> *The Waiter takes two banknotes from the top of the*
> *pile.*

Waiter My service is free
I take only the wage of a waiter.

> *The Waiter places the rest of the money on the table.*
> *He bows to the stricken guests.*
> *He leaves.*
> *Silence.*

> *Blackout.*

DYING FOR IT

a free adaptation of
The Suicide
by Nikolai Erdman

Dying For It was first performed at the Almeida Theatre, London, on 8 March 2007. The cast was as follows:

Semyon Semyonovich Podsekalnikov Tom Brooke
Maria Lukianovna, 'Masha' Liz White
Serafima Ilyinichna Susan Brown
Alexander Petrovich Kalabushkin Barnaby Kay
Margarita Ivanovna Peryesvetova Sophie Stanton
Yegor Timoveivich Paul Rider
Aristarkh Dominikovich Grand-Skubik Ronan Vibert
Kleopatra Maximovna, 'Kiki' Michelle Dockery
Father Yelpidy Tony Rohr
Viktor Viktorovich Charlie Condou
Stepan Vasilievich Dominic Charles-Rouse
Oleg Leonidovich Gil Cohen-Alloro

Director Anna Mackmin
Design Lez Brotherston
Lighting Neil Austin
Music Stephen Warbeck
Sound John Leonard
Choreography Scarlett Mackmin
Casting Julia Horam

Characters

Semyon Semyonovich Podsekalnikov
an unemployed man, aged twenty-seven

Maria Lukianovna, 'Masha'
his wife, a worker, aged twenty-five

Serafima Ilyinichna
her mother, a cleaner

Alexander Petrovich Kalabushkin
their neighbour, a fairground stallholder

Margarita Ivanovna Peryesvetova
his lover, owner of a coffee shop

Yegor Timoveivich
a postman

Aristarkh Dominikovich Grand-Skubik
a member of the intelligentsia

Kleopatra Maximovna, 'Kiki'
a romantic

Father Yelpidy
a priest

Viktor Viktorovich
a writer

Stepan Vasilievich
Oleg Leonidovich
undertakers

Two Beggar-Musicians

Russia in the late nineteen-twenties.
An urban slum.

Act One

In the darkness, we hear:

Semyon Masha
Masha
Are you asleep?

There is a sharp intake of breath as Masha starts into wakefulness.

Masha What?

Semyon Shhhh, it's just me
Sorry, sorry

Masha Semyon

She returns to an exhausted sleep.

Semyon Masha
Have we got any food left?
I need some blood sausage

Masha What?

Semyon Did we eat all that blood sausage?

Pause.

Masha Did you look?

Semyon I thought you might just know
You served it and
I thought you might remember

Masha You wake me
In the middle of the night
For this?

Semyon I was just asking –

Masha Your own feet won't carry you?

Semyon It's cold. I thought if you remembered it would save a wasted journey

Masha How could you?

Semyon I'm hungry

Masha Go to sleep

Semyon Masha

Masha Don't you dare wake me up again

She turns from him. He sighs.

Semyon I won't

We hear them both bitterly try to settle. Pause.

Masha You've killed me with that blood sausage, Semyon. You've destroyed me. I get up at five in the freezing dark. I'm at work at six every day for hour after hour after hour; a mind-numbing, gruelling slog – and when I finally fall into bed, shattered, what d'you do?
   What d'you do, Semyon?
   Are you asleep?

Semyon (*waking*) What?

Masha I was talking to you

Semyon What did you say?

Masha I said the least you could do is let me sleep

Semyon But

Masha But no, you wake me up to chat about blood sausage

Semyon Is there some left?

Masha Yes, yes there is
Yes, there's blood sausage
Because you didn't eat it at dinner

Semyon Don't start, Masha

Masha That's why you're hungry now

Semyon I can't stand / this

Masha My mother and I go out of our way to prepare everything you love / especially for you

Semyon Yes, and that's the point; / that's the point

Masha We put more food on your plate than / on our own

Semyon Yes, you do and that's the point –
You do it to humiliate me!
It's psychological

Masha What?

Semyon No wonder I can't eat. I'm a parasite. I'm a bloodsucking leech. I haven't got a job; I bring in / no money –

Masha Now is not the time for this

Semyon You pile my plate like that to rub it in to demean me
It muddies my soul
That food's like ashes in my mouth. And in the middle of the night when I'm lying in bed starving to death –
you crucify me with blood sausage

Masha I crucify you with blood sausage?

Semyon Yes

Masha Well, I'm sorry. (*She is getting out of bed.*) Let it never be said that I crucified my man with blood sausage. I'll get you some now. You eat your fill. Let me furnish you, Semyon

Semyon This is exactly what I'm talking about

Masha lights a candle. Her young, open features would look fine if they were better fed and had more sleep. Her nightwear would keep out a polar storm.

Can't you see what you're doing to me?

Masha holds the candlelight to his pained visage. He too is young: twenty-seven. His hair stands in tufts; he is flushed with stress. His eyes show great sensitivity. Masha pulls the candle away. It now lights her.

Masha God in heaven, this is no way to live.
Still, what can you do, eh?

She exits. Semyon lights a candle by the bed.

Semyon No way to live
No way to live

He catches sight of his reflection. It appals him. He turns from the mirror.

I am a maggot, not a man

Masha returns with a half-eaten blood sausage and some bread.

Masha Right; blood sausage

Semyon Look at you; eyes like a suffering beast. How can I eat food when it's served by an aching martyr?

Masha Why do I even bother?

Semyon You're playing all downtrodden, Masha, when we both know that you're really the man of the house. You bring home the money. It's you that wears the trousers, Masha, isn't it?

Masha Well, I wish I was wearing 'em now 'cause it's freezing out here

Semyon You'd squeeze the soul out of me and spread it on that bread, wouldn't you? You think that just because I'm unemployed I'm not a proper man.

Masha Is that what I think?

Semyon This life is destroying me

Masha Semyon, you can't talk like this. It's anti-revolutionary

Semyon I have betrayed the workers' revoliution. I have no work

Masha You're just hungry. Will you eat?

Semyon I fear for myself, Masha. I'm falling apart. Look what's happening to me. I've got a symptom. Look at my symptom

> *Semyon sits on the edge of the bed, throwing off his blankets. He crosses his legs. He hits his knee with the side of his hand. It jerks up in a reflex action.*

Did you see that?

Masha Yes

Semyon It's a chronic symptom. That never used to happen

Masha You might get a job in a circus with that, but it's no way to live

Semyon What do you mean by that? You mean that I should just die?

Masha I mean I've had enough

Semyon Well, let me set you free, Masha
  Let me take myself away
  Would you rather I cut my throat or hanged myself?

Masha Oh spare me please

Semyon 'Cause that's what you're saying isn't it?
  You want me to breathe my last

Masha Well, right at this moment / Semyon

Semyon I won't disappoint you

Masha Good

Semyon My God I won't

  Semyon blows out his candle.

I always knew you were a hard-faced troll

  *Semyon blows Masha's candle out. She squeals. The
  candlestick falls from her hand and breaks. The room
  is completely dark.*

Masha Semyon
  Semyon Semyonovich, where are you?
  Stop this

  *Serafima, Masha's mother, appears standing in the
  doorway. She is lit by a shaft of moonlight; a woman
  of no subtlety and indefatigable physical strength.*

Serafima Masha, you know I never intrude on your
private married life
  But the walls are like card in here.
  What's going on?

Masha Ask my husband

Serafima Are you crying?

Masha (*tearfully*) No

Serafima Semyon Semyonovich, what's going on?

Masha Semyon?

Serafima Semyon Semyonovich, Masha is crying

Masha Senyechka, talk to me

Serafima She's crying, Semyon Semyonovich. Are you stone?

Masha Where are you?

Serafima Perhaps he's had a stroke
Maybe his heart gave out
Or his brain

Masha Semyon, will you talk to me?

Serafima Semyon Semyonovich, is this your idea of a joke?

Serafima lights the candle. Masha looks around, fearfully.

Masha He isn't here. Something terrible is happening

Serafima He's probably fallen back asleep, the big ape

Masha (*pulling back the blanket*) He's gone

Serafima Gone where? What for at this time of night?

Masha Mother
I think he's going to top himself

Serafima What?

Masha He said I was crucifying him
He showed me his symptom

Serafima He never

Masha I said it was no way to live and he's gone

Serafima He's going to what himself?

Masha Top himself
Finish it
End it all
Self-murder

Serafima Oh

Masha Hand me my skirt
I've got to find him
This is a nightmare
Where are my shoes?

Serafima Here are his pants

Masha I don't need his pants

Serafima His pants, Masha. Jesus be praised

Masha What for?

Serafima He won't go far without them. A man without pants is like a blind rat; helpless and reluctant to leave the dark. He'll be lurking around here somewhere

Masha But the state he's in. Where can he be?

Serafima Perhaps he's on the toilet. Doing something

Masha He'll be drinking bleach

Serafima There isn't any

Masha Electrics in the bath

Serafima We haven't paid the bill; they cut us off

Masha He'll drown himself

Masha takes the candle from Serafima. She moves through the dismal space. We see it's not a proper room at all. Part of a hallway in a once fine but now semi-derelict house has been curtained off, giving

Masha and Semyon their bedroom. Serafima has the only private room on their floor.

It looks like a revolution happened in the building a decade before. It suffered serious damage that has never been repaired. What was once a bourgeois home now houses the very poorest.

Masha is making her way upstairs. We can just see the damaged staircase going up to the next landing, on which there are doors to the bathroom and Alexander's room. The rickety stairs continue up to an attic (where Yegor lives) and disappear down to the kitchen, the basement bed-sits and the front door. Masha is on the upper landing. We see her trying a door and pleading.

Masha Semyon, open the door. Talk to me / Semyon. Senyechka

Serafima lights another candle – under an icon of the Virgin.

Serafima Blessed Holy Virgin, I pray for the safety of my son-in-law. Preserve him from this lunacy and bring him on his knees safe before me, where I might blacken both his eyes and break his legs to restore him to your everlasting mercy. Amen.

Masha (*calling down*) He's locked the door. What if he's dead already?

Serafima I'll kill him

Masha I'm going to wake up Comrade Kalabushkin

Serafima You can't do that

Masha He can break the door down

Serafima Not Comrade Kalabushkin – Masha

Masha Why not?

Serafima He's in deep mourning. The poor man only buried his wife last week.

Masha Then he'll understand the meaning of my pain

Serafima I heard him through the ceiling earlier on
　　Moaning, roaring with grief

Masha We need a man, Mother. It's as simple as that. I can't break that door down alone

Masha goes to Alexander's door and knocks on it. Serafima starts to make her way up the stairs. When she gets to the bathroom door, she listens at it.

Masha Comrade Kalabushkin, Alexander Petrovich
　　It's me, Citizen Maria
　　I need a man
　　Comrade, I'm desperate
　　I need your strong arms
　　I have to break the door down

The door opens. Margarita appears in a pall of seedy light; a dishevelled woman, in a yellowing nightie; once beautiful, now sexy. She is one of life's survivors.

Margarita Break the door down?
　　You're more of a catch than I thought, Comrade Kalabushkin. There's a little floozy here who's desperate for your arms

Masha Look, I need a strong man, all right?

Margarita Remarkable behaviour, forcing yourself on a grieving man

Masha Alexander Petrovich, I'm in misery, please –

Margarita Here we are innocently talking about his poor, late wife – God rest her soul – when you start threatening to break down the door

Masha Not this door – what d'you take me for? I'm a respectable married woman

Margarita So am I, love

Alexander Leave it, Margarita

Alexander appears. He moves like a bear, with effortless strength. His humanity is often obscured by his bad behaviour. He is pulling his braces on over his vest.

Masha Alexander Petrovich, I need a man

Alexander Happy to oblige, Citizen Maria, but what about your husband?

Masha My husband has locked himself in the toilet to top himself

Margarita To what himself?

Alexander The stupid fool. Why didn't you say?

He barges past Margarita and approaches Serafima at the toilet door.

Serafima Knock this door down and save that idiot boy from himself

Alexander Comrade, open the door

Serafima Everyone knows how strong you are, Alexander Petrovich. I've seen you in your shooting gallery down at the fair, taking aim with your muscles, all taut, like a great big –

Alexander (*knocking*) Come on, citizen, what're you doing in there?

Margarita Knock it in then

Alexander Shh

Margarita What are you waiting for?

Serafima A shot

Alexander Has he got a gun?

Serafima I don't know

Margarita Who'd shoot themselves in a toilet?

Masha Where else can an unemployed man go?

Alexander If he's got a gun, or even a knife and I start breaking the door down, he might – (*He mimes.*)

Masha I hadn't thought of that

Alexander We have to be very careful

Masha Should I get the police?

Margarita *and* **Alexander** No!

Alexander Why don't you say something gentle and while he's distracted I'll – (*He mimes.*)

Masha God bless you, Alexander

Alexander slowly approaches the door, followed by Masha, then Serafima then Margarita. He prepares to break down the door and then gives Masha a nod.

Masha Darling, it's me, Maria Lukianovna
I love you
I revere you
I think you're handsome

Suddenly we hear a chain flushing. The door opens. Yegor Timoveivich comes out in his underwear, carrying a newspaper.

Yegor Can't an innocent communist
Take a dump in the night
Without a Red Guard battalion?

He creaks up the stairs to the attic: a small man in his thirties, whose hunched shoulders make him look older.

Masha Sorry, comrade

Yegor I love you too

Masha (*to Serafima*) You said he was in the toilet

Serafima So where is he?

Masha He's gone outside; I knew it
   He'll be running over the wasteland
   Finding a rope, slinging it over a tree –

Serafima Not without his pants
   Here, comrades, are his very pants
   And no Russian male would ever hang himself
without them

Margarita Have you looked in the kitchen?

Masha He'll have his head in the oven

Alexander Come on, Comrade Maria; we'll find him

Margarita is following Alexander. He stops her.

Are you my shadow or what?

Alexander and Masha hurry down the stairs.

Margarita Isn't that just like him
   Drinking my comfort all night long and then
   'You my shadow or what?'
   It's like a compulsion with him
   First one woman, then another
   And all of us at arms' length
   No wonder his wife croaked, the poor little wheeze-
bag

Serafima Do I know you?

Margarita No

*We hear a scream from Masha and a loud thud
coming from downstairs.*

Serafima He's dead
That's it
He's killed himself

Margarita I don't believe it

Serafima Heavenly God in your mercy pull him from the
flames of hell where he surely deserves to burn

Margarita It never stops, does it;
The train of horrible events
Only last week a customer of mine
Set his own beard on fire

Serafima I feel sick
I want to do something awful

Margarita And one night during the revolution
I was with this lad in a doorway
Celebrating the rise of the masses
When we'd finished
He kissed me
Stepped out into the street
And got his face blown off
It would have been me only I was still sorting out my
hosiery
My life's like that
Man in my arms one minute – face blown off the next

Serafima Who are you?

Margarita Never you mind

Alexander appears.

Serafima How did he do it?
  Was it gas?
  Has his skin gone green?

Alexander He wasn't there. Masha's lying in a faint

Margarita What have you done to her?

Alexander She saw a rat licking her pots. She screamed and hit her head on the cupboard door

Serafima Mother of God
  (*To Margarita.*) You look like you're useful with a rat
  Come with me and we'll kill the beast

Margarita All right, Grandma. I can see I'm not needed here

Margarita passes Alexander with a bitter look and follows Serafima. A grey dawn is beginning to come through the dirty skylight, casting gloomy light on the stairs. Alexander sits on them. He lights a cigarette.

Alexander Who'd blame anyone for ending it all?
  We are all worthless dogs

Semyon crawls out from under the bed. He pulls newspaper plugs out of his ears. He goes to the table and picks up the blood sausage. He puts it in his mouth. Alexander sees his silhouette.

Alexander Don't do it. Stop!

Semyon (*startled*) Shit on fire

Alexander Put that thing down

Semyon What thing?

Alexander Drop it, Semyon

Semyon Why?

Alexander You don't have to do this
We're all your friends here

*Alexander restrains him. Semyon puts the blood
sausage in his pocket.*

Semyon What are you doing, Kalabushkin? Let me go

Alexander I saw you with it in your mouth

Semyon So what?

Alexander Don't do it. There's always something to live
for

Semyon What are you talking about? Let me go

Alexander Those women are chewing their tails over
you
Think of them

Semyon I have been

Alexander Where were you?

Semyon Under the bed with newspaper stuffed in my
ears
I just wanted some peace
I wanted to think what to do – let me go

Alexander Promise you won't do anything until you've
heard me out

Semyon All right

Alexander (*releasing him*) I beg you as a friend, Semyon
Semyonovich
Just listen to me
Because what I have to say
Is very meaningful, all right?
Sit down. Look

*Semyon sits. Alexander opens a scrappy curtain,
casting sickly light over a dying rubber plant, Semyon's*

pathetic belongings on a cluttered table and the rest of
the depressing space. We can see overflowing rubbish
bins in the yard outside.

Life is beautiful, Semyon

Semyon Right

Alexander Life is a miracle, full of wonder

Semyon What has that got to do with me?

Alexander Everything. You're alive, aren't you?
Here you are, at the dawn of a brave new age
Age of industry and the working man
Age of medicine and electrics

Semyon Yeah, and what kind of age is it when they cut
us off because of an unpaid bill?

Alexander Good question. The Dark Age

Semyon It's like living in caves, isn't it?

Alexander I spent three weeks standing in line every day
to get them to adjust that bill

Semyon Yes

Alexander Some bureaucrat in a heated office saying this
regulation, that regulation and if it's not electric it's the
wording on the licence for my stall or a travel permit -
one form after another and finally as the line stretches
on before you through eternity you find you're tired of
living

Semyon Yes
Yes

Alexander Tired of living just for that
But
Life is beautiful, comrade. We live in a workers' utopia

Semyon You know I read that in the paper the other day and I'm sure that they'll retract it soon

Alexander You can't talk like that. You know what your problem is, Semyon?
You think too much

Semyon I know

Alexander You should get your head down.
Dignity of labour and all that
Only time you find a bit of peace is when you're working

Semyon I'm unemployed

Alexander Oh, it's vicious isn't it? What a struggle

Semyon It's killing me, I swear it.
Every job I go for
I stand in line with fifty other men
Who all look just like me
And forty-nine of us are turned away.
I have no dignity, no labour, no value at all

Alexander How d'you go on with a life like that?

Semyon I can't believe there's no work in Russia. There is so much to do. Why do they have no work for me?

Alexander Listen, citizen, you have to find a purpose. Even if you don't find a job you must find a purpose

Semyon That's just what I was thinking under the bed. What I need is a vocation, a reason for living and then, down between the floorboards, my fingers chanced on this. It seems like fate

Alexander What is it?

Semyon I hardly dare tell you. It's a manual for playing the tuba

Alexander The tuba?

Semyon Look; you can learn in only twenty lessons

Alexander (*reading*) 'For the first time Theodor Hugo Schultz, celebrated master of music, shares his knowledge with the masses'

Semyon I might be wrong but I bet you could make a mint. If I did twenty concerts a month at five roubles a go, plus tips –

Alexander That's a staggering fortune, isn't it

Semyon At least. I've got the will, I've got the time, I've got the manual; the only thing missing is the tuba

Alexander So a tuba would give you reason to live?

Semyon I guess it would, comrade

Alexander That's fantastic
I've convinced you
Life's amazing; a thing of beauty
Now give me the gun

Semyon What gun?

Alexander The gun I saw you putting in your mouth

Semyon Are you making a fool out of me?

Alexander You were trying to off yourself

Semyon To what myself?

Alexander To shoot yourself

Semyon Was I?

Alexander Everybody knows it

Semyon Everybody?

Alexander I can't say I blame you.
That mother-in-law
How d'you fucking endure it?
And living off your wife
The guilt must be terrible
That sweet girl looks old before her time
It's shameful

Semyon Get out
Leave me alone

Alexander Now come on, Semyon
In all the important ways
Your life is beautiful

Semyon Go to hell

Alexander I will, but give me the gun first

Semyon Are you absolutely mad? Where would I get a gun?

Alexander Anywhere; they're ten a rouble these days. Panfidich traded his razor for one at Borzov's round the corner

Semyon Borzov traded a gun for a razor?

Alexander It didn't have a permit. But then, if you're only going to use it once –

Semyon is suddenly rifling through the belongings on his table.

Alexander What're you doing? Semyon, hand it over

Semyon finds a razor. He brandishes it at Alexander, who backs away.

Semyon Swedish steel
My father's

Alexander What are you doing with that?

Semyon I won't be shaving in this world again

Alexander Semyon – God damn it – Life is wonderful

Semyon Thanks, Alexander
You've shown me the light
And here's my gun
A pretty tasty way to end it all

Semyon chucks the blood sausage at Alexander then exits out of the window.

Alexander If you wake Borzov at this hour he'll fucking murder you

Semyon (*off*) Save me the trouble then, won't he?

Pause.

Alexander I am a worthless dog

He takes a bite of the blood sausage. Serafima and Margarita enter, with the semi-conscious Masha.

Serafima Don't drag her, she's not a sack

Margarita She's an elephant

Serafima Get her thighs

Margarita I have

Alexander Give her here

Alexander effortlessly slings Masha over his shoulder.

She doesn't weigh anything;
She's like a little feather bed

He takes her to the bed and puts her on it.

Serafima It was a huge beast, Alexander Petrovich: a red-eyed, pestilent, pregnant bitch. We got it with the potato masher; pulverised its head. Very pleasant chicken flavour, rat

Masha Semyon

Alexander She needs air, poor girl. I'll unbutton her

Margarita *and* **Serafima** I'll do it

Masha Where's my Semyon?
  Is he dead?

Alexander Well not yet, no
  But he's gone into the night brandishing a razor.

Masha I was horrible to him. It's my fault

Alexander I tried to stop him

Serafima (*to Alexander*) You should have forced him to see reason
  We should get the police

Alexander *and* **Margarita** No!

Serafima They'd soon prosecute him
  And the court would sort him out

Margarita You can't sentence a man to live

Serafima Why not? He deserves it

Margarita What, the ultimate deterrent? The life penalty?

Serafima Who are you?

Margarita Just a stranger, freezing in the night

Masha What are we going to do?

Alexander Citizen Maria – get him a tuba

Serafima Don't be disgusting

Masha Get him a what?

Alexander A tuba

Margarita It's an instrument. Like a trumpet but bigger

Masha He wants a tuba?

Alexander It'll be his salvation
His eyes lit up when he spoke of it
He wants to play for money

Masha So how much do these tubas cost?

Margarita About fifty roubles

Masha If we had fifty roubles
My Semyon would never dream of taking his own life

Alexander Don't I know it, sweetheart

Margarita I've got a tuba

Serafima Well, I've heard it all now, I really have

Margarita If you're not interested –

Alexander Have you not realised who this is?

Margarita Shut it, Kalabushkin

Alexander This is Margarita Ivanovna Peryesvetova

Masha Who?

Serafima Her?

Alexander The very same

Serafima Holy saints protect us

Margarita Well, thanks a lot. Grandma here'll see that news gets back to my husband

Alexander He's eighty-three
You have to feed him with a spoon

Serafima You run that coffee shop. That used to be a decent place. I've heard about the way it's gone

Margarita I'm sure you have. It's a successful business now. A rare feat these days

Serafima I've heard that it's a decadent shebeen
A gambling den of smutty dancing girls
With party members, lice and drunken priests

Margarita And instruments for the Federated Socialist Jazz Quintet, including a tuba. Maybe even two

Masha Margarita Ivanovna

Margarita That is my name

Masha Comrade, it's a pleasure to meet you
Really
To have a genuine businesswoman in our humble home;
It's an honour and an inspiration

Margarita Yes it must be

Masha Would you take pity on a desperate wife and her poor old senile mother and lend us one of your tubas? We'd do anything

Margarita Well I was going to suggest a small rental fee but I can see you're a bit hard-pressed. So what I really need is someone regular to clean my gents' latrines. Perhaps your mother would oblige?

Masha Mother
This could save us

Serafima You think I'm shy of work?
You think I'm scared of your latrines?
I'm the woman who's cleaned where no one else would go. I spent fifteen years mopping gore off a bone surgeon's floor. During the war I put eyes and body parts in sacks and –

Masha Thanks, Mother

Margarita The tuba's yours then. Come and get it

Alexander I'll carry it for you, comrade. Least I can do

Margarita Isn't that nice? You can help her with your big, strong arms

Alexander (*to Margarita*) You think I'm a worthless dog, don't you?

Margarita (*to Masha*) Men are a burden, always

Margarita exits with Masha and Alexander.

Serafima (*calling after them*) What if he comes back before you do?
What if he tries something bad?
Hellfire I feel sick again
His future on earth might depend on me
I know; I could tell him some jokes

Serafima exits to her room. Semyon enters through the window. He has a gun. He goes to the desk and puts two bullets in it. He starts to compose a note.

Semyon In the event of my death –

Serafima enters

Serafima Semyon Semyonovich –

Semyon Could I be alone for a minute, please?

Serafima You don't want to be alone. I've got a joke for you
You'll die laughing
There were these Germans during the war –

Semyon What Germans?

Serafima Just Germans, you know, any Germans

Semyon What about them?

Serafima Well, they ate a pug. (*She laughs.*) My dead husband told me that. Oh, he was funny. A pug is a dog, Semyon

Semyon They ate a dog?

Serafima Never mind, I've got another

Semyon I'm busy, can't you see?

Serafima You'll love this one; it's a true story
During the war in our village
We had a Turk in jail
A little guy, shell-shocked because of our troops
His head used to shake all the time like this
We used to go and peep at him – so comical

Semyon Will you go away?

Serafima Anyway, one night we took him bread and meat
Now this Turk is starving, desperate for food,
But he can't speak Russian, so he jumps up
And his head's still shaking so we say
'Don't you want it? Don't you want it?'
And he goes – (*She mimes.*)
So we take it all away again

She roars with laughter

Semyon Will you get out?

Serafima Holy Jesus, did we ever laugh about that Turk

Semyon OUT, OUT!

Serafima goes to her room. She turns in the doorway, inspired.

Serafima I've got another –

Semyon starts throwing things at Serafima's door.

Semyon OUT

Serafima exits. Semyon continues his note.

In the event of my death
  No one is to blame
  Signed Semyon Semyonovich Podsekalnikov

Semyon puts the gun to his temple. It is a revelation.

Act Two

The winter afternoon light has managed to find its way into the space. Semyon is sitting on a stool holding a tuba. The manual is in front of him. Masha and Serafima are watching with anxious interest.

Semyon (*reads*) 'Chapter One. How to play. The tuba is played with three fingers. Put the first finger on the first valve, the second finger on the second valve and the third finger on the third valve'

> *He looks up, holding his position. He looks handsome, confident.*

How's that?

Serafima You're a natural

Masha (*coyly*) You look amazing

Semyon 'Upon blowing into the mouthpiece, the note "B" is obtained'

> *Semyon blows. He blows again. Nothing.*

It's not doing it
    Why isn't it doing it?

Serafima Oh Masha, hold on tight. If he gives up on this one we're lost

Semyon Hang on, hang on a minute: 'How To Blow'

Masha You look really gifted
    Really elegant Semyon, really

Semyon 'In order to blow properly, I, Theodor Hugo Schultz, internationally renowned concert tubist, suggest a simple and economical method.

'Tear off a little piece of yesterday's newspaper and place it on the tongue.' Newspaper – we need paper

Serafima and Masha start hunting through the clutter of the room.

Serafima Does it have to be yesterday's?

Semyon No

Masha (*finding one*) Here. Here

Semyon Right. Tear off a bit. Smaller than that; do you want to choke me?

Put it on my tongue

Masha does so. Semyon mumbles unintelligibly.

Masha Pardon?

More unintelligible mumbling. Masha looks blank. Semyon spits out the paper.

Semyon I said will you read the next instruction? God!

Semyon puts another piece of paper in his mouth.

Masha 'Tear off a little piece of yesterday's newspaper and place it on the tongue'

Semyon Uhhhhh

Masha 'Then, spit the paper on to the floor

'While spitting, try to memorise the position of your mouth.

'Having mastered it, blow, just like you spit'

Semyon Uhhhhh

Semyon prepares himself. He spits. Without moving his mouth, he puts it over the mouthpiece. He blows. Nothing.

Masha Dear God in Heaven
If you exist
Please let him make a sound

Semyon blows. A loud, shattering bellow from the tuba.

Serafima I told you God exists – there's your proof

Semyon Masha, hand in your notice. Your working days are over

Masha embraces him.

Twenty concerts a month at five roubles each plus tips. In pure earnings per year, that's . . . Hang on, I wrote it down (*He rummages in his pocket.*) 'In the event of my dea—' No! (*He chucks the paper on the desk.*) Here it is. Per year, at least one thousand three hundred and twenty roubles

Serafima But you haven't learnt to play it yet

Semyon Are you deaf?

He blows the instrument again. A loud bellow.

Masha It's beautiful
You're brilliant

Semyon Just think, just think Mashenka, how good it'll be.
Imagine it, me coming home from a weekend concert
Applause still ringing in my ears
Pockets stuffed with money
You waiting on our doorstep, dressed in fine cotton prints

You'll sit me on our chaise lounge and I'll say
Has your mother polished our floors today?
And you'll say

Masha Yes, Senyechka
With our polishing machine

Serafima You'd better learn to play it first

*He blows another bellowing note. Yegor appears on
the stairs.*

Yegor What in hell's name is that?

Semyon Get used to it, comrade. It's your new neighbour

Yegor You're not playing that in here

Semyon Yes I am

Yegor It's bourgeois

Semyon It's honest labour

Yegor It's anti-revolutionary noise

He blows another bellowing note.

I'll complain about you
The housing committee will hear about this
The rooms are like gold dust you know

Semyon Shut up

Yegor I'll fill in a form about you

Semyon blows. Yegor disappears, slamming his door.

Semyon And then I'll say 'Where's my eggnog?'
I'll have eggnog with every meal

Masha It's a sin, the way you love eggnog

Semyon And your mother'll bring me one on a tray
And I'll say 'Mashenka, is the nursery decorated yet?'

Masha And I'll – (*She is choked.*) Oh Senyechka

Serafima Will you learn to play the thing?

Masha We'll have a nursery

Semyon Silence and focus, please. These are vital moments of creativity.
(*He reads*) 'Scales. The scale is the umbilical cord of music. Once you have mastered the scale, you are a born musician.' Well it can't be that hard

Masha And my fine cotton prints will get bigger and bigger until one day –

Semyon looks at his wife, full of love. For a moment they hold each other's gaze.

Learn your scales, Senyechka

Semyon turns back to the book. He reads:

Semyon 'In order to conquer the scale, I, Theodor Hugo Schultz, internationally renowned concert tubist, suggest the following cheap and easy method. Go out and buy yourself a . . .'

He turns the page.

'Piano'

Serafima *and* **Masha** A piano?

Semyon That can't be right
What's he talking about?
(*Reads*) 'Buy yourself a . . .
(*Checks to see if pages are stuck.*) Piano'

Masha Read on. It can't be right

Semyon 'Check the appendix for more information on the piano'
Appendix, appendix

(*Reads*) 'Play the scale on your piano according to the
diagram below and then copy it to your tuba'
No, no, it can't be.
Mashenka, Serafima
What are we going to buy a piano with?

Masha Oh no

Semyon Theodor Hugo Schultz you villain
You scum

Masha Where will we get a piano?

Semyon is tearing up the manual.

Semyon World renowned concert tubist?
You're a swindling bastard
Cheat and bastard
Bastard
May you and your scales rot in hell
I could see my future through this tuba

Serafima Never mind. It made a shocking racket, anyway

Semyon This is the end
How will we live?

Masha is trying to comfort him.

Masha We'll manage

Serafima We always manage

Masha We can get by on my wages

Serafima Like we always have

Semyon Meaning I don't count!

Masha What else are we to do?

Semyon It's killing me
What about if we break a cup?
Have we got enough to replace it?

He breaks a cup.

No. Can we afford a new plate? NO

He smashes a plate. Yegor Timoveivich comes out of his room to watch.

Masha Stop it. Stop

Semyon Can we afford your mother? NO

Serafima I have a job cleaning toilets now

Semyon Why don't I have a job?

He picks up a vase.

Masha No, not that vase –
That's mine
It's mine

Semyon Can we buy another on your shitty wage?

Serafima (*to Masha*) Say we can't!

Masha Semyon, don't!

They fight for the vase. Semyon smashes it. Masha lets out a howl.

Serafima Now look what you've done

Masha That was mine
I made it at school
When I was a little girl
When I still had hope
And now you've ruined it

Semyon Just like I've ruined you; that's what you're saying

Masha Stop telling me what I'm saying

Semyon I wish this was my skull

Semyon smashes another plate.

Masha You want to smash things? Let's smash them.
Can we afford a new mirror? – NO

Masha smashes the mirror. Semyon is shocked.

Semyon What are you doing? That's seven years' bad
luck

Masha Everything shattered
Plates, cups
My human life
And you don't care

Masha is sobbing. Semyon is completely taken aback.

Semyon Mashenka
Since the day we married I've let you down
You'd be better off without me
I'll disappear

Masha You'll what?

Semyon I'll vanish
Blow away like a smokewreath
Extinguish myself

Masha How dare you say that
Me and my mother
We are the only two people in the world
Who would stand by your grave and weep for you
You go ahead and kill yourself.
But know this; I won't be there and neither will she

Semyon Are you leaving me?

Masha Do it and you die alone.
You're a selfish bastard, Semyon

*Pause. Yegor exits. Semyon and Masha are both
devastated.*

Serafima Are you leaving him then?
  Is that the plan?
  (*To Masha.*) We could go back to the village
  The bone surgeon wouldn't let me starve
  And there's work digging turnips out of the frost
  Come on now
  Come on

Serafima escorts Masha into her room. She closes the door. Semyon is alone.

Semyon Two people standing over my grave
  Only one of them cares
  And I have shattered her.
  Set her free
  There will be one less flea in the fleapit
  Split me with a fingernail and wipe me away

He takes up his gun.

Count to ten and the torment's over

He puts the gun to his temple and closes his eyes. Alexander enters, leading a dapper man in his forties up the stairs. This is Aristarkh Dominikovich Grand-Skubik, a member of the intelligentsia.

Semyon One, two, three –

Alexander He lives up there

Aristarkh I can't thank you enough

Semyon Four, five –

Alexander The small fee we talked about then, for arranging the meeting

Semyon Six

Aristarkh Of course

Semyon Seven

Aristarkh That should cover it. Where is he?

Semyon Eight, nine –

Alexander He lives in the hallway; can't afford a room

He exits back down the stairs.

Semyon Ten –

Aristarkh (*calling*) I say, comrade

Semyon is utterly startled. He hides the gun and draws back the curtain.

Semyon Shit on fire

Aristarkh Sorry to interrupt. I hope you weren't busy. Do carry on

Semyon That's all right

Aristarkh Well, I shan't keep you for long. Do I have the honour of addressing Semyon Semyonovich Podsekalnikov?

Semyon Yes, sir

Aristarkh Oh, don't call me sir. Here we are, two ordinary thinking chaps, no difference between us

Semyon Right

Aristarkh Are you the same Podsekalnikov who has declared an intention to kill himself?

Semyon Who told you that?

Aristarkh Well, I was taking my coffee at Margarita Ivanovna's – as is my habit, being a keen observer of the proletariat – and it was the topic of all the conversation

Semyon No way

Aristarkh That fairground chap Comrade Kalabushkin had us all enthralled. You pulled a razor on a him – good for you; shows a fine spirit

Semyon Look, if you're looking for unlicensed firearms I can't help you. And I don't know anything about anyone trying to kill themselves

Aristarkh Ah.

He picks up Semyon's discarded note from the table and reads.

'In the event of my death, no one is to blame.' Well this is interesting, you see, because it looks like a suicide note. And then you've signed it, haven't you?

Semyon I haven't done anything wrong, sir

Aristarkh My dear equal, I haven't come here to persecute; on the contrary; I'm here to assist you

Semyon How?

Aristarkh Are you determined?

Semyon Uh-huh

Aristarkh Well then. This note is based on an entirely faulty point of view

Semyon What do you mean?

Aristarkh Semyon Semyonovich – I may call you Semyon, mayn't I, in these egalitarian days?

Semyon Yes

Aristarkh I have bolted down my coffee, so keen was my desire to meet you

Semyon Why?

144

Aristarkh Because you are shooting yourself. You have an opportunity here that cannot be wasted. It is wonderful

Semyon Is it?

Aristarkh But I fear you are shooting yourself as an individual. You must shoot yourself as a responsible member of society. Know, comrade, that you are not alone. You are one of us; you're a thinking man. So think, Semyon, think. Why is this a useless note?

Semyon Er

Aristarkh No one is to blame? – Poppycock; of course someone is to blame

Semyon But

Aristarkh Look around you; what do you see?

Pause.

Russia. You see Russia. Look at her finest men; the intelligentsia. What do you hear?

Semyon Nothing

Aristarkh Precisely; they are silent. Why are they silent? Because they have been silenced, like white slaves in the proletariat's harem. But you, Semyon, can speak

Semyon Can I?

Aristarkh You are in a position of great power

Semyon Am I?

Aristarkh You are a dead man

Semyon Well, not yet –

Aristarkh Nowadays, only the dead may say what the living think. I come to you as to a dead comrade. I come to you on behalf of Russia's thinking men

145

Semyon I'm not anyone important, sir

Aristarkh You could be. My dear citizen, you're right to take leave of your life. It's not worth living; of course it's not; it must be simply ghastly. But someone is to blame. I cannot speak without restraint but you can. You have nothing to lose, nothing to fear. You are soon to be free. And so, Semyon, tell me, who do you blame?

Semyon Who do I blame?

Aristarkh Don't be afraid, hold nothing back

Semyon Theodor Hugo Schultz

Aristarkh Well, I don't know him personally but I'm sure the Comintern is full of chaps just like him. So . . .

Semyon What?

Aristarkh My dear fellow, I'm afraid you still don't understand why you are killing yourself. Allow me to explain

Semyon Go on

Aristarkh The circumstances of your life
    The grinding poverty, your unemployment
    Have led you to despair.
    Now these circumstances are a result
    Of certain political and economical factors.
    Who controls these factors?
    Come on Semyon spit it out.
    (*Prompting him.*) The g—
    The gov—

Semyon The government?

Aristarkh Just to hear you say it sends a thrill right down my spine. Semyon, I can see the intelligence shining in your eyes. I know you want to die a meaningful, heroic death.

Semyon That does sound good

Aristarkh It is good; a more magnificent death could not be found. But you must act quickly. Tear up this useless note and write another. Blame sincerely everyone who should be blamed

Semyon Blame the government?

Aristarkh If you feel that's appropriate – and defend us, defend the intelligentsia. And end by asking them the ultimate question: why has a loyal and sensitive citizen like Aristarkh Dominikovich Grand-Skubik not been employed in the construction of humane socialism?

Semyon Who?

Aristarkh Aristarkh Dominikovich Grand-Skubik
  That's me
  Sorry, didn't I say?

Semyon You are not employed either, sir?

Aristarkh Not in the way I would wish. Semyon Semyonovich, when you have written this note, I will personally ensure that the bullet you shoot through your brain will be heard through all Russia

Semyon But why would anyone be interested in me?

Aristarkh Because you will have spoken

Semyon That simple?

Aristarkh Speak and you're a hero. Men like me will honour you for your courage. You will be a legend. I'll make sure that a portrait of your corpse – providing it's not too disfigured – will be on every front page. Russia's intelligentsia will gather round your coffin, and your hearse will be drowning in erudite tokens of respect

Semyon What a death

Aristarkh I would have such a death myself only, alas, I'm needed alive. So, are we agreed?

Semyon A useful, courageous, meaningful death

Aristarkh You need to compose your new suicide note, along the lines that I've suggested. Better still, I could write it – then you have only to sign your name and shoot yourself

Semyon I'll write it myself, sir, if you don't mind

Aristarkh And shall we arrange a time?

Semyon A time?

Aristarkh Would tonight at midnight suit you?

Semyon Oh

Aristarkh You are a true Russian hero and you are my equal. In the name of the intelligentsia, allow me to embrace you.
    I find myself overcome
    I didn't cry when my mother died
    Oh, my poor mother

    Aristarkh sobs. Semyon comforts him.

Until midnight

    Aristarkh exits, deeply moved.

Semyon My name will be remembered
    My life will have meant something
    I'll give them the truth all right
    I will pour my blame all over Russia
    I need paper
    What kind of life is this?
    Truth and no paper to write it

    Serafima and Masha enter from Serafima's room. They are dressed to go out.

148

Where are you going?

Masha Never you mind

Semyon Are you leaving me?

Masha None of your business

Semyon Well, if you come back, will you bring me some paper?

Masha Get your own

They exit down the stairs. Semyon shouts after her.

Semyon It's not just the government, it's you!

The door slams.

My death will teach her to respect me
She will realise who she married then
My death will show them all my mettle
I am not a maggot. I am not a flea
And I am not alone

Alexander appears at the window with Kleopatra Maximovna, a striking young woman dressed in bohemian style. She is flushed with anticipation.

Alexander Semyon Semynovich

Semyon (*opening the window*) Have you got any paper, comrade?

Alexander Paper? Waste of time. Got someone here who wants to meet you

Kleopatra Hello

Alexander Come on, girl, have a leg up

Kleopatra Are you Semyon Semyonovich Podselankalov?

Alexander Podsekalnikov

Kleopatra Him

Semyon is gazing at her.

Alexander Well, answer her, comrade

Semyon Oui. C'est moi

Alexander lifts Kleopatra through the window.

Kleopatra I asked for a clandestine meeting

Alexander Kiki, the small fee I mentioned?

Kleopatra Oh yes. This should cover it

Alexander Clandestine is extra

Kleopatra (*reluctantly giving him some coins*) Outrageous

Semyon What are you doing, Alexander?

Alexander What a friend should

He goes.

Kleopatra I'm Kleopatra Maximovna
But people call me Kiki

Semyon Bonjour

Kleopatra I've heard about what you're going to do

Semyon Have you?

Kleopatra Are you fully committed? To die at your own hand?

Semyon Yes

Kleopatra Oh, you're so tragic and so brave? I have to beg you, I implore you, do not throw away your beautiful death

Semyon Kiki

Kleopatra I plead upon my knees. I understand how you must be feeling

Semyon (*moved*) Do you?

Kleopatra Yours is not the only heart to succumb to pain. My own breast is a victim of it too. We are similar, Comrade Potsedonkalov –

Semyon Podsekalnikov. Semyon

Kleopatra Semyon, my own breast burns with scorching flames
   And sometimes the heat of my emotion is so raw
   That I find myself crying out in solitary pain
   With no one to hear me but an imaginary love,
   'Now, now, end it all
   I can't bear living with a heart this full'
   I'm a Romantic you see

Semyon That's nice

Kleopatra And when I heard what you were doing – killing yourself in your youthful prime – I knew you must be a man of huge sensitivity. Are you a man of great soul?

Semyon Yes

Kleopatra I knew it. Men look at me and they just see a face, they see Kleopatra Maximovna; face, face, face, and when they pursue me they just want my body, they want to take my body and make love to it like a senseless thing, as if my body was just a body alone without a thinking, feeling soul, but Semyon, you wouldn't be like that, would you?

Semyon No

Kleopatra You would understand me, You would value me

Semyon Yes

During the following, Yegor leaves his room in his postman's uniform. He walks down the stairs, watching the scene in bewilderment.

Kleopatra I've been a prisoner of my body all my life. I knew I was in trouble at fifteen, when my mother took me to buy shoes and the shop owner lost control of himself. The sight of my stockinged foot was too much for him and he sunk his teeth into my toe. It was just a little bite really but my mother thought I had provoked him and she sent me away. From then I have limped from one man to another. There was my airplane pilot who said 'Your body is my sun and my moon and without it, I am without light' and when I left him, he flew his plane over the city in spirals crying my name, then there was my communist who said my body was his supreme soviet – but he was nothing but a penile imperialist, then there was the writer who called me his perfect muse and then said I drove him distracted but none of them, none of them has ever truly found me, or owned me or even come close. All my life I've searched for the man who would understand my soul and now I think I've found him, found him in you, and it's too late. You are to kill yourself

Semyon Yes
But
Maybe not yet

Kleopatra I've come here to plead. You must end your life only for the purest of reasons
Listen to the turmoil in your soul. What is it telling you?

Semyon Er –

Kleopatra Look at my eyes. Take my hands. You're an aesthete, a prince of emotion. Don't resist, let the pain flow out of you

Semyon Right

Kleopatra Love is agony

Semyon Yes

Kleopatra Can you feel it? Here?

Semyon Yes

Kleopatra I knew it. You feel it. Don't kiss me – you're too pure

Semyon Sorry

Kleopatra Semyon, angel, if you are truly determined on this course of action – and how I revere you for it – then kill yourself for the one woman who appreciates the beauty of your soul. Kill yourself for Kleopatra, for Kiki and for love. I'll make a fool of myself at your funeral. My body will be useless for any other man. Hundreds of girls will gather by your grave. We will carry your coffin on our fragrant shoulders. My remembrance will make you one of Russia's great lovers

Yegor You lucky dog

Semyon notices Yegor.

Semyon Is nothing private in this house?

Yegor This stairwell is a public thoroughfare

Semyon I'm asking you nicely to leave

Yegor And I am exercising / my right as a resident –

Semyon Get out –

Yegor As a resident and as a citizen / to be here

Semyon is rummaging for his gun.

Semyon Yegor Timoveivich, I am armed and desperate and I don't care what I do

Yegor You can't threaten me. My mettle was tested in the workers' civil war for freedom

Semyon shakily points the gun at Yegor.

Semyon Go away

Yegor Have you got a permit for that?

Semyon Get out of here, you sneaky little shit

Yegor runs downstairs and exits. Meanwhile, Kleopatra is swooning at the sight of the gun.

Kleopatra Semyon, I'm overcome. Hold me

Semyon Kiki, hang on

Kleopatra Listen to your heart

Semyon I am. But I'm not free –

Kleopatra We are both in chains
This is an age when love is despised, trampled
In Russia our souls have been silenced, but you can speak

Kleopatra kisses him. He is dazzled.

Semyon What do I have to do?

Kleopatra I need your note

Semyon What should I say?

Kleopatra Write down the way you feel. Stand up for the soul

Semyon Yes

Kleopatra Make it profound

Semyon In Russia, there's no room for love?

Kleopatra Yes, yes. Mention my name several times

Semyon Yes

Kleopatra Say you were overwhelmed –

Semyon Yes

Kleopatra Because you are overwhelmed, aren't you?

Semyon Yes

Kleopatra And then after your death, my inconsolable grief will move a nation and your name, Semyon Semyonovich Puntsalopalov –

Semyon Podsekalnikov

Kleopatra Yes – will never be forgotten

   We hear Masha calling from downstairs.

Masha Semyon? Semyon

Semyon Shit on fire

Kleopatra What is it?

Semyon My
   Oh God
   It's the cook

Kleopatra The cook?

Semyon Quick –

Masha Semyon?

Semyon (*to Masha*) Get down to the kitchen and make me some soup

Masha What?

Semyon I said make me some soup
   And an eggnog

Masha Who do you think you're talking to?
  I'm not your dog
  Or your slave
  You ungrateful bum

Semyon Quick –

Masha How dare you talk to me like that?
  You pathetic turd

Kleopatra What an uncouth person

Masha I was all for getting straight on a train but my mother said we should give you one more chance

Semyon She sometimes brings her mother who is vicious and a hag

  He is taking Kleopatra up to the landing.

Kleopatra Let's defy her with our love. Kiss me

Semyon No – look – please hide
  Just for a minute
  I'll get rid of her

Masha (*off*) Mother, he's still here
  He hasn't done it yet - worse luck

Kleopatra Where are you taking me, Semyon?
  To your bedroom

Semyon No

Kleopatra Oh I am weak
  My body is so weak

Semyon Better go in the toilet then

Kleopatra No, don't make me
  I'm scared of toilets
  I'm too sensitive

Semyon Well go in there then – quick

He bundles Kleopatra into Alexander's room. She is barely out of sight when Masha appears with Serafima.

Serafima Prepare yourself, Semyon Semyonovich

Semyon What for?

Serafima This is our last act of kindness towards you
Come on up, Father Yelpidy

Father Yelpidy enters: a man steeped in bitterness and alcohol. His thoughts, at this time of day, are as black as his robes.

Semyon Oh, hairy Mary
I don't believe it

Yelpidy I hear you're contemplating a mortal sin, boy

Semyon Listen, Father,
I don't believe in God

Yelpidy Well, believe in Him or not, He has no forgiveness for those who despair

Semyon Then why did He create a world like this?

Yelpidy He didn't. He gave us the Garden of Eden. We created this world through our own sinning natures

Semyon Masha, I can't believe you've brought him here

Masha I'm clutching at straws

Semyon How could you do it?

Masha Where else can I turn, Semyon?

Yelpidy You don't believe in God; that's fine. But think of the horrible shock when you wake in your coffin and instead of rising up to heaven your soul is pulled by clawing demons down to the murk of hell. That'll be the moment that you realise He exists – when it's too late and He's abandoned you. Because believe me, if you take your own life that is what will happen

Semyon Great

Serafima Watch your language in front of the priest, you dirty little boy

Alexander enters. On his way up to his room, he stops to listen. He is amused.

Yelpidy Let me tell you, you'll suffer agonies so extreme they cannot be described. Imagine all your extremities being slowly fried while demons blow poison in your ears. Imagine the pain as it scalds and eats your brain. Imagine them peeling your blistered skin off and bursting your eyeballs with skewers. Imagine them raping you over and over with hot metal implements of every kind

Semyon Oh for God's sake

Yelpidy Yes, for God's sake! For God's sake it'll happen, for you are committing the foulest sin

Semyon Will you get him out of here?

Serafima He hasn't had his tea yet. He's not going until he's had his tea

Yelpidy And do you have a little biscuit, Serafima Ilinichna?

Serafima I'll find you something tasty, Father

She runs down to the kitchen. Alexander is at his door.

Semyon Alexander, don't go in there

Alexander Why not?

Semyon Stay down here
  Join in the fun

Alexander No thanks

Semyon Wait – you're a far worse sinner than me. He can save us as a job lot

Alexander I'm a Marxist

Semyon So?

Alexander Fuck off

  He exits into his room. We hear Kleopatra squeal.

Masha Who's up there?

Semyon Mice

Yelpidy Have you listened to anything I have said?

Semyon Yes. You're enough to make anyone kill themselves

Yelpidy God hears your insolence
  He hears all in these godless times
  And he is storing up his vengeance

Masha Father, is there a different tack you could try?

  Yelpidy sighs. He sits.

Yelpidy I should be used to ridicule and rejection by now but it always stings. I spread my pearls before swine every day and no one listens any more. Why do I bother? Why?

Semyon I don't mean to be rude, Father, but I don't believe in God

Yelpidy Then abandon hope. Kill yourself

Masha Pardon?

Yelpidy Go on ahead. Slice your throat, shoot yourself, throw a rope from that landing there and swing from it

Semyon Right
Well, thanks

Yelpidy Nothing I can do with a godforsaken suicide
(*He is suddenly inspired.*) Except
Will you be writing a note, boy?

Semyon Yes

Yelpidy Will you be mentioning despair?

Semyon Don't know yet. Maybe

Yelpidy Then give it to me. Let me read it to the people. Tell them how you turned your back on God. Say how I, Father Yelpidy, begged you to hear His word and save yourself. Tell them how you pushed me away. Then drink poison; blow your head off, drown yourself

Masha Father, what are you saying?

Yelpidy No other sermon I could preach would have more power
To turn the wayward millions back to God
The lesson of your terrible despair
Your vision of Russia as an empty, godless universe
Will freeze men's hearts. Their terror
At your fate will rip desperate prayers
From out their mouths, like screams. Your suicide
Desolate boy, will fill my church
And I, Yelpidy, will gather my new flock
And nurture them within these humble robes

Semyon So, if I kill myself, I'm doing it for God?

Yelpidy He works in magnificent and enigmatic ways.
Write your sad defiance down
And sign it with your wretched name.
Your lost soul might save ten thousand others

Serafima enters.

Serafima Father, I poked around and found a little bit of meat. I know you'd rather have a biscuit but it's chicken-style stew

Yelpidy You didn't need go to trouble over me

Serafima I've also got a little bit of this

She holds up a flask of vodka.

Yelpidy The feast at Cana

Serafima Come on down

Yelpidy Think upon my words, young man. Repent and turn to God – or write that note

He exits with Serafima.

Masha I thought he'd speak more kindly
But he hasn't had a drink yet, I suppose

Semyon What are you trying to do to me?

Masha I'm trying to save your life

Semyon Well, don't bother

Masha I won't

Masha starts putting a few of her pathetic belongings in a bag. There are not many.

Semyon Are you going then?

Masha Not hanging round here to be the weeping widow

Her bag is ready. She shuts it.

Semyon Good luck then

Masha Thank you

Neither of them can move. They are verging on reconciliation.

Semyon Mashenka

Masha Yes?

Semyon I

Masha Semyon

Semyon I

Margarita (*entering*) Sorry to disturb you little turtle doves, but is Alexander Petrovich here?

Semyon No, he's not

Masha (*puzzled*) Yes, he is

Semyon No he's not
He just went out

Masha No, he didn't

Margarita I see. Who's he up there with?

Semyon No one

Alexander's door opens. We see him with Kleopatra in the doorway.

Kleopatra You savage. Your room smells like the cage of a beast. There's vodka on your breath
Your hands
Are huge

Alexander I'm here later on if you want to tame me

Kleopatra You barbarian

Kleopatra runs downstairs. Alexander stays on his doorstep, quietly laughing. He lights a cigarette. The sun is now setting.

Kleopatra Semyon, how could you force me to hide in there?

Semyon Kiki

Margarita (*directly beneath Alexander*) What slut are you chasing now?

Alexander There's only one slut for me, Margarita

He winks at her and returns to his room, leaving the door open. Kleopatra throws her arms around Semyon, who is mortified.

Kleopatra He is a blot on the world
And you, you are the bravest man I've ever met
I'll revere you for ever

Semyon That's great, Kiki

Kleopatra Remember my note

She releases him. Masha is disgusted.

Masha Kiki?

Kleopatra Is this your cook?

Semyon Er –

Kleopatra You should sweep up. There's a lot of broken crockery around. Adieu

She blows Semyon a kiss and leaves.

Masha Your cook?

Semyon Well –

Masha slaps him round the face.

Masha Useless lying pig

She thumps him, then storms up the stairs. She locks herself in the bathroom.

Margarita Semyon Semyonovich

Semyon Go away

Margarita Come on now
It's just a little marital
It won't last

Semyon I know
I'll be dead

Semyon starts to cry.

Margarita Are you serious?

Margarita puts her arms around him and comforts him.

Oh come on, sweetheart, pick yourself up.

Yegor enters. He slowly walks up to his room, watching and listening.

I've thought about ending it from time to time
When it just seems stupid going on
But I haven't got a bone in my whole body
That could harm itself
You need to dig into adversity and grip it till it squeals
Because in doing that
You'll find out how strong you really are

Semyon I want to make a difference in a way I can't alive

Margarita Has Kalabushkin got you in this state with all his visitors?

Semyon I never want to see the dawn on another day.
Come midnight – bang

Margarita is shocked. Alexander has wandered out of his room again.

Alexander (*to Yegor*) Can't you give him some privacy?

Yegor This is a public stairwell

Alexander You're like a little rat, you
Peering out of corners at other people's lives
Haven't you got one of your own?

Yegor Course I have. I live for the struggle

Yegor runs up to his room. Alexander now watches the scene. Semyon is drying his eyes.

Margarita Well, if you're that set on it there's nothing I can say.
You'll be an ideological corpse all right, Semyon
And a very cute one
If you don't mind my saying

Semyon At least I'll be a corpse; that's the main thing

Margarita Well what do you want to do, then?
If this is going to be your last night on earth
We'd better make it special.
What d'you feel like?

Semyon Don't know

Margarita You tell Margarita. What would you like to do?

Semyon Have a laugh?

Margarita We'd better throw a party then
To see you on your way.
Least they can do is raise you a glass.
Hold off till midnight
And who knows
I'll bet you wake up hungover in the morning
And decide that life's all right

Semyon nods. Margarita gets up. She notices Alexander.

Give Alexander Petrovich a message from me.
  Tell him he's a goat and a pornographer
  And a lumpen, savage beast
  Tell him he's a worthless dog
  And he's to come and help me carry all the booze

Alexander goes into his room. Yegor, seeing the coast is clear, immediately comes out of his room. He creeps down the stairs, watching.

You've a face like an icon, Semyon
  It seems a shocking waste

Margarita kisses Semyon; a long kiss.

Midnight

She exits.

Semyon The zero hour
  Between day and night
  On the strike of twelve
  On the final tock of the final tick
  I'll leave through a gap into silence

Yegor tries the bathroom door. He peers through the keyhole. Semyon looks up.

Hey, pervert
  That's my wife in there

Yegor Semyon Semyonovich
  I am looking through this keyhole from a Marxist
point of view.
  There is nothing perverted about it

Masha comes out.

Masha Yegor Timoveivich, do you see any worth in me?
  Any value or beauty?

Yegor Maria Lukianovna, you are so lovely

You are such a proper fine young woman
That when I pass you on the stairs
I often find myself looking away
Glancing aside in case I am dazzled
And occasionally when you smile at me
Or make a kind remark –
As you did when I got my People's Award
For Speed and Diligence in Postal Deliveries –
I find I am so moved I have to shut my eyes and
breathe

Semyon Unbelievable

Yegor And the only way forward then, is to see you
from a Marxist point of view – when suddenly, you're
safely drab and sexless

Masha Thank you, Yegor
I'm going to the station now
Would you ask my husband to pass me my coat?

Yegor Your wife would like her coat, Comrade
Podsekalnikov

*He hovers in the bathroom doorway, watching the
scene. Semyon gets Masha's coat. She walks to him.*

Masha (*to Semyon*) Are you going to stop me?

Semyon It's up to you

*He holds the coat out for her. Masha puts it on. Their
eyes are locked throughout the following exchange.*

Yegor That unlicensed gun you pointed at me, comrade

Semyon What about it? You going to fill in a form?

Yegor Are you going to shoot yourself with it?

Semyon I'm a man who doesn't care

Yegor Well, I hope you're doing the decent thing

Semyon What decent thing?

Alexander enters.

Yegor You've got to do it for the Party. The Party needs you. People are losing their fervour now we're not in active revolution any more. There's something in the air, a sense of – I don't know – (*He whispers.*) Disillusionment

Alexander (*to Yegor*) If you want to talk to him, you come through me, all right? You want to enter the lottery for his fate? It'll cost you five roubles

Yegor Do it for the Party, Semyon. You owe them everything

Threatened, he goes into the toilet and locks the door. Semyon and Masha are still staring at each other.

Semyon You don't believe I'll do it, do you? You don't think I'm man enough

Masha Goodbye

She leaves. The light is beginning to fade into dusk.

Alexander Call her back

Semyon hangs his head. Alexander comes downstairs.

I reckon that means you're serious.
You'd better have this then

He puts a handful of banknotes into Semyon's hand.

Semyon What's this?

Alexander About thirty roubles

Semyon Where did you get it?

Alexander Five roubles for a personal meeting – clandestine extra – and three for a written suggested cause

Semyon What?

Alexander Here are your written suggested causes. This is from Pugachev the butcher: 'Commerce is dying. Do it for meat'

Semyon What's going on?

Alexander Here's one from Raisa Filipovna – great stomach on her. Biceps like a poster girl

Semyon Who are these people?

Alexander She says 'Semyon Semyonovich, blah blah blah . . . sacrifice yourself for the sexual emancipation of all Russian women . . .' (*Handing the letter to him.*) If you fancy it

Semyon What are you talking about?

Alexander (*looking at the next*) Viktor Viktorovich – he's a writer. He's actually paid to meet you but I haven't fitted him in yet. He goes on and on and on about samovars and troikas and broken guitar strings. I can't work out his cause; he just wants to write about you once you're dead. Look through the rest at your leisure

He hands the rest of the letters to Semyon.

Semyon What is all this money for?

Alexander Whatever you like. It's poverty that's brought you to this. So I thought I'd alleviate your poverty

Semyon is moved.

Semyon You did this for me?

Alexander I took a massive cut, obviously

Semyon People really paid you?

Alexander Yes

Semyon Like I'm somebody important?

Alexander Well, you are. You're a hero to them. Nice idea of Margarita's, throwing you a party.

Semyon You're a pornographer

Alexander And a goat. I'll go and help her with the booze

Alexander moves away. Semyon opens one of the notes. He reads.

Semyon 'Comrade Podsekalnikov
Shoot and your soul flies out of its cage
Like a wild bird on the wind.
Hosanna it will cry; hosanna . . .'

Alexander (*stopping*) Oh yes, I didn't charge him
I didn't feel I could.
He's got no legs
Or fingers
And he's blind.
I had to write it down for him

He exits.

Semyon 'God calls to you, like he calls to all
The lost and those tormented in the mind.
Break the bonds of pain that hold you here
We will exalt you
Hosanna
We are the only voice of truth on Russia's streets
Do it for us, your brethren in the gutter
Do it for the beggars
And the mad.'

Semyon stands alone in the fading light.
He stares into the darkness, a look of determination growing on his face.

Midnight

Act Three

Guests have assembled in Semyon's dingy living space: Margarita, Serafima, Alexander, Aristarkh, Kleopatra and Father Yelpidy. Semyon has been covered in streamers and confetti. Everyone is singing. Two Beggar-Musicians play. Candlelight and gas lamps light the scene. Huge shadows.

All To us has come our very own
  Semyon Semyonovich
  Dear Semyon, Semyon
  Semyon, Semyon, Semyon
  Drink, drink, drink, drink
  Semyon drink it up

Margarita hands Semyon one of his last remaining cups, filled with wine.

Drink, drink, drink, drink, Semyon, drink it up!

Semyon drains the cup.

Semyon Can I afford to replace it? Who cares?

He smashes it. The guests cheer wildly.

Kleopatra What a man

Aristarkh Such proletarian passion

Alexander You're a fucking hussar, Semyon

Serafima That's why we all love you, darling. Father Yelpidy has explained why you're doing what you're doing and I must say I'm impressed. I never thought you had such strong religious feeling in you

Yelpidy (*to Kleopatra*) Have you heard the one about the monk in the bath house?

Kleopatra Don't talk to me about monks. I don't like smut

Yelpidy Ah go on, you do

Aristarkh Ten to midnight

Margerita It's nowhere near

Aristarkh Your moment looms

Margerita You've got all the time in the world

Semyon gives the Beggar-Musicians a handful of notes. Alexander notices. It troubles him.

Serafima It's only a pity my fool of a daughter isn't here to support you. And it's the first opportunity you've ever given her to be proud of you

Semyon Thanks for that, comrades. You keep playing

Yelpidy I just want to say, brethren, comrades, this young man's death will have an impact on every Russian

Aristarkh You are quite correct. Semyon Semyonovich is a catalyst

Serafima Don't be disgusting

Yelpidy Here's to him

Alexander Speech! Speech!

Margerita Tell them whose note you're going to run with

Kleopatra Speech!

The other guests join in, calling Semyon to speak. Semyon falters. Pause.

Viktor (*entering*) You are Semyon Semyonovich?

Semyon is startled. He cries out.

May I shake your hand?

He shakes Semyon's hand.

Comrade Kalabushkin promised a meeting and I was worried that the sands of time would run out before we'd had a chance to speak

Semyon Who are you?

Viktor I'm Viktor Viktorovich

Semyon What do you want?

Viktor You might have heard of me; I've been published in seven different publications. I'm the people's poet

Kleopatra The people's pest

Viktor Kiki

Kleopatra The people's pipsqueak

Viktor You must be here looking for a new victim

Semyon She's my guest; the only woman who cares two kopeks for me

Serafima I care

Kleopatra Be warned, Semyon Semyonovich

Viktor Yes, be warned

Kleopatra Viktor Viktorovich is not a true poet. He loves only the body and not the soul

Viktor I am the voice of the Russian man

Aristarch The Russian man is not dry and unreadable

Kleopatra The Russian man is silent. Completely silent, even when he makes love. He just snorts

Aristarch Semyon Semyonovich – (*Referring to Viktor.*) This is the state-paid drummer of the revolution

Kleopatra The state, the dictatorship, the revolution, who needs it?

There are shocked intakes of breath in the room.

I didn't say that! I didn't say anything

Viktor There is a way the state requires me to write. Art is now a commerce

Margarita Really? Because I can tell you
Commerce is now an art

Viktor I'm a slogan-writer but I could be so much more. I could be Tolstoy! I want to be in a fur coat, on the steppes, in a troika, with the ringing of bells in the morning light, a grey beaver hat perched on the back of my head, with gypsies all around, embracing my favourite dog, measuring the miles of my hapless homeland. I want to throw my fur hat up in the air, swear and drink, sing and fly, and write poetry so beautiful that the earth spins, so that the troika isn't a troika anymore, it's Russia. Russia, you need art. Semyon Semyonovich, this artist begs you to say so in your note

Semyon Oh

Viktor May the troika of literature speed like a comet through our streets

Yegor Straight to the police station

Viktor (*afraid*) What? . . . I didn't say anything

174

Yegor You can't drive a troika like that. The speed
limit's thirty

Semyon This is Yegor, everybody
  To us has come our very own
  Yegor Oh-what's-his-name?

*The Beggar-Musicians start to play. Alexander joins
in, singing.*

Dear Yegor, Yegor
  Yegor, Yegor, Yegor
  Drink, drink, drink, drink
  Yegor drink it up

Margarita hands Yegor a bottle. He drinks.

All Drink, drink, drink, drink, Yegor drink it up!

Yegor Thank you, comrades. I don't usually take alcohol
  But I like it when people drink to me –
  As they did when I won my People's Award for Speed
and Diligence in Postal Deliveries

Semyon This man has won a People's Award
  What do you say to that, people?
  He is a model postman
  And a very handy man with the ladies
  Isn't that right, Yegor?

Yegor Well, I'll try to deny it, Semyon Semyonovich

Semyon You wouldn't be believed

Viktor (*to Semyon*) Comrade Podsekalnikov, I've written
extensively about the character of the Russian; That this
character has cracks is deeply moving to me. You
embody those cracks

Yegor The character of the Russian has been created
by historical materialism. How can it have cracks? It
simply is

Viktor Let me write about you. We artists have become red slaves in the proletariat's harem –

Aristarch No, you haven't. It is we, the intellectuals, we're in the harem

Yelpidy What harem? Where?

Viktor Semyon Semyonovich
My poetry will cry out to the world
Let me write your obituary
If it were printed alongside your note
I guarantee it would make the strongest statement

Semyon You can write what you like. I won't be here. Can I get some more of that booze?

Margarita You'll laugh about this in the morning, Semyon

Semyon I'm laughing now

Yegor I'm fed up reading things about the Russian character, as if we're still peasants painted on a biscuit tin. I'm a postman and I want to read about postmen

Viktor I've written about foundry workers

Yegor Then let the foundry workers read it.
I want to read about the postman's toils
His heavy load
His beating heart

Kleopatra Well, that's an audience of one

Yegor There are ten thousand thousand postmen in this Soviet Union, lady. And not one of us has a crack

Aristarkh Ladies and gentlemen –

Yegor And people

Aristarkh We are here to accompany Semyon Semyonovich to . . . dare one say 'the next world' in these secular times?

Semyon I've got something to ask you; all of you. What is there after?

Aristarkh Well obviously there's a lavish funeral with invitations to all our premier citizens; graveside orations from myself and other interested parties –

Semyon I don't mean for you, I mean for me

Aristarkh For you?
My dear citizen

Semyon Is there life after death? That's what I'm asking. Is there anything out there after this?

Pause.

Aristarkh Well, Father, I rather think this might be one for you

Yelpidy God, I hate that question. I'd rather tell a joke

Alexander Yes, tell a joke

Margarita Let's have a bit of life before death

Yelpidy One night, after a long day's godless theorising, Marx and Hegel decided to visit a den of iniquity

Yegor You cannot joke about them

Yelpidy Why not?

Yegor Because communism isn't funny

Alexander I've got a joke. A young man with no money and no prospects decides to end his life –

Semyon I need an answer!

Yelpidy Well, of course there's life after death

Semyon You look as if you want to say 'but'

Yelpidy But
Well
You know now
Your corpse will be water for the great mill of life,
that's all we can say. Fill me up there now, Margarita

Margarita It'll make you a lion in the pulpit

Yelpidy And a lamb in your bar

Viktor I'll tell you what your corpse will be

Kleopatra His corpse is not important

Viktor What's important is what will remain

Semyon What will remain?

Viktor The worm
And that is where your power is, Semyon Semyonovich
The worm toils eternally
The worm crawls out and starts to gnaw

Margarita Come on, boys, keep playing

Alexander Let's have a fucking tune

Margarita This is supposed to be a party

The Beggar-Musicians play.

Semyon Wait!
The worm
What does it gnaw on, comrade?

Viktor Let's say it starts with the weakest, with the little
men, the model workers, the Party ants and the splendid
types, those who have never thought, but have a sort of
sadness in them –

Kleopatra The soulless

Yelpidy The godless

Viktor The hollow ones, the empty ones. I'm saying this to comfort you. You will put your worm in them. And how your worm will multiply

Serafima Has he got worms?

Margarita Drink

Aristarkh Many fine young heads will follow the trail of suicide that you are blazing. And the pile of ideological corpses will grow. Their fathers and mothers will cry over their graves, and then our great homeland will start to shake. The gates of the Kremlin will open wide, and our government will come out to see us. And our leader will extend his hand to the merchant, and the labourer, and the landowner. And the landowner will be given back everything he's lost! I didn't say that. I didn't say anything . . .

Alexander So anyway, this young man decides to kill himself
But he can't decide on a cause
So this pack of vultures hears about it

Semyon Are you laughing at me?

Alexander No

Margarita Drink

Kleopatra You're a hero, Semyon

Alexander Fill him up

Margarita If you feel the room spinning, your bed's right here

Kleopatra Your soul will never die

Semyon You're right
Drink to me, comrades
Drink to Semyon, friends
Drink, you bastards, drink

*The company drinks, shouting Semyon's name.
Semyon and Alexander start a wild dance. The music
becomes frenzied. All the others join in.*

Aristarkh Semyon Semyonovich, hero of our times.

Yegor To the people

Alexander May you live for ever

*The Beggar-Musicians finish to loud applause and
cheers. Semyon gives them more of his roubles.*

Semyon Take it, comrades

Alexander What are you doing? That's ten roubles

Semyon They can have it

Alexander Don't give them your money

Semyon I'm about to die
(*Turning from him.*) People, listen
My life is just beginning as it ends

Viktor Speech – he makes a final speech

Semyon So who's to blame? All of them.
Comrades, I am now going to telephone the red heart
of the Soviet Republic. I'm going to phone them and –

Aristarkh Sorry, phone who?

Semyon The Kremlin. I'm going to phone the Kremlin.
And I'm going to swear at someone

There are shocked intakes of breath in the room.

Serafima No, you're not

Semyon I'm going to tell them my name and I'll say
openly that I, Semyon Semyonovich Podsekalnikov, have
read Marx and I didn't think much of him

More shocked intakes of breath in the room.

I thought he was boring

More shocked intakes of breath.

Then I'll ask to speak to the man at the top
  Not just anyone; I'll get the top man
  And I'll ask him, telephone to telephone,
  What did you ever do for Podsekalnikov?
  And he won't answer
  Because he doesn't know that Podsekalnikov exists
  And I'll tell him to go and f—

Serafima Semyon Semyonovich

Aristarkh Such courage

Viktor He's a fighter

Margarita This is the drink talking, Semyon

Semyon Shit on fire
  How can I say anything?
  I haven't written my note

Viktor Dictate it, comrade

Aristarkh Excellent idea. Time is ticking on

Viktor I am poised

Pause.

Semyon You're so good to me, all of you, coming here
  I am a man alone and you have shown me that
  You care about me, all of you
  Look at you
  You care about my words, my thoughts
  And to my surprise, dear comrades

I find that I am not afraid
My fear has gone
Yes, I'm going to die
And for the first time in my life
I'm completely unafraid.
I feel a power growing in me
Like a blaze in my head
There are two hundred million of us
In this Union of Soviets
A huge mass of masses
And I'm the only one
Not cowering in fear
I'm going to die
Hold me down before I start to fly
To think I finally have power
I can do anything, anything
Hold me back
I'm a colossus, I am Caesar
You will see me everywhere
And I'm doing this for us
For all of us
This is me, Semyon, truly me
Shit your pants, you, cowering in the Kremlin
I am the arrow of disillusionment
The meaning of me
Will terrify you
I matter
I matter
I am the genius I always could have been
My life will not insult me
I will not have lived a mockery
Today, tonight, this minute
This second of slippery time
My turn has come
I am
I am

The clock begins to strike twelve. A deathly hush.
Viktor finishes scribbling. Semyon takes Viktor's page.
He signs his name.

Semyon Semyonovich Podsekalnikov

He picks up his gun. He takes his bottle, holding it up
to the company.

Margarita Semyon, what are you doing?

Semyon Life, I challenge you

He bows. He exits. Silence.
   A round of stunned applause from the company –
apart from Alexander and Margarita.

Yegor He told them to shit their pants
He said it
He told the Kremlin to shit their pants

Kleopatra My love, my beautiful love
I love him, I really do
Look at me, I'm feeling

Viktor 'This second of slippery time'

Aristarch 'Arrow of disillusionment'

Viktor Can you believe he came out with that?

Aristarkh This boy; a starving proletarian. What
unexpected quality

Serafima He's not really going to do it, is he?

The feeling of discomfort grows.

Aristarkh My brother-in-law
Has sat in jail
For five years now

Kleopatra There is another

Wonderful splendid life
Somewhere

Serafima What am I feeling? Will somebody tell me what I'm supposed to be feeling?

Alexander We are all worthless dogs

Margarita Go after him

Alexander It's gone far enough

Alexander exits, following Semyon.

Semyon!

Pause. We hear a distant gunshot.
  Reactions range from stricken (Serafima) to relieved (Aristarkh).
  Aristarkh shakily pours himself a glass.

Aristarkh To Semyon Semyonovich Podsekalnikov
He made his choice

Yelpidy May he rest in peace

They drink. Aristarkh brutally smashes his glass.

Act Four

Dawn, growing into a sunny morning. Masha enters.
As well as her belongings, she carries a loaf of bread and
some cheese. There is a figure sleeping in the bed.

Masha Semyon?
I knew you wouldn't do it
Just like you knew I wouldn't get on any train
I've always believed in you
I walked instead
I walked and walked
And at first light a feeling came on me
Like I was floating inches off the street
I joined a queue for bread.
It brought me back to earth, the smell of food
I watched the daylight soak the city
And I thought about your face
And thinking of it made me warm
We're hungry; that's all that's wrong with us
Would you like some bread?

She gently lifts the sheet. Serafima is lying there in a
stupor.

Mother! What're you doing in our bed?
Where's my husband?
Come on, move it

Masha roughly shakes her. Serafima moans. The
remains of the party slowly become apparent to Masha.

What's been going on?
Mother, where's Semyon?

185

Serafima I can't bear it
They're out on the wasteland looking for his body

The shock hits Masha.

They had to wait for dawn so they could see

Masha falls to her knees.

Where were you? Why did you go? I came running after
you to try and bring you back but you were gone

Masha Semyon
No

Serafima I'm sorry
It's like a bad old dream
I'm sorry, Masha

*Serafima takes Masha in her arms. They hold each
other. Enter Yelpidy, Aristarkh and Viktor.*

Yelpidy Weep, weep, young widow. Hold your little ones
close and weep, weep for their daddy

Aristarkh What daddy?

Yelpidy The little ones' daddy

Aristarkh What little ones?

Yelpidy His little ones

Aristarkh There are no little ones

Yelpidy Well that's fate then; he missed his chance.

Aristarkh Thank you, Father, for those comforting
words from the church. My dear young widow, it is true.
Your husband is dead

Viktor And yet he lives. His image is shining with life.
The departed Semyon Semyonovich is a poetic symbol of

our disenchanted times. And as this symbol, he will never die

Masha emits a terrible cry of grief.

Aristarkh Goodness me

Serafima Where did you find him?

Aristarkh Under a tree

Serafima Is he a mess?

Aristarkh From compassion, I couldn't look

Serafima Where's the body?

Aristarkh Those endowed with strength of arm are bringing him. We are the advance party. Madam, we have little time to lose. The corpse must be prepared

Masha emits another terrible cry of grief.

Heavens above

Viktor He died an honourable death. You should be proud

Aristarkh His funeral will be inspired by that of Lenin himself. Obviously we don't have the same budget but Semyon Semyonovich deserves nothing less

Masha DEAD
HE IS DEAD

Serafima Masha
Masha

Viktor Wife of Semyon Semyonovich. We honour you, we glorify you

Aristarkh Widow, stand with your head held high. He died a hero

Masha MY LIFE IS OVER

Aristarkh Come on now
You do understand what he was doing?

Masha SENYECHKA

Yelpidy Why do women always make this racket?
Time to clear off
We'll come back when she's in the stupor that comes
next
Then the mother might be in the mood for making tea

Viktor Wait; he comes. Our fallen comrade

*They stand back respectfully. Alexander, Yegor and
the Beggar-Musicians enter, carrying Semyon's body.
Margarita and Kleopatra follow behind. Semyon has a
wound to the head. The sight of him horrifies Masha
into silence.*
   Yelpidy starts to pray.

Yelpidy Soul of Christ, sanctify him
Body of Christ, save him

Alexander and Yegor lay Semyon on the bed.

Blood of Christ, inebriate him
Water from the side of Christ, wash him
Passion of Christ, strengthen him

Alexander Masha
I'm sorry
I ran after him too late
Masha
I'm sorry

He goes up to his room and shuts the door.

Yelpidy Oh good Jesus hear us
Hide this man within thy wounds
Defend him from the wicked enemy

Kleopatra People followed us asking who he was / I –

Margarita Shut it, can't you?

Yelpidy Call him at the hour of his death
And bid him come to thee
That he may give thee praise for all eternity, Amen.

All Amen

Kleopatra I told the bystanders what Semyon had done
and why
They were deeply moved
And now a crowd is gathering outside

Yegor Maria Lukianovna
He was curled up on the wasteland
Eyes closed in peace
I've brought you back his gun
I didn't know Semyon Semyonovich that well – not
until the day he died. In fact, I thought him lazy – and
a yob

Aristarkh This man is one of life's natural fools

Yegor As you know, I am a model worker; recipient of
a People's Award for Speed and Diligence in Postal
Deliveries. But Semyon Semyonovich put into words
thoughts so secret I would never have dared think them.
If those in the Kremlin could have heard, they would
indeed have shat themselves –

Serafima Yegor Timoveivich, now is not the time

Yegor There are hundreds of men like him
With secret thoughts locked in their breasts
He said he was the genius he always could have been.
That's true of all of us

Aristarkh Another time, comrade

Yegor This humble postman asks if there is anything
that he might do
    I would lay myself down flat
    In your dear service
    If you would let me kiss your hand

Masha Fuck off

Yegor Thank you

Masha All of you, fuck off
    Get out of here
    I hate you

    Yegor makes his way upstairs.

Yelpidy I think it's time we took our leave

Masha I want to die
    I want to die

    Upstairs, Yegor quietly exits.

Kleopatra (*to Viktor*) That girl is devastated, is she not?

Viktor She is indeed

Kleopatra Semyon Semyonovich inspired love. Even his
domestics loved him

Serafima Father, how will we bury him?
    We've not a kopek to our names

Aristarkh Good woman. Do not fear. We have taken it
upon ourselves to pay for everything

Yelpidy With the generosity of the church

Aristarkh And the last of my mother's bone china, we're
providing top quality undertakers, wreaths

Yelpidy Sung mass with a full choir

Viktor The poem I'm composing, for which I'll take
no fee

Aristarkh A camera, a new suit of clothes for him to
wear

Kleopatra And something for you women too. I'm sure
he'd want you in his retinue – however poor and humble
you may be

Masha Get out

Yelpidy I'll go and book the choir

He exits.

Kleopatra You shall have a hand-made hat, perhaps the
latest thing in felt, something elegant to lift your features

Serafima That's lovely; what a lovely girl you are

Kleopatra exits.

Aristarkh I took the liberty of ordering his coffin
yesterday. It's made of oak, with fittings in a modernist
style; quite the finest

Serafima Thank you, sir. It's wonderful that Semyon's
getting all that, but can I put in a request for the living?

Viktor The living?

Serafima We haven't got any food

Aristarkh Food

Viktor We must start a fund

Serafima A fund

Aristarkh Of course; a fund

Viktor I'll see to it myself

Aristarkh We shall return before you know it

Viktor and Aristarkh exit.

Serafima What lovely, educated men; so clean

Margarita A fund? You don't miss a trick, you

Serafima You look after her while I wash the carcass.
He's going to be on show. We don't want him dirtying
his coffin. I'll work like a machine on him

Margarita (*to Masha*) You poor love

Serafima (*examining the body*) Now I saw a lot of head
wounds in the war
At this close range the brains would usually slide out
With little bits of skull lodged in the mess.
That's very neat
Just a little hole above the ear.

*Serafima climbs up to the bathroom. We hear her
filling a bucket of water.*

Masha Put me with Semyon
I want to hold him

Margarita I never thought he'd do it
I can't believe he did.
Masha, I'm so sorry

Masha I want to die with him

Margarita No, you don't

Masha I'll kill myself

Margarita No, you won't

*Margarita puts Masha next to Semyon. Serafima is
coming down the stairs with a bucket and cloth.*

Serafima Everything taken care of
A fund for our expenses
A decadent hat

Margarita You're like your mother. You'd survive an
arctic storm

Serafima On every cloud a silver lining
   We'll be all right, my girl
   His death will give us life
   I wish we had a clean dishcloth; never mind
   (*To Margarita.*) Roll your silky sleeves up then

Margarita I'm no good with corpses
   My vocation's always been with men who are alive

   She climbs the stairs.

Alexander needs me

Serafima You know for all your fancy business talk,
you're still a fool

Margarita I know. But I've never seen him look like that

Serafima Like what?

Margarita Seems Comrade Kalabushkin's got a heart
   Beating somewhere, after all

   *Margarita knocks on Alexander's door. Alexander
   takes her into his room. He shuts the door on their
   emotional embrace. Masha is clinging to Semyon.*

Masha He always kept me warm and now he's cold

   She kisses him. She is bewildered.

But not that cold

   *She sits up. She pokes him. Semyon suddenly snores
   loudly.*

Bastard

Serafima Holy Jesus

Masha makes her hands into a single fist and hits him in the heart. Semyon starts.

Semyon Dead
I'm dead
Hosanna
The pain
I'm flying

Masha Semyon Semyonovich

Semyon Angel, I hear you
Take me to God
The light hurts me
Hosanna

Masha slaps him round the face.

Masha Wake up

Semyon Pain
I'm dead
Am I in hell?

Serafima You're here

Semyon Serafima
Where are we?
Are you dead too?
Am I with you for ever?
This is awful
This is hell

Masha hits and punches him as she speaks.

Masha Wake up, you idiot
You're not dead; you're drunk
You're stinking of it
You bastard
How dare you, I've been half dead with grief
I thought you'd gone

Semyon Masha
   Am I alive?

Masha Yes

Semyon I'm alive

   She hits him again.

Mashenka, I'm alive

   *Masha starts to cry. Semyon holds her. Serafima
   wearily picks up the bucket.*

Serafima Well, we'll not be needing this. You can wash
yourself

   She starts back up the stairs.

Semyon I'm alive

   *We hear the sound of Margarita and Alexander
   making love.*

Serafima They've no respect for the dead

   She locks herself in the toilet.

Semyon I left here with my gun. I saw a beggar on a
trolley by the wasteland. He had no fingers and no legs.
He couldn't see me; both his eyes were white. I gave him
all my money. He gripped it pincer-like, thumb against
his ruined hand. I said: 'Take it, brother.' 'Don't insult
me with your litter; curse you,' he replied and he let it fly
away. I saw it sail up through the street light and the
ground started shifting like thin ice. I ran. I stumbled
over clumps of grass and wire and frozen shit. I didn't
stop until I hit a tree. I knew the place; the tree that
blossoms during May and for a fortnight every year
looks like a piece of heaven; but last night it was freezing
barren black. I held the trunk with one hand and I put
the gun in my mouth. Turns out it was the bottle so I

drank until the stars all burst and everything went dark.
Then my fingers closed round metal and I brought it up
to see and bang

Margarita and Alexander finish.

Masha You missed

Semyon Guess I did

Masha You stupid idiot

Semyon Can't even kill myself

Masha You're useless, you

Semyon (*putting his hand up to his wound*) Look at
that. I got a wound though

Masha Missed by a mile

Semyon Nice to know you're glad to see me anyway

Masha Well. Better luck next time, eh?

Semyon Mashenka

Masha Am I really so horrible to live with?

Semyon No
I am

Masha Senya
Senyechka

Serafima emerges from the toilet.

Serafima Jesus of Nazareth, save us or we perish!
What'll we tell those people?
They've gone to plan your funeral

Masha So they have

Serafima They're modelling it on Lenin's

Semyon Shit on fire

Serafima We'll take care of all the bills they said
They're making me a hat

Semyon I'm supposed to be dead

*Stepan Vasilievich and Oleg Leonidovich enter – two
undertakers. They are carrying a coffin and some
wreaths.*

Oleg Is this where the dead man lives?

Semyon What?

Oleg The dead man. Does he live here?

Stepan To you, Oleg, to you

Oleg Mind that thing; hang on

Semyon Who are you?

Stepan We've come from 'Eternity'

Masha Pardon?

Stepan From 'Eternity'

Oleg You know, the funeral parlour

Stepan Right, where do you want it?

Oleg Come on please, comrades; it's heavy. We've
carried it all the way from the workshop

*Pause. Semyon, Masha and Serafima are staring at
them in horror.*

Stepan Look, I know it's a bit of a shock when you first
see it, but please take comfort from the fact that it's the
very best one we do

Oleg Fantastic coffin, this. I'd have one myself if I could
afford it – and if I was dead, obviously

Stepan Oh Jesus, let's just put it down

Stepan and Oleg put the coffin on the table.

Right, where's the incoming occupant?

Semyon What?

Stepan The incoming occupant. You see they make us say that, as if obscure language makes losing your loved one easier or something.
    But that's 'Eternity' for you; full of obscurity. I say 'Why don't we just say the body?'

Oleg The corpse. Where's the corpse?

Stepan What's its name?

Oleg (*consulting a clipboard*) Semyon Semyonovich Podsekalnikov

Semyon Here

Oleg Where?

Serafima He's not ready yet. We haven't finished him

Stepan We're supposed to lift him in for you

Semyon No thanks

Stepan It's part of the service. We're supposed to do it

Oleg Once the *mortis* sets in, it's a tricky job

Serafima We'll manage

Oleg It's upsetting, comrade. They don't bend

Masha We'll look after him ourselves, thank you

Serafima We like a challenge

Stepan You sure?

Masha Yes thanks, comrades

Oleg Right then

He hands Semyon a clipboard.

Sign for it, will you?

Semyon takes up the pen. He falters.

Semyon You do it

He hands the clipboard to Masha. She signs.

Oleg And there for the wreaths, please

She signs again.

Stepan There's a lot of folk out there; quite a crowd. Was he well known?

Semyon Not really

Stepan Must have been a party member, or something. What was he, a people's commissar?

Semyon He was just a
Nothing really

Oleg Well, first-class coffin. I hope he gets good use of it

Serafima Thanks, boys.

Stepan I feel great compassion for the dead

Oleg So do I

Semyon Thank you

Stepan We take tips

Masha comes forward rummaging in her pockets. She finds a tiny coin.

Masha Good luck

Stepan and Oleg leave, insulted. Masha picks up one of the wreaths. She reads the dedication.

Masha 'For my beloved Semyon. A fighter, a hero and an unforgettable son-in-law.' (*She looks at Serafima.*) It's from you

Serafima Did I write that?

Masha No, they did

Serafima We haven't got a body

Masha What are we going to do?

We hear the front door opening.

Serafima It's them

Semyon I've let them down. They trusted me. They were banking on me

We hear Aristarkh off, speaking through a loud-hailer.

Aristarkh (*off*) Comrades –

Semyon They're the only people who've ever had time for anything I've said

Aristarkh (*off*) In a few moments we shall escort Semyon Semyonovich Podsekalnikov to his final resting place –

Semyon I thought I was a maggot. They made me feel a man

Yelpidy (*off*) – Saint Josef's on Zverkov Street where you are welcome to reacquaint yourselves with God

Semyon Look at that thing. It's fit for a prince

Aristarkh (*off*) Await us here, comrades.

Masha We'll tell them the truth. How hard can that be? We'll tell them you're alive

Serafima They were going to start a fund for us, a fund, Semyon

Semyon My death would have provided for you?

Serafima We were going to have an income

Semyon Where's my gun? I'll kill myself.

Masha I've got a better idea; I'll kill you

Serafima You won't have to; they'll kill him
Holy Virgin, pray for us

*Aristarkh, Yelpidy and Viktor come up the stairs.
Masha and Serafima turn to face them. Behind
them, Semyon panics.
He jumps into the coffin and lies there, as if dead.*

Aristarkh My dear young widow, the crowd is growing,
swelling, multiplying beyond our wildest expectations

Masha There's been a terrible mistake

Yelpidy I have preached the parable of / Podsekalnikov

Viktor I've managed to compose his praises in this verse

Masha It's a mistake

Aristarkh I've also contacted the press. / His fame will
spread

Viktor Revered widow, here is our collective effort to
replace your husband. It's just the beginning

He hands her a collection of money.

Masha We can't take this

Serafima Holy Jesus, I can't bear it

Masha Thank you but
He isn't dead
It's a mistake
He's still alive

Aristarkh (*looking at Semyon in the coffin*) Well, I'm
rather confused that you should say that, my dear

Masha We thought he was dead
And so did he, actually
But as you can see –

*Masha turns. She sees Semyon, corpse-like in the
coffin.*

Serafima Has he died?

Masha Semyon, what are you doing?
Get up out of there

Aristarkh Oh no, she's hysterical

Yelpidy (*going to Semyon*) Look at him. Dead

Masha Semyon
GET UP I SAID
He's alive

Aristarkh My dear widow

Masha I'm not a widow; he's alive

Viktor She's trapped in her moment of nemesis
Unable to face her tragic hubris

Masha Mother, tell them

Serafima (*taking the money from Masha*) Masha, when
you see it from their point of view –

Yelpidy I've seen this happen before. She'll either come
round in an hour or two or she's a case for the asylum

Viktor Tragedy

Alexander and Margarita appear on the landing.

Masha Semyon, I'm warning you. Get up or I'll murder
you

She goes to shake him. Yelpidy and Aristarkh stop her.

Yelpidy (*stopping her*) Widow, do not defile the dead

Aristarkh We can't let you do it

Masha Semyon

Viktor You must face the truth

Masha Get up you idiot. You're making it harder for yourself

Yelpidy Your husband is dead

Masha Semyon Semyonovich –

Alexander What's going on?

Masha Comrade Kalabushkin, Semyon is alive

Margarita Oh no; poor girl

Alexander Mashenka

Margarita I once had a neighbour who kept his dead mother sitting at the table for sixteen days. It was the smell that convinced him in the end

Masha He was talking to me five minutes ago

Serafima (*hiding the money in her apron*) You know, Masha, you never can tell with these head wounds. You can be walking around one minute, telling a fine old joke and next minute – gone

Masha What are you saying?

Serafima I'm saying brain explosion. Look at him

Masha Alexander Petrovich, he's not dead

Yelpidy She needs rest
Seclusion in a dark place
Possibly restraints

Alexander Masha, I carried him home. He was frozen to the touch

Masha Well, he thawed

Aristarkh Is there a dark room where she can get some rest?

Margarita Bring her up here

Alexander Come on, Masha

Masha You wouldn't. Comrade Kalabushkin, you couldn't

Alexander I'm sorry, Mashenka
I'm so sorry
But you'll thank me for it, sweetheart

He puts Masha over his shoulder. He carries her up the stairs.

Masha Semyon Semyonovich Podsekalnikov, I will get you for this. You toe-rag. You coward. Why is life so difficult to face?

Margarita Come on, girl

Masha Let me go
Put me down

Alexander I'm sorry

Margarita Leave her with me

Masha All right, all right, he's dead
I believe you
Just don't bury him
Don't bury him

Semyon sits up in a panic. No one is looking at the coffin; all their eyes are on Masha. She is the only person who notices Semyon.

Semyon, you *fool*

Margarita closes the door. Semyon hurriedly lies down.

Viktor Her grief is epic
Cassandra tormented
Andromache at the gates of Troy

Aristarkh (*setting up the camera*) Now, without wishing to ride roughshod over the needs of the bereaved, I'd like to point out that the crowd should not be kept waiting. They have come to see a suicide and a suicide they'll have. (*To Viktor.*) Have you sent his final words to the printer?

Viktor Of course

Yelpidy One has to admit that this dead man is not the finest choice

Alexander What do you mean?

Yelpidy Well, it's a pity that a people's commissar or a society figure hadn't decided to shoot himself in the head

Aristarkh I disagree; his obscurity is his perfection

Yelpidy How?

Aristarkh Because we can mould him. In our careful hands, he will become the model dead man

Viktor You're right. We can construct a truth. Listen to my poem

Aristarkh (*to Serafima*) Madam, could we have you by the coffin?

Serafima Here?

We hear a plaintive melody, coming closer.

Viktor
A young working man, without job or means
Found his life was a series of frustrated dreams
But the path he was given he chose not to tread
For society's sake, he chose death instead

Aristarkh Madam, forgive me, but I don't think a smile is appropriate

The photograph is taken.

Viktor
When we climb up snowdrifts or lie in the grass,
Betraying his pain with our carefree hearts
Let us think of that second of slippery time
When death drew him forwards at midnight's slow
   chime

Aristarkh This is Tolstoy?

Viktor
His body now crumpled, the gun in his hand
They killed him – the philistines – no more could
   he stand!

Aristarkh Doesn't scan

Viktor It's for the peasants, you pedant

Kleopatra enters followed by the Beggar-Musicians, who are playing the plaintive melody. She speaks over the last verse of Viktor's poem.

His coffin will / lead us through life from this day

Kleopatra The crowd is enormous. We had to fight / our way through

Viktor
The ultimate price he paid, I would say /
Our hopes are now with him buried below

Kleopatra I told them 'Love killed Semyon Semyonovich'
'I am a murderer!'

Viktor Kiki, I'm reciting!

Kleopatra He wanted me body and soul and when I said
'Darling we can't; our feelings are reactionary'
He ended his life. I murdered him

Kleopatra signals the musicians to stop playing.

Viktor You?

Kleopatra Yes

Viktor Your body is made entirely of lies

Kleopatra My body is his! They've been moved by our
tragedy

*Masha comes out on to the landing. Margarita follows
her.*

Viktor By your what?

Kleopatra By the tragedy of our great love

Viktor That's quick work, even for you. You only knew
him a day

Kleopatra It was long enough. He took his life because
of me. If only you were man enough to do the same

Viktor Oh, if only

Kleopatra Ah, you have a camera –
Let me throw myself upon him

Masha (*running down the stairs*) Over my dead body

Yelpidy Why do these women insist on hurling themselves
at corpses?

Masha and Kleopatra meet over the coffin.

Masha He's mine, you stupid, stuck-up slut

Kleopatra How dare you, you cleaner

Masha I'm his wife

Kleopatra You're quite mistaken

Masha No I'm not

Margarita She's his wife

Kleopatra Well, what does it matter? He wanted me, me

Masha Semyon, sort this out

Kleopatra He died for my love

Masha He will in a minute

The men restrain Masha and Kleopatra.

Aristarkh Ladies, please, this is not a personal drama. Semyon Semyonovich died so that others could act for him. / His death is clarion call to Russia's intellectuals

Viktor He had a poet's sensibility. He died because the state had no faith / in him

Yelpidy He died because he had no faith. / Perilous is the godless path he trod

Margarita He died because he'd had a fight with Masha / and he thought she'd left him

Alexander He died because he didn't have a fucking job / and it sent him twisted

Masha HE ISN'T DEAD

Pause.

Serafima Is that my hat?

Kleopatra Yes

Serafima (*taking it*) Thank you so much

Aristarkh Gentlemen – and people – there is no reason why Semyon Semyonovich could not be poet and lover, political thinker, unemployed worker, religious devotee – and immortal to those who loved him. Our model dead man could be all of these things

Viktor You're right

Yelpidy I'll put the lid on, shall I?

Alexander I'll put the lid on –
When his wife is ready
Masha?

Masha You take him. Put him on show and then shove him in the ground. God help you, Semyon

Alexander picks up the lid. He raises it over the coffin.

Alexander I was no friend to you
Forgive me

Semyon holds back the coffin lid.

Semyon No, no, you forgive me

Aristarkh screams. There is pandemonium.

Forgive me, comrades. All of you, forgive me

Yelpidy Get thee from me

Alexander Shit on fire

Kleopatra The living dead

Aristarkh Get back! Get back

Margarita Semyon Semyonovich

Serafima It's a miracle! A resurrection, look!

Semyon I can't go on. Sorry but I've got to live

Viktor Alive

Semyon Yes

Masha I tried to tell you

Aristarkh You were supposed to kill yourself

Semyon I meant to

Serafima He only missed by an inch

Margarita We wept for you

Alexander Actually, I just got dust in my eyes

Semyon I'm sorry

Kleopatra I have wasted my suffering

Viktor You Judas

Aristarkh You have put your own interests before society

Semyon My society is here, with her, and her, and them

Aristarkh I thought you were a hero and I find you are a worm. How can you go on living?

Semyon I don't know; thoughtlessly
    Like a chicken with its head cut off perhaps
    I don't want to die. Not for you, not for them, not for clever men or the masses, not for romance, not for art, and not for God himself

Yelpidy Blasphemer

Viktor We were going to make you a symbol

Semyon You could have made me a bearded lady
    What would I care in that box?
    I am alive and well
    And nothing on this earth has ever scared me

Like the thought of lying there for ever
With the lid nailed down

Yelpidy He has made fools of us all

Masha I tried to tell you

Viktor Are you laughing at our expense?

Aristarch Our literal expense. My mother's china

Kleopatra Semyon, you lied

Semyon I didn't lie. I meant to do it
But I can't be your model dead man
I can't set the world ablaze
I'm not a multiplying worm
All I want is a quiet life and a decent wage

Viktor That's bourgeois

Aristarkh That's reactionary. Listen to him

Viktor Everything he says is counter-revolutionary

Aristarkh You're right

Viktor Why didn't we realise before? He's a traitor to the revolution

Semyon What have I ever done against the revolution?

Aristarkh You spoke

Semyon You all wanted me to speak

Aristarkh But only as a dead man. I told you from the start that there are things the living cannot say – and you have said them, citizen

Viktor Words are frightening. They will lock you up for your words

Semyon Then let me whisper.

Let me sometimes whisper 'It's a hard life'
Because we need to, people like me with not enough
bread.
Leave me free to whisper.
I will live my whole life in that whisper

*The noise of the crowd is growing louder. Funereal
hymns are being sung.*

Kleopatra Listen

Viktor The crowd

Yelpidy We have promised them a suicide

Aristarkh And we cannot deliver

Semyon It's a hard life

Kleopatra Viktor, what'll we do?

Viktor Kiki

Semyon It's a hard life

Yelpidy The merciless masses

Viktor They'll tear us apart

Kleopatra Save me from the crowd

Kleopatra throws herself upon Viktor.

Viktor My perfect muse

Aristarkh You have exposed us to the rage and ridicule
of all those people

Yelpidy We must have a body

Aristarch They'll tear us apart

Kleopatra Shoot him

Masha Shoot her

Aristarkh Recant and shoot yourself

Yelpidy I could get him with this shovel if you held him down

Semyon No need; I still have a bullet left
Take the gun, comrades
If I've committed any crime
If I've brought death or misfortune to a single soul
Then take your shot

Aristarkh Huh

Semyon Come forward, Aristarkh Dominikovich Grand-Skubik. If you can name my crime, then take the gun and shoot me

Serafima is hiding the money. Aristarkh takes the gun.
He aims it at Semyon.

Aristarkh You cheat, you utter nonentity
You gave us *hope*
You have dug us a grave with your own hands
And you dare to survive?
I might destroy myself but I'll make sure you're shot
You THIEF

Margarita is at the top of the stairs. She lifts
Serafima's bucket and holds it over the heads of
Aristarkh, Viktor, Yelpidy and Kleopatra.

Margarita Anyone thinking of firing that gun should know that I have a bucket of shit up here, from the toilet of this slum. He who moves, gets it

Aristarkh lowers the gun.

Aristarkh I wasn't going to fire. How could you think that? I'm a civilised man. I just wanted to teach him a lesson

Margarita Take it off him, Masha

Masha takes the gun and aims it at them.

Kleopatra (*trying to hide herself in his jacket*) Viktor, shelter me

Masha Get back

Yelpidy I'm a / humble man of God

Viktor We're peace-loving artists, men of the people
We believe in humane socialism

Aristarkh We always put the proletariat first

Kleopatra Spare me

Masha Shut it, slut

Margarita Semyon, get out of that coffin. Kalabushkin, put the lid on it

Semyon and Alexander obey her commands.

Viktor Kiki, you smell like a meadow

Kleopatra I belong in your jacket

Margarita Right, there's your body
There's your hollow truth
Take it and go

Aristarkh But it's empty

Alexander Who's to know?

Margarita Tell them he shot his head off and you can't show the corpse. Now pick it up. All of you

Alexander You heard the lady

Viktor Come on, Kiki. We'll get through this

Kleopatra I can't
I'm too sensitive

Serafima Chuck the shit on her

Kleopatra moves with a squeal and takes her place as pall-bearer.

Margarita And if any of you ever bother this man or his family again, I'll tell the world that coffin's empty and I'll ban you from my bar

Kleopatra / No

Yelpidy Margarita, / you couldn't. I'm just a lamb

Aristarkh Dear lady, it's my / window on the world

Viktor No, please. We're all friends here. All civilised friends

Alexander Play them out, boys

The Beggar-Musicians play an inappropriate tune.

Semyon (*waving them off*) Good luck with the funeral
Hope they like your poem

The four pall-bearers leave with their coffin.
The remaining five celebrate.

Masha Thank you

Alexander You've really got style, Margarita
A bucket of shit?

Margarita It's only water

Alexander Beautiful
Beautiful

Serafima Look at them go
The crowd parting like the Red Sea
Their heads bowed in respect.
Amazing what people will believe.

Margarita I'll open a bottle, shall I?

Alexander Music to my ears

Margarita goes into Alexander's room.

Masha Alexander, go and fetch Yegor –
Tell him what's happened.
Let him come and share

Alexander goes up the stairs.

I told him to fuck off when I thought you were dead
I was horrible to him

Semyon I am in love
I'm in love with my hands, with my feet, with my legs
With this bed
With my wife
With the hawthorn tree
And the blue sky
With that crowd
With the music
And more than anything, I have fallen in love with my
stomach
My poor stomach
It was all I could think of in that coffin

Masha Senyechka, I got bread

Semyon I haven't eaten for a whole day
And a night and another endless day
Not since that blood sausage
Mashenka
You best of all wives
I am wildly in love with that bread

Masha Let me furnish you, Semyon

Serafima You can eat the lot. Here, we can afford plenty
more. Five thousand loaves

She puts the collection of money on the table.

Margarita uncorks a bottle.

Margarita You can afford some glasses too

Masha Mother, we have to give that back

Serafima How can we? It's Semyon's. He earned it by dying

Alexander comes out of the attic. He is ashen.

Margarita What is it?

A hush falls.

Alexander, what's happened?

Alexander Yegor Timoveivich
Yegor has hanged himself

Serafima Holy God, why?

Silence.

Alexander He left us a note

Semyon What does it say?

Alexander 'Semyon is right. Why live?'

The End.

A VAMPIRE STORY

For Bridie

A Vampire Story was written for the National Theatre's Connections programme 2008. It has been performed by schools and youth theatres all over the world.

Characters

Ella

Eleanor

Claire

Clara

Frank

Briggs

Moon
schoolboys, present day

Debit

Point
schoolgirls, present day

Mint
a drama teacher

Fillet
a food technology teacher

Marianne
a child prostitute

Ruthven
a gambler

Darvell
a stranger

Tina
Frank's mother

Geoff
Frank's father

Letty and Harriet
schoolgirls, nineteenth century

Bettina
a maidservant

Mint and Fillet can be played by male or female actors

A town, somewhere in Britain. Present day.

SCENES

SCENE ONE

*Eleanor is sixteen. She is dressed in a costume of 1822.
She is on stage almost all the time. There is a small
writing desk where she occasionally sits and writes,
although her focus should always be on the action.*

Eleanor People will always believe the most fabulous tale
you can tell. It's the one that they secretly long for. It
must be unprovable, impossible, fantastical. To believe it
then becomes an act of faith. An act of faith. Scene one.
A train.

> *Ella and Claire are dressed in modern-day clothes. Ella
> is sixteen, Claire, twenty-one. Claire is very
> fashionably and stylishly attired. Ella dresses as if the
> whole concept of fashion is confusing and alien to her.*

Claire Guess what your name is

Ella I can't

Claire Go on

Ella Just tell me

Claire You'll never guess

Ella Don't make me

Claire It's fun

Ella Janet

Claire No

Ella Karen

Claire Come on, it's interesting

Ella Beelzebub

Claire I'll give you a clue. My name's Claire

Ella Claire what?

Claire Wythenshawe

Ella Claire Wythenshawe

Claire And you're my little sister. We're the Wythenshawes. What's your name; go on?

Ella Something ironic; Joy

Claire No. It's Eleanor

Ella Oh

Claire Isn't that great? I thought you'd be pleased with that

Ella Eleanor Wythenshawe

Claire That's right. And I'm Claire

Ella You found two sisters called Eleanor and Claire?

Claire Fancy that

Ella What happened to them?

Claire Killed in a car crash. Identities there for the taking

Ella What about their parents?

Claire They only had a dad. And I'm afraid he recently died

Ella How?

Claire blandly shrugs.

Don't you feel anything?

Claire Like what?

Ella For them

Claire I feel glad we got away. You didn't think we would, did you?

Ella One day, we won't

Pause.

So where are we going, Claire?

Claire A lovely smalltown

Ella I told you; no more smalltowns

Claire They're the best places

Ella They're a nightmare

Claire We're going to a lovely British smalltown surrounded by beautiful countryside

Ella I'll be sick

Claire No you won't

Ella I'll go mad

Claire You always say that

Ella I'll kill myself

Claire You could try

Ella I could kill you

Claire Then you'd be all alone. I love these smalltowns, Ella. The people are wonderful. Really lovely, so trusting

Ella So gullible

Claire I've rented us a nice little flat and I'll get a job in a bar or something

Ella You're a very sad person

Claire I thought you had doubts as to whether I was a person at all. (*She looks out of the window.*) Look at those lovely little gardens. The way the sun dapples the patios. They've planted magnolias in the multiplex car park – and look at the bins; they're rainforest green. It's going to be good for us here, I can feel it

Ella You said that about the last place

Claire That town we just left? I've already forgotten it

Ella How can you do that?

Claire Because it's over; it's gone

Ella You can't keep discarding the past like litter

Claire It kills me the way you cling on to things. You've got to live for now, Ella. That's what life's about; the rush of the present

Ella So what am I going to do in this dump?

Claire There are two schools –

Ella Not school again!

Claire What else can I do with you? You refuse to grow up; you won't behave like an adult –

Ella I feel ancient

Claire Well the effect is utterly teenage. You don't know how lucky you are to be at school; all that knowledge you've got, all that education. One day, Ella, you'll put it all together and you'll calculate the most important thing. How to survive

Ella Fine. School then

Claire Don't do English Literature again. It makes you depressed. Take nice, practical subjects. What about computing?

Ella Done it

Claire Music then

Ella No thanks

Claire Art

Ella Done it

Claire Or that subject where you make benches

Ella That is not a subject

Claire Can you do espionage at A Level?

Ella No

Claire What about cooking?

Ella You mean food technology?

Claire About time you learnt to cook

Ella What's the point?

Claire Ella, you don't have to eat all the stuff. It might just awaken something, some buried

Ella What?

Claire I don't know; life force. Do it for me

Ella Food technology

Claire And what else is there? A nice, light subject. You could do with a laugh. I know –

Ella I won't do it

Claire What's wrong with you?

Ella You can't make me

Claire I haven't even said / what it is yet

Ella I know what you're going to say. And how can I do that? It's all about laying yourself open to vicious attack, exposing your soul, performing like a flea in a / flea circus

Claire Oh come on. What subject can be so terrible?

SCENE TWO

Eleanor Scene two

Frank A-level Drama

Frank has sensitive eyes and a nervous demeanour. Mint is full of fervour and frustration. Mint's students Briggs, Point, Debit and Moon have perfected an air of cultivated boredom. They look as if they haven't had any fresh air in years. They look, in fact, like detached, fashionable, effortlessly nonchalant vampires.

Mint So, same old spoilt rebels and fashion victims as last year. Not allowed to swear with disappointment or I would. Briggs

Briggs Mint

Mint I'm gutted to see you; I thought you'd be shovelling fries for the rest of your life. And Debit

Debit Hello Mint

Mint You actually passed an exam then?

Debit Might have

Mint So there's a brain somewhere under all that hairspray

Debit It's mousse

Mint Well, let's see how long you last

Point No Mint, why don't we see how long you last?

Mint Well, we're off to a great start already. Now, I'm more than delighted to see that we have two new faces; some new blood. What are your names?

Ella Eleanor Wythenshawe

Mint And?

Frank Frank Adam Stein

Mint OK, Ella and – one name will do – Frank. I'm going to throw you in at the deep end. Either of you ever been in a play?

Ella/Frank No

Mint What do you know about Brecht?

Ella Um

Mint What's the first rule of making drama? Come on! First rule of making drama?

Debit Just say 'yes'

Mint Thank you, Debit. Being involved in making theatre involves being able to say 'yes'. Yes to an idea, yes to each other, yes to the energy, to the communal experience, yes to the mighty, universal 'yes'. That's what we aspire to in this class, isn't it?

Moon No

Mint So here we are. Four students who know each other inside out and two complete strangers. We've got to even that up, OK? I'm not going to suggest that we play name games or do trust exercises because that's Drama For Babies. So. The hot-seat. Frank; let's start with you

Frank What?

Mint takes Frank to a seat apart from the group.

Mint We're going to put you on the hot-seat

Frank What for? Why?

Briggs To scald your arse

Mint The hot-seat, guys, is a place of discovery, OK? Now we usually use it when we're 'in character', but I don't believe in having things all mapped out. So, I'm going to do something we've never tried before. I'm an instinctive teacher and my instincts are saying 'Go, Mint, go.' So I'm going to throw away the code of good practice and hot-seat you as yourself

Moon That's psychological torture, Mint

Mint It's going to be fun, OK?

Moon You could leave him permanently scarred

Mint Frank, the rest of the group will ask you questions

Moon You're infringing his human rights

Mint And your only job is to be truthful

Moon These are torture chamber conditions

Mint Oh that is ridiculous; it's a simple question and answer exercise. Are you being tortured, Frank?

Frank Um

Mint Eleanor, am I torturing you?

Ella Er

Mint By the end of the lesson, you'll be part of the gang. Now, think about everything that has brought you to this moment in time. People, when I clap my hands we're going to begin – so have your questions for Frank ready

Frank is full of dread. Mint claps.

Moon Do you feel that in doing this, Mint is infringing your human rights?

Frank Um

Briggs What's your name?

Frank I've already said it

Briggs I didn't listen

Frank Frank

Briggs Frank what?

Frank Stein

Briggs What's that short for?

Frank Franklin

Moon Your name's Franklinstein?

Briggs (*laughing*) Are you lying?

Frank My dad thought it was funny too. In fact, it was his last big joke before his sense of humour calcified and had to be removed

Point Are you a monster?

Frank Probably

Briggs Are you a wanker?

Mint Briggs!

Debit What school were you at before, Franklin?

Frank I'm home educated

Debit What?

Frank My mum and dad have been teaching me at home

Briggs How long for?

Frank Since I was a foetus

Moon You've never been to school?

Frank No

Point Why not?

Frank Well you'll have to ask my parents that really

Point No thanks

Frank Perhaps they were worried that I might grow up normal if I went to school so they decided to concentrate all their efforts on turning me into a freak

Point Why?

Frank Well, they're freaks, so I expect they just wanted me to fit in

Mint Frank, I can understand your defensiveness but just try to be open. No one is judging you here. Try and tell us how it really is being Frank

Frank Well to be fair on my mum and dad – that's Tina and Geoff – I think they had high hopes. They wanted me to fulfil my potential

Point What potential is that, Franklin?

Frank Well Tina and Geoff thought that if I learnt everything there is to know by the age of sixteen I might turn out to be a leader of men or a genius or something but I eventually had to point out the flaw in their plan and say 'Tina and Geoff, if you don't let me go to school and talk to some other people I'll end up in a nut house before I'm twenty' and to drive home my point I painted my bedroom black and drowned Tina's pot plants so, given that I've got four 'A's at A-level already, they decided to let me come. They see it as a bit of a gap year I think

234

Moon Did you say you were a genius?

Frank No, I'm a great disappointment

Point So what's your ambition, Frank?

Frank To get through the next half hour, really

Briggs Are you gay?

Mint Question not allowed

Point What medication are you on?

Mint Question not allowed

Moon Is God a man or a woman?

Frank Pardon?

Mint I think he means are you religious?

Moon No, I mean is God a man or a woman?

Frank Um, if there was a deity or creator I'd say it would be unlikely to have recognisable genitalia, so it would be hard to tell

Debit That's rude

Frank God probably transcends gender. The deity is probably asexual or even polysexual

Point Is that what you are, Frank?

Frank It may even be formless, without substance or indeed, dare I say it, non existent and therefore imaginable in any form

Debit I think you're shy about sex

Frank Is that a question?

Debit That's cute

Mint Only questions please

Debit You got any diseases?

Mint Not allowed

Debit Have you got a girlfriend, Frank?

Frank No

Briggs Have you got any friends at all?

Frank Yes, no, well it depends what you mean by friends. If you mean actual living people who like me, then no

Debit That's a bit sad isn't it?

Frank Well I used to have an imaginary friend but he moved out. He was great; really funny; much more daring than me. He used to subvert Geoff's quizzes and put lighted matches in the bin but in the end he had to go

Moon Why?

Frank Um, it turned out he was hiding pornography under the bed and Tina found it. She had a massive row with him and he came in to tell me he was leaving and I haven't seen him since

Ella Do you miss him?

Frank Yes

Debit So what d'you do for fun, Frank?

Frank Fun?

Moon Apart from the pornography

Frank That wasn't mine. It was imaginary

Mint One last question: what made you choose Drama, Frank?

Frank Um, my parents think it's a totally useless subject so it seemed like the obvious choice

Mint OK. Well done. Respect. Round of applause

Only Mint and Ella clap.

Briggs Frank

Frank Yes?

Briggs I love you

Frank flinches as if he's about to be hit.

Mint Eleanor, we're going to do something different with you, OK because asking intelligent questions is obviously beyond this group. We're going to play 'Lifegame'. Are you ready?

Ella No

Mint Learn to say yes. OK you barbarians, get off your chairs. Eleanor, I'm going be 'in role' as the interviewer. I'm going to try to find out who you are. (*To the rest of the group.*) And from what I glean in the interview, you lot are going to act out episodes in Ella's life

Point Bore me to death

Mint Someone's already beaten me to it, Point. Move these chairs

Ella and Frank move their chairs.

Ella That was brave

Frank No it wasn't

Ella I've never told the truth about myself

Frank Why not?

Ella Because no one would believe it

Mint I said move your chairs

The others move their chairs.

Frank I would

Ella Would you?

Frank Yes

Mint Right. Welcome to 'Lifegame'. Today we have as our special guest Eleanor Wythenshawe

Moon (*without enthusiasm*) Yo

Mint And we're going to be recreating before her very own eyes, episodes from her true life story. Eleanor, let's take a journey back to your early childhood. Can you share with us one of your earliest memories?

Ella Yes. I'm at Miss Skullpepper's school. It's a rainy night. I'm about six years old and I'm in bed with two of my friends

Point What sort of a school was this?

Ella It was a private orphanage. We all had benefactors who paid our fees. Most of us didn't know who they were. It's hard to describe really; such places don't exist any more.

Mint When was this?

Ella Must have been 1812

Mint Eleanor, I think I can feel some improvising going on here, which, in a different exercise would be totally cool but as this game's about the Real You, just stick to the truth for now, OK?

Ella I'll try

Mint So, take us back to your childhood

Ella I have a clear memory of celebrating the rout of Napoleon in Russia, that's why I'm so sure it was 1812. It was night

Briggs What were you doing in bed with two girls?

Ella Space was short and in winter the house was so cold

Briggs Were you naked?

Ella No

Debit What were your friends called?

Ella Harriet and Leticia

Mint OK, in the spirit of saying yes, we're going to go along with Ella's impro

Ella It's not an impro; it's a memory

Mint Point, you play Eleanor, Debit, you play Harriet, and Briggs, you're Leticia

Briggs No way

Mint I beg your pardon?

Briggs I'm not playing a girl

Mint Get over it, or get out. You're three in a bed

Briggs Tell me about my character

Ella Well, Leticia was very shy and sweet

Briggs Was she buff?

Ella Pardon?

Briggs 'Cause I'm not playing a dog

Ella She was dark and slight. I thought her beautiful. Her mother had died on her way home from the Gold Coast, after giving birth to her child of shame

Briggs Her what?

Ella Leticia was a child of shame. We all were. Harriet was the daughter of a tea merchant. Her mother was a whore, like mine

239

Debit Did you just say my mother was a whore?

Mint Eleanor, this certainly shows you've done some very interesting reading

Moon Listen, if this was 1812, how come you've not decomposed?

Ella I freely confess that I have stayed alive for all these years by drinking human blood

This causes a sensation; from shock to laughter.

Moon Yuk

Point Oh my god

Briggs That's disgusting

Debit You fucking weirdo

Mint Language

Point That is so freaked out

Moon Are you saying you're a vampire?

Ella Yes

Mint Eleanor, you know sometimes, when we've gone through a traumatic event, maybe bereavement or parental divorce, we retreat into fantasy to try to make sense of it all. Now, I don't think that's wrong. You've found a sympathetic ear here, / OK?

Debit No she hasn't

Point Is this supposed to be a drama lesson?

Mint Yes

Point So can we do some drama? Because this is like stepping into someone's nervous breakdown, Mint

Mint Let's have a tableau

Moon A tableau of what?

Mint Of Eleanor's story. She's at school, in bed with her friends, Leticia and Harriet

Moon What about me?

Mint You're the bed

> *They form a tableau. Point, as a vampire, is trying to suck Briggs' blood. Briggs swoons, girlishly. Debit does Munch's 'scream'. Moon attention-seeks as the bed.*

Mint Eleanor, is that how it was?

Ella No. We were six years old. They were asleep

Mint You two; you're asleep. You're six years old.

Briggs What is the point of being asleep? Are we supposed to learn something, being asleep?

Mint I ask myself that question every time you enter this Studio

Point We've spent enough time on this freakish shit

Mint Language! Eleanor, you've got a great imagination – and that's a vital tool for making effective theatre. Now, I don't want to finish yet, OK? I don't want you to walk out of here feeling that you've failed

Ella I won't

Mint I want you to leave this studio with your head held high, OK?

Ella I will

Mint Let's fast forward to the present, to the twenty-first century here and now and find out about the real Eleanor

Debit How many people have you drunk?

Briggs Do you suck anything else apart from blood?

Mint Who do you live with, Eleanor?

Ella Claire

Frank Who's Claire?

Ella She's my legal guardian

Debit What about your mum and dad?

Ella My father was a sperm. I never knew him

Mint And your mum?

Ella My mother is a vampire

Point She is a mental emergency, Mint

Mint OK, thank you Eleanor. One final question: what made you choose drama?

Ella giggles at their consternation.

Ella My hilarious sense of fun

Fillet Scene three

SCENE THREE

Moon Food Tech

Fillet And so, we begin our exploration with the humble root vegetable. They grow and thrive in the darkness, down in the rich heart of our mother earth. Gastronauts, have your peelers at the ready. Today, we're going to discover the science of mash

The students start peeling their root vegetables. Ella is working next to Frank.

Frank One thing's puzzling me; it's daylight

Ella Yes

Frank So if you were a vampire you'd be a little pile of dust. And I'm surprised you haven't cringed away from me shrieking by now

Ella Why's that?

Frank Because Tina made me garlic sandwiches for lunch

Ella True vampires live and move in society just like everyone else

Frank You haven't even got pointy teeth

Ella We don't die in daylight. We're not scared of garlic. We need only one victim a month. We can use our teeth but we find it more effective to let the blood with a knife

Frank You don't look like someone who's committed countless motiveless killings

Ella I do have a motive; my own survival

Fillet Make sure every blemish is removed. We need perfect specimens

Frank Eleanor, why on earth do you want to be a vampire?

Ella I spend most of the time wishing I was human

Frank But if you really were a vampire, why would you tell us?

Ella I've carried the secret for so long. When I told it I thought – I don't know – the walls would come crashing down. I might have known that no one would believe me. It was a mistake. No one usually notices me and now I've put myself in their sights

Fillet As we boil, we are going to observe the physico-chemical alterations of cell-wall constituents. What is the behaviour of the vegetable during cooking? Does it scream with pain?

Frank Well if it cheers you up I don't think I made any friends either. I don't know how to be in groups. I bring out the worst in people. They can probably sense that there's something not quite right about me

Fillet Let us meditate on the fate of the potato

Ella What's not right about you, Frank?

Frank I see the world too clearly

Ella Do you?

Fillet This humble tuber will lead us to ponder the morals of the food chain

Frank It's all in fragments but I see everything all the time, splintered, fractured, all of creation, the beauty, the horror, the madness, the inescapable ride towards destruction

Ella Yes

Frank The, the machinations of far-off power, the monsters of –

Ella Yes

Frank The terrible and ridiculous monsters of –

Ella Monsters of what?

Frank Sorry. Monsters of my own making. My own thoughts

Ella That's not what you were going to say

Frank No. Some days I think we're so monstrous that we'll destroy this earth, that's all

Ella You think humanity is monstrous?

Frank I don't know. Just asleep, maybe. Otherwise they'd do something

Ella They're happy, Frank; that's what it is. They appear asleep because they're happy

Frank How can you be happy in a world like this?

Fillet The subject of food on this planet is like a door, a metaphysical door opening between worlds; the scientific, the political, the environmental, the culinary and yes, the spiritual. Gastronauts, today, by peeling and boiling this potato, you will be taking your first step into a bigger universe

Frank So, where d'you keep your coffin, anyway?

Ella smiles.

Ella No one ever got around to burying me

Frank smiles.

Frank They're giving me an appointment to see the school shrink

Ella Me too

Eleanor comes forward.

Eleanor 1812. I am six years old. At night, I sleep in a bed with two other abandoned girls. They are my friends, Letty and Harriet.

Clara enters. Claire enters.

One night, I wake up in the dark to see a lovely woman in a shining dress sitting on our bed. She is staring at me, as if I am something precious. 'Who are you?' I say

Clara/Claire I'm your mother

Eleanor She replies and I am glad because my mother is dead and now I know she is an angel

SCENE FOUR

Clara Scene four

Clara exits.

Claire Happy hour

Claire's bar. A spectacle in which the whole company excepting Ella and Eleanor can take part: The bar staff are busy, the dance floor already crowded. Friday night Happy Hour. Socialising, hedonism, drink; male behaviours and female behaviours. The spectacle is full of energy and charge. People are already dancing. Moon plays the fool, Briggs shows off his wares, Point plays hard to get and Debit is drunk.

Claire watches from behind the bar, pulling a pint in slow motion, her serenity a counterpoint to all the movement – as if time is standing still for her. She focuses on Briggs, taking note of everything he does. Point tries to attract Briggs' attention. But Briggs has seen Claire staring at him – and now he's staring back. Point becomes angry. She yells:

Point Let's go

Briggs I can't

Point Why not?

Briggs I'm staring at her

Point looks at Claire and back to Briggs. Briggs ignores her.

Point Loser. Boy band loser

Point throws her drink at him. She exits. Briggs tries to wipe the alcopop off his face. Claire holds out a napkin. As Briggs takes it, the bar falls silent and all the movement continues in slow motion – as if Briggs has joined Claire in her pocket of time.

Claire What's your name?

Briggs Dave Briggs

Claire Well Dave Briggs, I'm Claire Wythenshawe

Briggs Wythenshawe? Shit; have you got a sister?

Claire Might have

Briggs What's her name?

Claire Eleanor

Briggs I don't believe it

Claire D'you know her?

Briggs She is something else, isn't she?

Claire Is she?

Briggs Well, you know; she's a bit

Claire Bit what?

Briggs Well, not meaning to disrespect your family but she's a fucking mentalist

Claire Oh

Briggs I'm not knocking her but

Claire Yeh, she's a strange one

Briggs What a looper. I can't believe she's got a sister like you

Claire How d'you know her then, Dave? You at school with her?

Briggs We both do drama. Man, she is so crap. I mean I know she's your sister and everything but you should see her trying to act. It is like watching a door trying to walk. Honestly, every week we have such a laugh at her. What a freakoid

Claire Well that's strange because Eleanor's only in Year Twelve

Briggs Yeah?

Claire So, you're in here underage drinking aren't you, Dave?

Briggs No

Claire I take a very dim view of that

Briggs How dim?

Briggs has one of his hands spread out on the bar. Claire leans forward, digging her elbow into the back of it. It brings her very close to him. The action in the bar has been going slower and slower. It now freezes.

Claire I could lose my job for serving you

Briggs I'm eighteen

Claire Show me some ID

Briggs I haven't got any. I never get asked cos I look so mature

Claire Get out

Briggs You see, you're saying that, but then you've got your elbow digging into the back of my hand so I can't actually move and so I'm getting mixed messages, you know? You smell lovely. What did you say your name was again?

Claire Claire

Briggs Claire, I know there's an age difference between us, but –

Claire You going to give me some bullshit, Dave?

Briggs Yeah, I was going to try

Claire About how you could prove you were all grown up by giving me the shag of a lifetime?

Briggs I was going to put it nicer than that

Claire Shall we cut to the chase?

Briggs Are you chasing me, Claire?

Claire I'm always in pursuit of pleasure, Dave. I like to live in the moment, in the eternal second of present time

Claire clicks her fingers. The bar suddenly empties. Briggs and Claire are alone.

D'you get me?

Briggs Yeh

Claire It's what I exist for. The present that I seek is random and indiscriminate and when I find it, there is no guilt or consequence. Just gratification and a moment of bliss

Briggs Wow

Claire Do you consent?

Briggs To what?

Claire To be my next pleasure

Briggs I think that's the best offer I've ever had

Claire Is that a yes, then?

Briggs You don't mess about, do you?

Claire Never

Clara takes the tray of drinks from Claire.

Clara Scene five

SCENE FIVE

Ella is sitting at a small desk.

Eleanor Coursework

Ella Write a short scene incorporating some of Brecht's techniques of alienation. Subject matter: a secret

> *Ella starts to write. Characters enter and position themselves as she speaks.*

A smoky, opulent room. Bodies lie drunkenly scattered in slumber. Ruthven, a gambler, and Darvell

Eleanor It is him

Ella Are at a card table. They are deep in their game. Clara Webb serves them with drinks.

> *Ruthven and Darvell are at a card table. Clara serves them with drinks.*

Clara, to us:

Clara This game of cards has been going on for the last five hours

Ella Ruthven:

Ruthven (*to Darvell*) I'll see your hundred and add two

Ella Darvell:

Darvell As you wish

Ella Darvell puts the last of his money on the table.

> *Darvell puts the last of his money on the table.*
> *Marianne, little more than a child, is cradling a drunk.*

Marianne (*to us*) You're in a house of ill repute. That's to say a brothel. That's to say a whorehouse, a fleshpot, full of sluts, trollops, tarts, strumpets, whores / and men

Eleanor And men

Ella writes, concentrating deeply.

Marianne You're lucky to be here – and so am I for that matter because it's one of London's finest. It is run by a woman called / Clara Webb

Eleanor Clara Webb

Marianne That's her. She survived her brutal childhood to become at the age of just twenty-one, London's pushiest and most ambitious whore

Clara Have you given that man what he's paid for?

Marianne I don't think he's capable really

Clara Chuck him out on the street then, and see to someone else

Marianne Clara Webb is a hardfaced slag if ever there was one but she pays all right. She won't let them beat us and there's always a doctor on call for our clap. What more could a prostitute ask for? It's 1816 after all; our life expectancy's just twenty

Ella Marianne exits, dragging the unconscious lord

Marianne What do I say next?

Ella Nothing

Marianne Is this it? Is this the whole of my part?

Ella Yes

Marianne But I'm an interesting character

Ella This story is not about you

Marianne exits, dragging the unconscious lord.

Clara My business turns over two thousand a year; all of it tax free. I plough a lot of it back in, providing the gentlemen with the very finest service in the most decadent surroundings. The profits I make, I secrete in a trust for my daughter

Ruthven has put more money on the table.

Ruthven So what are you to do, my lord? Where do we go from here?

Clara My daughter is the only thing in the world I love. When the midwife put her on my chest it was like a revelation. I had never known what love was until I felt her thundering heartbeat and smelt her tiny, bloodied head. Everything I have done since then has been for her

Darvell You'll need to accept a credit note. I've no more cash on me

Ruthven You're mistaking me for an idiot

Darvell Then what will you accept?

Ruthven Admit defeat. To go on is past reason

Clara My daughter's at a little school, where she'll learn how to marry and have a safe life. She's been told that her mother is dead. And the fiction will soon be true. In my profession we don't last long; even us clever ones. My lungs are rotting by inches – and I'm so angry about it I am spitting blood

Darvell I have something far more valuable than cash. Perhaps we should play for that

Ruthven What is it?

Darvell I have a secret

Ruthven Don't waste my time

Darvell I am offering you Time. I possess the knowledge, Sir, of a place where one can find life everlasting

Ruthven I'm insulted

Darvell Lord Ruthven, I can give you immortality. Where is the insult in that? I have seen it

Clara remains in the shadows, watching, fascinated.

Ruthven Immortality?

Darvell I was travelling through Asia Minor

Ruthven When?

Darvell Last spring. I was with a companion, an old friend of mine. We were nearing Byzantium,

Ruthven Constantinople, surely?

Darvell Byzantium, when he caught a fever and fell gravely ill

Ruthven What companion? His name, please

Ella/Darvell I have sworn never to reveal his name

Ruthven Then your story is full of holes

Darvell We were up in the mountains when his fever heightened and I knew that he would be dead before I could get him down. We came upon a high, deserted cemetery overshadowed by an ancient ruin; a temple with a half-blasted statue – of Artemis the huntress I think. In the heat of the day, with the birds circling above us, I laid him down to die

Ruthven Your powers of fiction are truly compelling, my lord

At some point during the next speech, Ella stops writing. She looks up, as if she is seeing what Darvell describes. Some of the sleepers begin to wake and listen.

Darvell He begged me for water. I went to look for it and when I returned, I saw on a rock nearby, a great bird with a serpent writhing in its beak. I shouted a curse at it. The bird tossed the serpent into the air and devoured it. Then it spread its great wings and flew with slow grace over the graves.

Ella and Eleanor spread their arms as if they are wings.

I gave my friend water. Upon his neck was a mark; red and angry – like the two-pronged bite of a snake. 'A miracle,' he whispered. With the last of his strength he made me swear to tell no one of his death – an oath that I am breaking now – and he said that in a month's time, when the moon rose –

Ruthven (*laughing*) Oh this is fabulous. This is too fantastic!

Darvell stands.

Darvell You don't deserve my secret. The thought of bestowing that priceless gift on you; you'd waste it.

Darvell looks straight at Clara.

I'd do better offering it to one of these girls. It'd be a fine thing, don't you think, to have an immortal whore? She could reap vengeance on mankind forever more

Ruthven This secret; have you taken advantage of it yourself? Are you immortal, sir?

Darvell I cannot describe the terror I felt in that place

Ruthven That's not an answer

All of the sleepers are now awake, listening.

Darvell My friend died

Ruthven He whispered the secret and died; perfect

Darvell I held him until he was as cold as the rock he lay on

Ruthven And then what?

Darvell I dug a shallow grave with my bare hands. The bird watched as I worked, perched on the broken goddess, a hunched silhouette. In the shadows, it seemed to have a human shape. I buried him, and then ran, stumbled through the night. At first light I saw the coast and found a town. I lay in a fever for a month, hallucinating terrors. I sent letters to Byzantium requesting aid

Ruthven Constantinople surely

Darvell And then, the evening that my boat was due to sail, I saw him – my friend – walking down by the harbour. At first I thought it was an apparition but he approached and gripped my arm. A strange light was in his eyes, a cold burning as if everything he looked upon was a source of wonder

Ruthven A cold burning; very nice

Darvell He shook me by the hand and thanked me for my care of him. He was freezing. I almost collapsed

Ruthven What a fabulous tale. I don't believe a word

Darvell That's because you have no faith. But you're longing for it to be true. My secret for your fortune. I will tell you all; the location of the cemetery, the significance of the bird and what befell my friend

Ruthven Where is he now?

Darvell Do we play?

Ruthven We play

Clara I hardly dared breathe, hoping that the stranger would –

Frank has entered. He stands just behind Ella.

Frank Hi

Ella startles. The characters in her scene freeze.

Ella, sorry did I scare you?

Ella No

Frank What are you doing?

Ella Drama coursework.

Frank Oh, how's it going?

Ella Fine. I'll put it away

She closes her book. Eleanor clicks her fingers. The characters in the scene disappear – except Clara.

Frank Mine's crap. I don't know what the hell he's talking about

Ella Who?

Frank Brecht. I mean, what's alienation anyway; will you go out with me?

Ella What?

Frank Don't say yes. Forget I asked. I've just come from my session with the shrink

Ella Oh

Frank Yes, he wants to refer me

Ella To whom?

Frank More shrinks. Have you seen him yet?

Ella No

Frank Don't tell the truth, will you? It's a bad mistake

Ella Thank you

Frank I've been watching a lot of vampire films

Ella What for?

Frank Oh, you know, thought I'd try and get to know you better. They say some great stuff. I mean once you get past the cape era you start wondering what they're a metaphor for; you know, it might be AIDS, heroin, anorexia, it might be the whole spiralling chaos of western society; not knowing the difference between good and evil any more – I mean not even being able to define the terms. And they're sexy and heartbroken and mostly Californian and they keep coming out with fantastic clichés like 'it's easier to succumb to the darkness within you than to fight the darkness without' and you get the feeling that if it wasn't for their nihilistic disregard for human life, they'd be the nearest thing we've got these days to gods

Ella Could you say that again?

Frank They used to be there just to terrify, as if the forces they represented had to be crushed by the righteous but we don't want to crush them now. They fascinate us. Perhaps we are all becoming vampires. I mean the way we devour everything. (*Pause.*) Can you see your reflection in a mirror by the way?

Ella Not properly, no

Frank That must be disturbing

Ella It was at first. I'm used to it now

Frank I love your psychosis, Ella. It's epic. It's amazing

Ella You don't listen

Frank I'm having a party. It's not really a party. I'm only inviting you. But it's my birthday. Will you come?

Ella Yes

Frank Great

Ella Frank, I love the way you speak

Frank Do you?

Ella You're so human

Clara The great thing about being a whore is that no one remembers you're there. I could have been furniture that night. The stranger lost. He forfeited his secret – and it fell right into my eavesdropping ear. Lord Ruthven soon departed for the East. I said that if he took me with him, he would get my constant service, free. By the time we reached Byzantium, my lungs were seeping blood. I prayed that I would live to see my daughter grow

Eleanor Scene six

SCENE SIX

Geoff Franklin's party

Tina Every year, since Franklin was five, he's had a geography quiz on his birthday

Tina is offering Ella a plate piled high with Jammie Dodgers.

Geoff Which African nation was known until recently as Zaire?

Tina makes a buzzing sound.

Tina

Tina The Congo

Geoff I'm sorry it's the Democratic Republic of Congo

Tina Silly me

Geoff What phenomenon produces opposite weather conditions to El Niño?

Tina Don't you like Jammie Dodgers, Eleanor?

Ella No thank you

Tina picks up another plate. Frank makes a buzzing sound.

Geoff Franklin

Frank La Nina

Geoff Ten points. Name two languages of Eritrea

Tina These are luncheon meat wraparounds. I made them myself

Ella No thank you

Geoff Come on, languages of Eritrea

Tina Oh!

Tina makes a buzzing sound.

Geoff Tina

Tina Tigrinyan and Arabic

Geoff Correct. One step closer to those chockies, Tina

Tina How exciting

Tina exits with her plates.

Geoff If I was looking at a Sprite, where would I be?

Frank sighs. He buzzes.

Franklin

Frank You'd be in the middle of a lightning storm above the clouds

Geoff Ten points. Name the debris deposited by a receding glacier

Ella Terminal moraine

Geoff I'm sorry; strictly speaking it's just moraine

Ella Oh

Frank Will you give her the points?

Geoff I was looking for the generic term

Tina enters with a plate piled high with tinned peach halves

Frank Give her the points, Geoff

Geoff Besides, I can't give her the points because she didn't buzz. You've got to buzz, Eleanor

Tina (*to Ella*) Do you like tinned peach halves? Franklin only gets them as a very special treat

Frank Dad, will you please give Ella the points?

Tina Have a peach half

Geoff Look, I'm the / quizmaster

Frank You're being totally unfair

Ella It doesn't matter

Frank Yes / it does

Geoff I can't award points unless they've been properly won according to the rules

Tina Go on, Eleanor; they're yummy

Ella No thank you

Tina Why not? What's wrong with them?

Geoff Name three different / kinds of –

Frank Right, I'm not playing

Geoff Franklin, I've bought these chocolates specially and I've spent time and effort compiling a question list. We do a geography quiz every year and we do it because you like it

Frank But I'm seventeen –

Geoff And I've taken that into account with my choice of questions. Now pull yourself together and name three different kinds of igneous rock

Frank I've had enough

Tina Pumice

Frank I don't want to play

Geoff Buzz, Tina, buzz

Tina makes a buzzing sound.

Tina

Frank Shut up

Tina Pumice, soapstone and –

Frank Shut up now or I'll swear

Geoff How dare you

Frank I don't want to do a geography quiz. I don't want peach halves. I don't want you or Tina at my party

Tina Franklin, how could you say that? I've made all your favourites

Geoff You are so ungrateful. We did everything right

Frank Oh, not / this again

Geoff We devoted ourselves to you. We could have had careers, holidays, fulfilling adult lives but no. We exhausted ourselves ensuring your development. You had a reading age of twelve by the time you were six years old and one day you'll appreciate what that meant

Frank It meant I was alone, always

Ella Let's go for a walk in the car park, Frank. The magnolias are coming into bloom

Frank Yes

Ella And the bins are rainforest green

Frank takes Ella's hand.

Frank Eleanor's a vampire

Tina Are you?

Ella Yes

Frank She's been alive for over two hundred years

Tina Have you?

Ella Yes

Tina I thought there was something about you, some whiff of depression

Frank Let's go

Tina I know what it is. You're an anorexic

Ella No

Tina I've got no patience with anorexics. I think you're rude and freakish. What's wrong with food?

Frank Come on

Ella I'm coming

Geoff Wherever you're going young lady, whatever weird starvation-induced visions you might be having, don't pull our son down with you

Tina Frank, she won't even eat peaches. She is embracing death. Keep away from her

Frank Scene seven

SCENE SEVEN

Claire Car park

Ella Embracing death?

Frank They won an award for designing this car park. I'm not surprised; if it wasn't for the cars you'd think you were in nirvana

Ella I'm not embracing death

Frank That was my best party yet

Ella I feel alive. I feel like I'm burning all the time. I feel raw with it

Frank Yes

Ella Something's going to happen. I can feel it coming; some terrible change

Frank What if it's not terrible? What if it's good? What if it's amazing?

Frank tries to kiss her. Ella breaks away.

Ella I have to go

Frank Where?

Ella Back to Claire

Frank I'll come with you

Ella You can't

Frank Why not?

Ella Claire won't like you

Frank Doesn't matter

Ella You won't like her

Frank Why not?

Ella Because she'll tell you lies. Claire will try and tell you that I'm only sixteen. She'll try to tell you that our mother died three years ago of cancer. She'll try to tell you that they couldn't trace our useless sperm of a father so they put me in a care home. Claire will tell you I got raped there. She came and found me all withdrawn and suicidal. She'll tell you how she fought for me, rescued me, breathed her life force into me. Since then, she has been my mother. She'll tell you that we go from town to town avoiding social workers and police, and that she sticks at low paid jobs because they give her opportunity to steal. She'll tell you how her magpie heart is satisfied by simple, little pleasures. She'll say she lives each moment to the full – and so she does. My sister-mother is ruthless Frank, and so am I

Frank You're not ruthless

Claire enters laden with bags from fashion stores.

Ella Why don't you believe me? I keep telling you the truth

Claire So who's this then?

They startle.

Frank Hi

Ella This is Frank. He's my friend

Claire Your *what*?

Frank Are you Claire? Great to meet you. I hear you're really good at shoplifting and identity theft

Claire (*to Ella*) They've called me into your school. Why would that be?

Ella I expect it's because someone tried to put a stake through my heart

Claire Come indoors. Now. (*Referring to Frank.*) And send that home.

She exits.

Ella You'd better go

Frank Why?

Ella She doesn't like you

Frank So what?

Ella Frank, I don't want to hurt you

Frank I wouldn't care if you did

Ella Scene eight

Frank Kiss me

Ella Scene eight

Frank That's what vampires do, isn't it?

Claire Scene eight

SCENE EIGHT

Mint Costume cupboard

Claire You can call me Claire

Mint Thank you so much for coming, Claire

Claire This is a nice classroom

Mint It's not a classroom, it's a drama studio

Claire Lovely and dark

Mint Yes, the darkness is a blank canvas upon which young imaginations can paint

Claire That's nice. What's this over here?

Mint The costume cupboard

Claire Oh, I like dressing up, don't you?

Claire picks up Marianne's costumes. Eleanor is watching from the shadows.

Mint Claire?

Claire These are super. Just like the real thing

Mint How long have you had sole care of Eleanor?

Claire Since I was legally able. When our mother died three years ago, Ella was put in a care home. I got her out as soon as I could and she's been with me ever since

Mint That's a great responsibility for someone so young

Claire There were monsters in that care home. I couldn't have left her

Mint Well; respect

Claire Sorry what's your name again?

Mint The kids like to call me Mint

Claire You've got very nice hands, Mint

Mint Thank you

Claire Can't help noticing. Very elegant fingers

Mint I'm sorry that I had to call you in

Claire What's she been up to, Mint? Because she's usually fine at school. Usually, I don't have to bother

Mint Well, it's hard to know where to start. As part of their coursework the kids have to write a short scene

> *Eleanor clicks her fingers. Ruthven enters. He is looking for something. He is not aware of Mint and Claire.*

Some kids just do little monologues but Eleanor's written the best part of a play – which is great / don't get me wrong –

Claire A play? Isn't she clever?

Mint The reason I've asked you to come in is the subject matter. Eleanor is quite convinced that she's a vampire

> *Clara enters. She watches Ruthven, unaware of Claire and Mint.*

Claire I'm sorry?

Mint Yes and not only that; she thinks you're a vampire too

Claire What??

Mint She says that you're not really her sister at all. She says you're her mother

Claire A vampire mother?

Ruthven (*to Clara*) What are you looking at?

Clara Nothing, my lord

Mint She says you were a nineteeth-century hooker

Claire You're joking

Mint And you became a vampire when she was just six years old

Claire I can't believe you're saying this

Ruthven (*to Clara*) Are you laughing at me?

Clara I wouldn't dare

Mint It's a really amazing story. I'm giving her an 'A'. She's got you eavesdropping following some lord to a ruined cemetery near Constantinople

Claire Istanbul, surely

Mint Lord Ruthven, she calls him. It's a name ripped off from an early vampire story. You're dying of consumption

Ruthven I've searched every rock and stone in this godforsaken ruin and no revelation has come. He lied to me. The secret is not here

Clara You don't see it, do you?

Clara is laughing. She is physically frail.

Ruthven Why are you laughing? What did he tell you? Where is it?

Clara shakes her head. Ruthven grabs her, furious.

You know how to get it, don't you? You'd better tell me, or by god you'll regret it

Mint He becomes totally incensed

Ruthven If you make a fool of me I swear I'll kill you

Mint And he strikes you – very violent, quite disturbing actually – In your weakened state, he kills you

Clara is dying – but smiling, triumphantly.

Clara Eternal life will only come to those prepared to die

Ruthven Then die

Mint He lobs you into a tomb and leaves you. By the next full moon, he's preparing to sail for home and you find yourself reborn

Claire Wow

Ruthven has picked up Marianne's costume. He embraces it, as if it is a girl.

Mint You wake with a terrible thirst and set out to find Lord Ruthven. He's in a hotel room with a little girl he's paid to entertain him

Clara My lord

Ruthven Clara

Clara touches him. Ruthven is terrified.

You're cold

Clara I'm burning

Mint You realise that the worst fate for him would be to die slowly of all the sexually transmitted diseases he's picked up over the years

Clara takes Marianne's dress from Ruthven.

Clara Your own corruption will kill you. You'll never be immortal – But this girl will

Mint And you kill and drink his innocent prostitute right in front of him. Just to show him how powerful you are

Claire I'd never do that. No way. I'd never kill an innocent

Mint Eleanor says you're indiscriminate

Claire She must hate me

Mint You show no mercy

Claire Mint, I'm stunned

Mint Can we come out of the cupboard, please?

Eleanor clicks her fingers. Clara and Ruthven exit.

Claire How could she write about me like that?

Mint The trouble is, her vampire delusion is so carefully maintained and so convincing that the rest of the group has completely rejected her. It doesn't help that one of them recently disappeared; a kid called Dave Briggs – ran away from home, we think

Claire Dave what?

Mint Briggs. D'you know him?

Claire Never come across him

Mint Eleanor had taken an active dislike to him and now the others are accusing her of macabre and outlandish crimes

Elsewhere. Point, Moon and Debit enter. They are wheeling a trolley on which Ella is tied – Hannibal Lecter style. She has a sock shoved in her mouth.

Debit What have you done with him?

Point Where's Dave, you freak?

Point is brandishing a wooden stake. Ella tries to speak.

Debit Don't lie to us you bloodsucking bitch – where's he gone?

Point He'd never disappear like that

Moon He was too boring

Point And we were in love

Debit So tell us where he is before we put a stake through your heart

Ella is furiously trying to make herself understood.

Moon Look, if you took the sock out of her mouth she might talk. Otherwise it's just mindless torture and I'm a member of Amnesty, OK, so I'm a bit uncomfortable with this?

Point (*pulling out the sock*) Where's Briggs?

Ella You have no idea how hard I'm fighting not to use my powers, not to tear through these bonds and make a bloodbath of your flesh. You have no idea how much self-control and godlike compassion I am exercising

Debit That is so pathetic

Point What did you do to Briggs?

Ella Nothing

Point He was beautiful

Ella He was an idiot; just the kind of conceited moron I'd love to have killed, but I didn't

Point Then where is he?

Moon Look, there's a very real possibility that he just ran away. You know how much he wanted to be interesting

Point He'd never have gone without me. We had dreams. We were going to live in a van and write songs about meaningful sex

Ella I wish I had claimed him as prey, I wish I'd gorged on his every last corpuscle – but I didn't

Point Something terrible has happened to him, I just know it

Ella I'd feel I'd done humanity a service in culling him, but I didn't

Debit You're going to pick us off one by one aren't you?

Point Unless we finish you off first – you mutant

Debit Stake her

Point Watch her age two hundred years. She'll decompose before our eyes

Debit And her scream will rip out her throat

Point raises the wooden stake.

Moon I'm freaking out! I'm freaking out! I don't know what to do! We need a teacher

Moon hurriedly wheels Ella off.

Debit Bring her back here, Moon

Point I want violence! Violence!

Point and Debit exit after Moon.

Mint We found her outside the staff room, still tied to the trolley. There was a wooden stake shoved down her cardie

Claire My poor baby

Mint Obviously we had to get you in

Claire I've tried so hard to be a mum to her – and a sister

Mint I'm sure you've done everything you could, but Claire –

Claire She's my whole life, Mint. Everything I do is for her

Mint I've been speaking to the head teacher and to her counsellor. He's keen to refer her to psychiatric services who –

272

Claire You're not sending her to shrinks. They'd split us up

Mint Maybe a short stay in a residential –

Claire NO WAY

Mint Look, we're very sympathetic but we can't ignore her problems. Eleanor needs more help that this school can currently offer

Claire Mint, they might try to take her away from me – and then my heart would break; right here

Claire has taken Mint's hand and put it on her heart.

Mint What are you doing? Let go of my hand please, Claire

Claire moves closer.

Claire You want to help me, Mint; you know you do. Look at me

Mint Claire, I made a decision a long time ago that relationships, feelings, human interaction; these things would only happen in the theatre for me – because real emotion doesn't come near the wild spectacle of the stage. I live for creating drama. I've made it my life

Claire That's terrible. You must be so alone

Mint I'm never alone. Anything can come out of this darkness, any character, any marvellous scene. I've been happy to wear down my health in the service of theatre

Claire You're so devoted

Mint Yes – and the pinnacle of my achievement is A-Level Drama. It sustains me every year. Claire, the worst thing about all of this, about your sister's breakdown, Briggs disappearing, the traumatising bullying, the very worst thing

273

Claire What is it?

Mint The group won't work together. They are saying 'no'. Please try to understand

Claire I'll try

Mint If I don't get Eleanor out of my class, they'll get a bad mark in their practical. They might even get 'D's

Claire looks at Mint in utter disbelief. She moves closer.

Claire My heart bleeds for you. It really does

Eleanor Scene nine

SCENE NINE

Eleanor is sitting at Ella's desk. Ruthven is behind her.

Ruthven Education

Eleanor writes.

Eleanor 3rd of January, 1822. Beloved diary, I love your clean white pages. They're like sheets in which my lonely thoughts can lie. Today I am sixteen

Ella enters. She is wearing a modern, pink nightdress.

Ella Sixteen

Eleanor rises. Ella sits in her place and starts writing.

Ella/Eleanor Perhaps I will prick my finger on a spinning wheel and die

Ella Leticia and Harriet enter. Bettina, a maidservant, follows

Letty and Harriet enter. Bettina, a maidservant, follows.

Letty Eleanor?

Harriet There's a gentleman to see you –

Letty A gentleman in our school

Eleanor A gentleman?

Harriet He said

Ruthven I'm here for Miss Webb

Letty For you, for you

Bettina (*taking Ruthven's coat*) I got to take his coat and as he gave it to me he said

Ruthven Thank you, child

Bettina And his hand brushed against my wrist, like a feather and Oh, it was like lightning, miniature lightning rushing up my arm

Eleanor Who is he?

Ella Lord Ruthven

Harriet/Letty Lord Ruthven

Bettina Him

Eleanor But I don't know him. I've never heard of him

Bettina Mrs Skullpepper led him into the library. She asked him the purpose of his visit. He said

Ella/Ruthven I have news of her mother

Bettina Mrs Skullpepper tried to question him but he sent her away

Ruthven My time is precious

Harriet He wants to see you alone

Letty Alone

Harriet/Letty We're so jealous

Eleanor He has news of my mother?

Bettina He touched me right there. I will never wash my wrist again

Eleanor My mother is dead

Letty Look at his jacket

Harriet The best tailoring – just the best

Bettina Smell it

Harriet Oh you can't!

Bettina It smells of late nights

Letty Tobacco, some kind of faint scent

Harriet Don't! He'll be able to tell

Letty It smells of male

Bettina Did you see his boots?

Harriet Spattered with mud from his manly life

Eleanor My mother is dead. Why is he here?

Harriet It must be something dreadfully important

Bettina His expression

Letty It was grave, Ella

Bettina Dark and brooding

Harriet As if he's prey to some cureless inquietetude of mind

Eleanor Some what?

Harriet He looks dangerous

Eleanor All men look dangerous when you're us. We've never seen any men

Letty He looks somehow blighted too

Bettina Like a poor, wounded beast

Harriet Full of dark mystery

Eleanor Oh, stop it

Bettina When he touched me, it was lightning I felt. I'll never, never be the same again

Bettina, Harriet and Letty exit. Eleanor approaches Ruthven.

Eleanor My Lord? I am Eleanor Webb

She curtsies.

Ruthven Eleanor Webb. Look at you

Ruthven stares at Eleanor. She grows uncomfortable.

I know your mother

Eleanor My mother is dead, my lord

Ruthven Nonsense. I've been searching for her this past decade – ever since she stole my secret – and last week I found her. She is living not two miles from here and doing what she does best

Eleanor My lord?

Ruthven Keeping a brothel, a kennel, a dungheap, a whorehouse – do you understand me, child? Your mother sells human flesh

Eleanor (*to Ella*) Stop writing

Ella No

Eleanor Stop now

Ella/Ruthven And she preys on her customers like a carrion crow; picks them off one by one

Eleanor You know how it ends; please stop

Ella I don't understand you. My mother is dead

Eleanor (*to Ruthven*) I don't understand you. My mother is dead.

Ruthven Is that what they've told you?

Eleanor (*to Ella*) Don't make me go on!

Ruthven My dear, they have nourished you on lies

Ella/Eleanor What do you mean?

Ruthven I'll be brief with you, Miss Webb. Your mother stole a secret from me and I'm here to steal something from her

   Ruthven takes hold of Eleanor.

Eleanor Let me go

Ruthven Imagine my delight when I discovered you existed. Her precious, treasured daughter, the jewel she's hidden away for all these years

Ella/Eleanor My mother is dead

Ruthven Your mother believes she is invincible. But I will cause her pain. I will make her rage – as I raged when she stole my secret

Eleanor (*to Ella*) Don't let him touch me

Ruthven I am dying, Miss Webb. I could have lived forever but I'll soon be dead. Your mother robbed me of eternal life and I will rob you. You will share my disease

Eleanor Mother

Ruthven A terrible disease for an innocent to catch. For there is only one way to catch it, Miss Webb

Eleanor Mother

Ruthven And when I have finished with you –

Ella and Eleanor close their eyes and put their hands over their ears. The action freezes. Claire enters.

Claire What are you doing? Ella

Claire takes Ella's hands from her ears.

I've just been to see your teacher. Why are you telling people that we're vampires?

Ella Leave me alone

Claire They will cart you away to the nuthouse

Ella Get out

Claire We were doing so well here

Ella OUT

Claire Why are you like this?

Ella YOU MADE ME LIKE THIS

Claire grabs Ella's script.

Claire You are condemning yourself. They will section you. And once they write personality disorder on your notes they will throw away the key. I am fed up trying to save you

Ella Suppose I don't want to be saved?

Claire Is this your play?

Ella Yes

Claire How dare you

Claire reads the scene.

Ruthven Eleanor Webb. I know your mother

Eleanor My mother is dead

Ruthven A dungheap. Carrion crow

Eleanor I don't understand

Ruthven Nourished on lies

Eleanor My mother is dead

Ruthven A secret

Eleanor Let me go

Ruthven Disease

Eleanor Mother

Ruthven Terrible for an innocent

Eleanor Mother

Ruthven And when I have finished with you –

Claire stops reading.

Claire Very clever. What comes next?

Ella I can't write it

Claire A rape scene without a rape?

She drops the script.

Why are you calling him Ruthven?

Ella doesn't respond. Claire exits. Ruthven releases Eleanor.

Ruthven Welcome to the adult world. Welcome, Miss Webb. Welcome to a slow death. Welcome, you whore

He throws a coin at her.

Give my regards to your mother

Ruthven exits. Ella goes to Eleanor. They cling to each other.

Ella Eleanor, he didn't kill you

Eleanor I'm still dying

Ella He didn't kill you

Eleanor I'm dying

Ella Why have you let him win?

Eleanor fights her way out of Ella's arms. She exits.
Ella is shocked that she has gone. Claire returns with a
suitcase.

Claire Right. Get packing

She starts putting Ella's things in the case.

Ella What are you doing?

Claire We have to go

Ella Why?

Claire Because you've been telling people we're
vampires!

Ella (*suspiciously*) What have you done, Mother?

Claire Don't call me that. I'm your sister

Ella What have you done?

Claire Nothing

Ella Then I'm not leaving

Claire We have to

Ella Why?

Claire Because you're right. This place is killing you.
You're going smalltown crazy. We'll go to London,
wherever you like –

Ella I want to stay here

281

Claire Why?

Ella Because the magnolias are blooming. The bins are rainforest green

Claire When did you last eat?

Ella What's that got to do with anything?

Claire When did you last feed yourself? (*Pause.*) You're so unique Ella, you're so amazing. When are you going to start living? Look at you, you're starving

Point Scene ten

SCENE TEN

Fillet The Beast

The students of A-Level Food Technology gather themselves. Ella is ill, withdrawn.

In order to do my proper duty to you as a teacher of Food Technology

Frank Eleanor

Fillet I have been trying to teach you about every edible thing on this planet. We've gone into the Earth and returned bearing fruits

Frank I'm leaving Tina and Geoff. Come to London with me. We'll find somewhere to live, even if it's a protest tent on Westminster Green

Ella I can't

Frank Yes you can

Fillet We've spent many weeks delving into the vegetable. And now we must encounter the beast

Frank We can get crap jobs and at nights we'll lie there

Fillet A new heading. Meat

Frank Trying to find stars in the light pollution, thinking up ways to attack the consumerist system

Fillet Franklin Stein! This lesson may bring you learning that will affect the rest of your life. I want you young people to leave my class secure in the knowledge that if society broke down and all the supermarkets closed, you could walk into a field, butcher an animal and prepare enough food to feed a village for a week

Debit (*to Point*) Have you heard about Mint?

Point What?

Fillet I'm harking back to a purer time, when we didn't consume meat from factory abattoirs, vacuum sealed in plastic, I'm harking back to a time when we stroked and petted every beast we ate

Debit Found this morning; dead as a doornail in the costume cupboard

Point No! Poor Mint

Fillet If we killed it, we'd respect it

Debit They're trying to tell us it was a stroke

Point No

Fillet I am going to teach you to respect the beast. And one day, when order breaks down into violence and chaos and starving hordes are roaming the land, you will be the one who can hold up your cleaver and say 'I did A-Level Food Technology. I can save humanity!' So today, adults of tomorrow, we shall begin our study of the beast by investigating its life force. We are going to make blood pudding

Moon faints. Fillet arranges the ingredients.

Onions finely chopped, a kilo of diced pork fat, two metres of intestine, a litre of double cream, oatmeal, barley, salt, mace

Fillet lifts a bowl filled with pig's blood on to the table. Ella stares at it longingly.

And here is our pig's blood, identical to human blood by ninety-eight per cent. Isn't that a strange fact? We are only two per cent different from a pig. Mint is dead. Mint, my comrade, your teacher, has fallen. We shall have a minute's silence at the end of the lesson but for now, contemplate this: GOD, WHY DID YOU MAKE US ONLY TWO PER CENT DIFFERENT FROM A PIG? Forgive me. I'm wreckage this morning. I loved Mint. Mint was an innocent. You get gallons of blood from each mature beast but here, I have just two litres

Frank Eleanor

Ella has walked up to the desk as if in a trance.

Fillet Now, the pudding sticks better if the blood is warm. Get back to your seat. Get back I said. What are you doing?

Ella Forgive me

Ella lifts the bowl. She puts it to her lips.

Starving

The class erupts into screams. Pandemonium, as Ella drinks the blood.

Point It's her!

Debit Her!

Point She killed Briggs

Debit She killed Mint

Debit/Point Vampire!

A cacophony of screaming. Frank is watching, aghast.

Blackout.

Clara Eleven

SCENE ELEVEN

In the darkness:

Ruthven Deathbed

Clara Eleanor

Eleanor Who's there?

Clara strikes a light. She is sitting on the end of Eleanor's bed. Eleanor is wearing Ella's pink nightdress.

Who are you?

Clara My name is Clara Webb

Eleanor I've seen you before. When I was a child

Clara You're right

Eleanor You are an angel

Clara I used to climb in through your window and watch you while you slept

Eleanor My mother

Clara My girl

Eleanor I'm dying

Clara There's no need to die. I'll take you away with me

Eleanor A man was here

Clara I'll teach you how to live

Eleanor He has killed me

Clara You shall not die

Eleanor Mother

Clara I'll never leave you. Never leave you again

Clara gently bares Eleanor's neck. She blows out the light.

Claire Scene twelve

SCENE TWELVE

Darvell Immortal

Ella Let me out of here! Let me out

Fillet You stay in that drama studio, down there in the darkness where you belong. My lab looks like carnage; it's apocalyptic. I'm not letting you out until they're here

Ella Who?

Fillet The mental healthcare professionals, those in authority, those with absolute power

Ella You've got no right to keep me

Fillet Mint had files on you. Mint knew something was wrong

Ella What files? I demand to see them

Fillet Mint was trying to help you and look what you did

Ella Nothing! I've done nothing

Claire is robbing a till.

Frank Claire

Claire Who's asking?

Frank I'm Frank, your sister's friend

Claire Her what?

Frank You've got to come

Claire Where is she? What's happened?

Frank They've contained her – locked her in the drama studio

Claire What's she done?

Frank She drank blood

Claire You're lying. You're sick for saying that

Frank She needs to get away. I want to take her to London with me

Claire You what?

Frank I'm running away from my parents

Claire How teen and cute

Frank I want to take Ella with me

Claire Well you're just her type, I must say. Earnest, clueless, about as sexy as a pair of sandals. But I know what's best for Eleanor and as a matter of fact I'm taking her away. We're leaving now. And no one at that shit-heap school will ever hear of us again

Claire slams the till and makes to go.

Frank Maybe that's why she did it

Claire Did what?

Frank Drank the blood – an act of protest

Claire Against what?

Frank Against you. Eleanor's written a story where she's spent two hundred years with you. So that must be what it feels like

Claire Ella couldn't survive without me

Frank I think it's the other way round. I think you rely on her for everything. You don't let anyone near her, do you? You're worse than my parents.

Claire Well right now, I'm all she's got

Frank No you're not

Claire If it wasn't for me she'd be dead

Frank Personally, I think you're slowly killing her

Claire Is that right? Is that what you personally think?

Frank Yes it is

Claire Are you in love with her, little Frank?

Frank That's none of your business

Claire And you're going to solve all her problems are you? A little no-brain schoolboy?

Frank Actually, I have the IQ of a genius

Claire Well you'll find your local asylum is stuffed full of people with the IQ of a genius. And I'm not about to let Eleanor join them

Frank Do you know anything about Mint's death?

Claire I beg your pardon?

Frank When we met you in the car park you were on your way to meet him. And next morning he was dead. And Briggs. Point saw you talking to him, the night he went away

Claire You're playing a very dangerous game, little Frank

Frank makes his fingers into a crucifix.

Frank Are you threatening me?

Claire I'm just giving you a warning. I am by nature indiscriminate. I learnt to be promiscuous when I was still a child. But with Ella, it's all about love

Frank What do you mean?

Claire It's tragic really. It's like the saying with her; 'each man kills the thing he loves'

Frank Ella's not a man

Claire When she's finished with you, you'll be left hanging like a cheap suit on a washing line. We use people up. That's what we do. We're survivors

The drama studio. Ella has dressed up in a costume from the costume cupboard.

Eleanor enters, wearing Ella's pink nightgown. She starts to write.

Ella I need a pen and paper. Every prisoner should have the means to write. It says so in the Geneva dramatic convention. I demand a pen and paper

Eleanor People will always believe the most fabulous tale you can tell. The fabulous tale is the one that they long for. It must be unprovable, impossible, fantastical. To believe it then becomes an act of faith

Ella An act of faith

Eleanor Enter Darvell. He is dressed as a doctor of psychiatry

Darvell enters. He is dressed as a doctor of psychiatry.

289

Darvell Eleanor? My name is Darvell

Ella What do you want?

Darvell I'm a doctor

Ella What kind of doctor?

Darvell The kind who seeks to heal

Eleanor Eleanor is looking at Darvell as if he stirs an ancient memory

Ella Do I know you?

Darvell I'd like to help you, Eleanor

Ella May I have a pen and paper?

Darvell In due time, you shall have everything you want

Ella I need to finish my story

Darvell Of course you do

Ella It's about a girl. She meets a boy. He's a genius, but every bit as friendless as she. The girl has been alone for a long time. The boy tries to bring her back to life. But her past is gone; the present hurts; she has no future. She is the beetle who crawled into amber

Darvell What do you mean?

Ella I cannot die, though I know I am dead. I am hungry all the time but I cannot eat. My desires are destructive. I live off others. I am alone. I am a vampire. / Do you believe me?

Eleanor Am I mad?

Darvell I don't know what madness is. There is only pain and our ability to bear it. Sometimes, when the pain is too great, the mind can no longer withstand and it breaks

Ella When we devour, it's because it's our nature

Darvell But our natures are able to change. Change can be painful. It can feel like a mortal blow

Ella It hurts

Darvell All pain can be relieved

Ella I feel immortal sir, but not alive

Eleanor clicks her fingers. Claire and Frank enter.

Claire She's sixteen. She's a sixteen-year-old kid. You can't legally section her; she's too young

Darvell In order to help her, I need to take her away

Frank Ella, he's from a secure institution. Don't go with him. There's nothing wrong with you

Claire (*to Frank*) Listen, you tank-topped desperado, you got no right to be here and nothing to say. This situation is none of your business

Frank Yes it is

Claire I'm her legal guardian. She's mine

Darvell Eleanor is free to come with me

Claire Ella, he thinks he's God in a white coat

Ella Mother

Claire I'm not your mother. Come away with me

Darvell Eleanor, you can let go. You can rest

Claire Don't leave me

Clara Please

Claire/Clara I got nothing else

Ella (*turning to him*) Frank

Frank I want nothing from you

Claire Come with me

Darvell You're under my protection now

Ella Frank

Frank Run. This way. Quick

Ella No; through here

Eleanor clicks her fingers. The action freezes, as if Frank and Ella are alone in a pocket of time.

Frank This isn't the exit

Ella I know

Frank Where are we?

Ella The costume cupboard

Frank Then we're stuck

Ella Lock the door. Keep them out

Clara, Claire and Darvell exit.

Frank We're trapped, Ella. Why didn't you run for the exit?

Ella I love it in here. You can be anything you like

Frank We'll get away somehow. Come to London with me

Ella We'll protest

Frank Yes

Ella Against what?

Frank Ella, unless we act, unless we stop devouring everything, unless we try to understand what it means to be human, in two hundred, a hundred, in fifty years' time . . . we'll be nothing. We must protest, even if we're inarticulate, even if our only word is 'no'. There's so much to do. Don't hide away in your pain

Ella I love the way you speak

Frank tries to kiss her. She stops him.

I'm writing a story, Frank. It's a vampire story

Frank I know. But it's just a story. It isn't real. You're real

Ella Frank

Eleanor (*writing*) Frank, you can't have a vampire story

Ella You can't have a vampire story

Eleanor Unless

Ella Unless there are vampires in it

Eleanor I'm sorry

Ella I'm so sorry

Frank Don't be sorry

Frank and Ella kiss. A beautiful kiss, straight from a dark Gothic tale. With one hand, Ella bares Frank's neck. Eleanor watches them.

Darvell Thirteen

SCENE THIRTEEN

Eleanor Byzantium

Morning light. Birdsong.

Darvell Good morning, Eleanor

Eleanor I've finished my story, Doctor

Darvell Well done

Eleanor I worked all night. Right though the darkness

Darvell That's very good. I look forward to it. You have a wonderful flair

Eleanor Thank you

Darvell Now, you've been alone in here long enough. It's time to come down. Your sister is coming to visit

Eleanor My mother?

Darvell Your sister. Did you forget?

Eleanor turns away.

Perhaps you'll try and eat a bit of something for her today

Eleanor nods.

That's very good. Now, what would you like to wear? Eleanor, will you choose some clothes?

Eleanor I'd like to wear my costume, please

End.

WELCOME TO THEBES

To Mihret Tekie
on her journey throughout the time of writing

Welcome to Thebes was first performed in the Olivier auditorium of the National Theatre, London, on 15 June 2010. The cast was as follows:

THEBANS

Megaera Madeline Appiah
Sergeant Miletus Michael Wildman
Junior Lieutenant Scud Omar Brown *or* René Gray

Eurydice Nikki Amuka-Bird

Prince Tydeus Chuk Iwuji
Pargeia Rakie Ayola

Haemon Simon Manyonda
Antigone Vinette Robinson
Ismene Tracy Ifeachor

Tiresias Bruce Myers
Harmonia Alexia Khadime
Polykleitos Daniel Poyser

Aglaea Aicha Kossoko
Thalia Joy Richardson
Euphrosyne Pamela Nomvete

Eunomia Zara Tempest-Walters
Bia Karlina Grace
Helia Clare Perkins
Eris Irma Inniss
Xenophanes Cornelius Macarthy

ATHENIANS

Theseus David Harewood
Phaeax Ferdinand Kingsley
Talthybia Jacqueline Defferary
Enyalius Victor Power
Plautus Daniel Fine
Ichnaea Jessie Burton

Director Richard Eyre
Designer Tim Hatley
Lighting Designer Neil Austin
Music Stephen Warbeck
Choreographer Scarlett Mackmin
Sound Designer Rich Walsh

Characters

Megaera
a soldier

Sergeant Miletus

Junior Lieutenant Scud

Eurydice
President of Thebes

Prince Tydeus
Leader of the Opposition

Pargeia
a senator

Haemon
Eurydice's son

Antigone
her niece

Ismene
her niece

Tiresias
a seer

Harmonia
his guide

Polykleitos
a mechanic

Aglaea
Foreign Secretary

Thalia
Minister of Justice

Euphrosyne
Minister of Finance

Eunomia
a student of law

Bia
Minister of Trade and Industry

Helia
Minister of Agriculture

Eris
Chief of Police

Xenophanes
Minister of Education

Theseus
First Citizen of Athens

Phaeax
his aide

Talthybia
a diplomat

Enyalius
Head of Athenian Security

Plautus
Athenian Security

Ichnaea
Athenian Secret Service

Aides, bodyguards, attendants, soldiers, citizens

A city named Thebes,
somewhere in the twenty-first century.

Prologue

Three Theban soldiers enter: Megaera, a woman of twenty, Miletus a sergeant of maybe thirty, Junior Lieutenant Scud, a boy of thirteen. It is dawn.

Megaera OK shut up

Miletus Anyone still talking now shut up

Scud SILENCE

Megaera Nobody make any sudden moves, nobody get up

Miletus Stay in your seats

Scud PHONES

Miletus Phones – any fucking disco tunes and I will not answer for my men

Scud You check them NOW

Megaera Put the booklets down. Don't read that shit

Scud All of you make sure those fuckers don't go off

Miletus Listen to the Junior Lieutenant – he don't like mobile phones

Scud They have bad energy and they affect your brain. I'm telling you for your own good

Megaera Anyone who wants the toilet I don't care. You missed your chance

Scud You've got to look for bomblets

Miletus I am insulted if the truth be known

Scud Get looking

Miletus Our orders are to search for unexploded sub-munitions. No equipment. For our mine detector we have got the Junior Lieutenant here

Scud They are called bomblets – and they're yellow.
Look like little cans of fizz
And children pull on them because their thirst is bad
BOOM
And you become a rain of meat
And women pulling bits of you from out their hair
And screaming oh disgusting get me some shampoo

Miletus What are you doing?

Megaera I'm sitting down here on my arse

Miletus Why?

Megaera I haven't finished with these people

Miletus What d'you want with them?

Scud jumps on some rubble.

Scud BOOM

Megaera To welcome them to Thebes

Miletus Don't tell them all your shit

Megaera Why not?

Miletus They'll leave

Megaera Are you the expert?

Miletus I would leave

Megaera I'm going to tell them Theban politics

Miletus No one understands that

Scud jumps on another pile of rubble.

Scud BOOM

Miletus Easy, son
Be easy
You stay right by my side

Miletus moves away, with Scud. Megaera holds up her gun.

Megaera The only politics in Thebes is this.
This has been the government for years.
I don't know how it started; I don't care
Some brother fighting brother for the power.
My politics began the day the soldiers came.
This is my shit and if you're scared to hear it
Close your eyes.
We heard their guns and ran.
I could feel bullets whooshing past my face.
I saw a man turn round and try to stop one with his
hand
Because he thought 'what's this?'
As if the bullet was a fly.
Whoosh
They trapped us by the river.
If I could describe you how it felt
They way they held me down and tore
You would be sick I know you would
Or scream and we'd be here all day
While you had counselling and cried.
After five or six I was unconscious I suppose.
The soldiers must have thought that I was dead
Because when I came to, I found myself
In a pile of bodies. My mother
And my sisters seethed with ants.
This is your introduction to our state
'Cause everybody has a tale like this.

I slipped into the river, floated to the fields
Time was not even. It was odd
It bends and it's misshapen in my mind
A day was like a month, a month a year
I don't think that I spoke one word.
I ate forest nuts and beetles, poor old me
My monthly bleeding never came again

Scud BOOM

Megaera And then Miletus found me
He's the sergeant there, my brother now.
He put this gun into my hand and
Made me human once again.
When we fall upon our enemies –
Always the men who did that to me –
Feelings come on me like I don't know
I am not scared of anything
No pain about my family
No cares
I am all powerful, all fire
I am revenge, Megaera; I am fury
Whoosh.
The furies have no laws other than their own
Which even Zeus himself has to obey.
These are my laws now
And this, my life of politics.
Peace?
Never, not for me

Miletus Megaera

Scud Dead bloke

*Miletus and Scud have discovered a corpse. Megaera
approaches.*

Miletus Look at that uniform
New boots, the golden braid

Scud spins, startled. He raises his rifle.

Scud Felt fingers down my back

Megaera Well, they ain't his
He's maggot food

Miletus This is Polynices

Megaera How do you know?

Miletus His necklace

Megaera Fuck

Miletus General Polynices

Scud Did we fight for him?

Miletus No. He's the one who pulled you out of school,
his men –

Scud reacts to this, the memory like a cuff.

When I picked you up I was with Creon's men, remember?
We fought for him till the stupid fucker got dismembered.
Then for Adrastus till he set himself on fire. Then we were
in the forest fighting everyone. Last we joined Eteocles.
He's the one who still had food

Scud Who do we fight for now?

Megaera That is the question, Scud

Scud I fought for you

Miletus I know

Scud The ghosts are grey

Miletus Come on

Miletus leaves with Scud.

Megaera Welcome
Welcome to Thebes

Act One

SCENE ONE

Enter Tiresias led by a Harmonia, a girl.
  Enter Polykleitos, a mechanic. He sits amid a pile of rifle parts, dismantling weapons.
  Enter Antigone, barefoot, objectless, alone.
  The sound of a helicopter approaching from afar.

Enter Thebans and Athenians, preparing for a state event.
  Antigone watches them as if their actions make no sense.

Talthybia runs on, an Athenian aide. Bottled water, paperwork, bad choice of footwear.
  Harmonia is begging. Talthybia declines to give her a coin and exits hurriedly.

Harmonia approaches Antigone.

Antigone I have nothing
  Nothing no

Tiresias You have not survived this war
  You're breathing but you're not alive

Antigone Don't speak to me, Tiresias

  Antigone begins to walk away. His voice arrests her.

Tiresias The dead see everything you do
  In darkness they have eyes that never close
  Up here, everyone is blind
  Think hard where you belong

  She turns to him, pained.

You and your sister
  Last remnants of a cursed house

Follow your destiny, Antigone

Antigone exits. The helicopter, louder.

Talthybia enters. A makeshift Theban choir begins to sing a national anthem.
Other Athenian men and women enter in silk and linen suits, Theban officials in cheaper suits or trying to hold together their national dress in the face of the helicopter's gale.

The helicopter becomes deafening. One of the choir runs. Harmonia seeks cover.
Tiresias remains, the only still point in the scene.

Helicopters are obviously beasts of terror in Thebes, for the makeshift choir has fled.
Talthybia loses her hair-do. Everyone crouches in the blast.

The blast dies down. Talthybia rushes off, followed by soldiers and aides.
Bodyguards and aides cross with all the luggage and paraphernalia of a diplomatic stay.
Harmonia stands up, trying to see.

Theseus enters, a confident man in his prime. Talthybia is at his side.

Theseus Thebes

Talthybia We have our people working on a new hotel and embassy but at the moment there's two options, sir: the compound where our military are, or there's an invitation from the president elect, Eurydice, to stay here at the presidential palace. We've checked it over; basic but OK. A lot of art and artefacts; no electricity. There is no national grid right now

Theseus I'm staying here?

Talthybia It's a building of historic interest and much cooler than the compound. It also gets the breeze; built by Cadmus and Harmonia who founded Thebes

Theseus Do they have internet?

Talthybia At the compound we have internet

Theseus They got a phone?

Talthybia Mobiles, yes, amazingly. They seem to go on working even when the power is down

Theseus I want to call my wife

Talthybia I'm sure they're setting up a private line

Theseus Right now
I feel like telling her I'm here

Talthybia Please borrow mine, sir. It would be such a privilege –

Theseus Sure

Talthybia To know that I've assisted with your communication

Phaeax joins them. Theseus dials.

Everyone has mobiles; it's astonishing. You go out to the villages and even in these little one-goat towns without a single flushing loo, everyone is talking on a mobile phone

Phaeax (*to Talthybia*) Excuse me, where's the band?

Talthybia Yes actually, there is no band

Theseus Hey, Phaedra – guess where I am
Oh – could you get her?

Phaeax Theseus was told there'd be a band. He is expecting one

Talthybia Well very / sorry but

Phaeax If there wasn't one I should have been informed

Talthybia I did my best to get a band. The Thebans / told
me this –

Phaeax He likes the music here

Talthybia The band are dead except the bass guitar
He's alive but only one hand left

Theseus / She what?

Talthybia So then I tried to organise a choral group;
Authentic local sound.

Theseus / OK

Talthybia But people don't like helicopters here. They've
gone

Phaeax Would you explain that to him, please?
Because this is insulting
I can't even see a fucking flag

  Phaeax exits.

Theseus Get her to call me on this number; thanks

Talthybia The city's still unstable, sir
We didn't think it wise to make a lot of fuss

Theseus Quite so. I'd better keep this phone; she's going
to call me back

Talthybia That's absolutely
What an honour
Sir, I did intend for there to be some music as a welcome
but –

Theseus No commotion. Good

Talthybia I'm glad you think so

Theseus Yes. I've come here in humility

I want to see first hand what we Athenians have done
We've given common people here control of their own
fate
The gift of democratic government

Talthybia The voting; frankly it was moving –

Theseus They need to see what democratic leadership
can be

Phaeax re-enters.

Phaeax Sir, they have some rooms prepared. Perhaps
you'd like to freshen up? Before you meet the president
elect

Theseus Just look at this old palace

Talthybia Soon to be renamed the congress

Theseus Dionysus – he was born here
The great god Frenzy

Phaeax Yes sir

Theseus Bacchus
Pulled from the thigh of Zeus
Maybe right where we stand

Phaeax Forgive me, sir, that's not correct
He wasn't pulled from the thigh here
He was sewn into it.
/ Zeus gestated the foetal god –

Theseus Dionysus comes from Thebes
That's what I'm saying

Phaeax Yes sir

Theseus Have they got plumbing here?

Talthybia We've been installing it. No hot water but

Theseus I like my water cold.
   So this is Thebes
   You can almost smell the history

SCENE TWO

Eurydice is dressing. Ismene attends her.

Eurydice First, I will express my disbelief

Ismene In what?

Eurydice Disbelief they voted for us
   I can't believe it

Ismene Well, they did

Eurydice I only fought because there had to be an
opposition
   We could not let the violence go on
   Could not have another Polynices
   So I found myself –
   It's literally like that
   Found myself with others
   Acting to oppose
   Speaking
   Words issuing from out my mouth
   In torrents
   A solace from the pain
   I never dreamt that politics would be my path
   I've always hated them
   Hated standing there at Creon's side
   Watching the ebb and flow of power from man to man
   The little games of consequence
   Experiments with human lives.
   Politics is what I've always fought against.
   But now I've won

I'm feeling sick
I've promised them pipe dreams, Ismene

Ismene You've promised peace

Eurydice I'm feeling I might actually throw up

Ismene Well, if you do, please miss the outfit

Eurydice Creon had principles until he was in power.
I saw what power did to him.
I watched the man diminish as it took its hold.
I watched his hopes and values all corrode

Ismene The people know you're different

Eurydice Am I, though?
Am I?
What will it do to me?
Ismene

Ismene Yes

Eurydice I'm meeting Theseus

Ismene I know; it's so exciting

Eurydice I look awful in this dress

Ismene I haven't finished yet
You need accessories
A scarf, you see?
Connotations of humility
But powerful mystique.
It softens all your lines
And then the architecture works

Eurydice Oh yes

Ismene You need an elegant but manly watch
To show that Time is your new god

Eurydice I love you

Ismene What about a bag?

Eurydice No bag

Ismene Athenians all have them
  This one is designer

Eurydice I'm walking out into a world of men
  Unadorned and empty-handed

  Ismene holds her.

Ismene Bring us justice

  Aglaea enters.

Aglaea He is here

Eurydice I'm ready

Aglaea You have made a terrible mistake

Eurydice Don't you like it?

Aglaea You have not invited Sparta

Eurydice Oh

Aglaea I assumed you'd have the sense to see they must
be here

Eurydice If I invite the Spartans, Theseus might leave. I'll
not antagonise him

Aglaea We need Sparta or he'll walk all over you. We
need a bidding war with Thebes as prize –

Eurydice Athens stands for everything we've fought for:
freedom and democracy –

Aglaea For their own citizens

Eurydice Sparta is secretive, oppressive and aggressive
  They want an empire here by stealth –

Aglaea So does Theseus
  We are staring at the Titans

313

> Monsters both –
> Both poised to scavenge us.
> Be practical
> We have to play them
> One against the other

Eurydice That's a dangerous game for novices

Aglaea It's the only way we stand to win.
> We need money, not ideals
> Stability will only come with economic growth

Eurydice I will not get into bed with a regime
> That uses fear and violence to control.
> In Athens human rights are shrined in law

Aglaea They are a luxury
> When we have food enough / and sanitation

Eurydice Our principles won us this election
> And in the ruins of this bleeding state
> They are the only shreds of dignity we have.
> I put my trust in Theseus – on principle

Aglaea Then go and kiss his hairy hand

Eurydice I'm sorry that we disagree

Aglaea Nice dress

> *She starts to go.*

> Be careful please
> I know he wears a splendid suit
> Sewn with a democratic thread;
> He's still a warlord with a warlord's heart

Eurydice All men are not so

Aglaea He fights his wars behind a desk
> But don't imagine that the beast is tame

Euphrosyne Eurydice, they've found a body by the walls.
It is the corpse of Polynices

  Eurydice and Ismene are profoundly affected.

Eurydice How do you know?

Euphrosyne His necklace

Eurydice I must see him

Euphrosyne Come, child

Aglaea Don't keep Theseus waiting

Eurydice (*going*) Nothing takes precedence

  Eurydice and Euphrosyne exit.

Aglaea Is this the way it goes?
  Already she has put her own needs first

Ismene Polynices killed her son

Aglaea I know

Ismene My cousin Menoceus. He was only just thirteen

Aglaea I know

Ismene Polynices pulled the brains from out his skull
while still he lived –

Aglaea Yes, Ismene, yes
  But it is past.
  Her job is to secure our future

Ismene Why don't you go and meet him?

Aglaea Because I am incapable of hiding what I think
  And I think Theseus a bag of wind

SCENE THREE

Theseus enters with Talthybia and Phaeax.

Theseus So on a scale of one to ten, exactly how fucked is this place?

Talthybia I'd say it's been up to eleven.
    Thebes is conflict-devastated

Theseus Currently around?

Talthybia Eight or nine
    Still very volatile

Theseus OK

Talthybia The election has improved things but there is no infrastructure whatsoever; thousands of displaced, traumatised people, destruction of homes, agriculture, industry. The violence was bestial. There were seven different armed militias all advancing on the city

Theseus I heard they ate each other

Talthybia Yes, combatants used to eat the brains of those they killed in order to inherit strength and skill. Apparently a custom from pre-Cadmus times. There has been indescribable brutality. I put accounts into my briefing, sir. Polynices said the violence would reshape the human soul

Theseus You wrote that briefing?

Talthybia Yes sir

Theseus What's your name again?

Talthybia Talthybia

Theseus That's right; nice piece of work, Talthybia

Talthybia Thank you

Theseus It almost put me off my in-flight meal

Talthybia May I say, on behalf of everybody working on the ground, how very glad we are to see you. Your visit's a terrific boost to our morale

Theseus They have democracy and now they can rise out of this disgusting quagmire

Talthybia That is our hope

Theseus So when do we begin to pull our peacekeepers out?

Phaeax In ten days' time

Talthybia But sir –

Phaeax Where is the president elect? She should be here by now.

> ELSEWHERE: *Eurydice is staring at Polynices' corpse. Euphrosyne and the soldiers accompany. She cannot tear her eyes away.*

Talthybia It's probably some urgent matter

Phaeax She can have no conception of your status, sir

Euphrosyne What shall we do with him?

Talthybia It's my belief that Thebes will need our presence here long term. There's a tremendous will for change but it won't happen overnight. In Eurydice, the people have chosen a leader / who –

Theseus Who is not here

Eurydice Do nothing
Let me think

Phaeax This is clearly someone, sir, with no experience

317

Talthybia She has experienced a decade of extreme and bloody war. When Creon died, the generals put her under house arrest. And even from her prison here she fought. She gave her strength to this amazing movement of women all risking their lives for peace

Theseus The women, right

Talthybia They would congregate in numbers and place themselves in the line of fire. During the peace talks they barricaded all the men inside the building, shamed them into peace. I find it deeply moving, inspirational

Theseus Yes, quite so

Talthybia She's given people hope.

Eurydice Polynices

Talthybia The leaders of this grass-roots movement; they are now the government

ELSEWHERE: *Eurydice and Euphrosyne exit.*

Phaeax The Minister of Finance was a teacher in a rural school

Talthybia Yes; she's incorruptible
She's sweeping out the toads, the ghosts, the layabouts
She'll spend our money on the people not on palaces
and cars

Theseus There's no such thing as incorruptible

Talthybia Eurydice has said that everything must change.
The men have shown what they can do for Thebes
And now the women will

Phaeax Whoa

Theseus But what do we think; do we trust her?

Talthybia Yes I think / she's –

318

Theseus Do we like her?

Talthybia – very good news

Theseus Because she isn't here. Why is that?

Tiresias Welcome, blind traveller

Theseus I'm sorry?

Tiresias is with Harmonia. She holds out a hand for money.

Phaeax What's this person doing here?

Tiresias Welcome to the country of the blind

Phaeax I thought we had secured this area

Talthybia He's a beggar. That's his place. We've checked him and he's not a threat. Don't look so scared; you don't have to give him anything

Theseus I don't have any Theban currency

Talthybia The begging's kind of overwhelming – so I've developed strategies. I only give to grandmothers; they're the poorest and most selfless. Sometimes I give to exceptionally hideous amputees but –

Theseus That is a grandmother

Talthybia No sir, excuse me; that's a man

Theseus It's a woman

Tiresias Give me your hand, King Theseus

Theseus Actually my title is First Citizen. We don't have kings in Athens; we're a democratic state

Tiresias The future holds my clear unblinking gaze
It's only in the present that I'm blind.
Why don't you let me tell you what I see?

Theseus Female, unquestionably

Talthybia Male

Tiresias I'm both.
I saw two serpents mating on a path

Talthybia We have no interest, sorry

Tiresias (*taking Theseus' hand*) Intertwined
Encoiled, jaws wrapped round each other
Poison dripping in mistrust even as
They slithered propagation

Theseus Oh, OK

Tiresias The sight disgusted me. It seemed too human.
I tore the slippery beasts apart
And crushed one with my heel. It was the she.
As punishment the snakes made me a woman

Theseus The snakes changed you into a woman?

Tiresias No punishment, say I, to be a female.
Lying back, my legs spread wide, I know
Ten times the bliss I suffered as a man.
We suffer pleasure as we suffer pain
You know this to be true. So does your wife

Theseus My wife?

Tiresias She's young; you married her last year

Theseus Good guess

Tiresias She harbours love for someone else.
She doesn't want to but it's there, a love.
It grows in her like cancer day by day.
It will consume her

Theseus pulls back his hand, deeply affected.

Theseus What the fuck?

320

Talthybia He's just a bullshit beggar, sir

Harmonia holds out her hand for money.

Move along now please. You get him out of here

Eurydice enters with Euphrosyne.

Theseus I want internet, hot water. I don't care if you drag the generator up the hill yourself. I want a private line, Phaedra on the end of it. And where's the fucking president elect? I've flown all the way from Athens to witness her inauguration and she doesn't have the decency to meet me

Eurydice Theseus
Hello

Eurydice takes his hand.

Welcome to Thebes

Theseus Eurydice

Eurydice We're thrilled to see you
Thank you so much for coming.
It means a great deal to Thebes and to me

Theseus Congratulations on your victory

Eurydice Thank you. My late husband Creon was a great admirer of all things Athenian. So am I, especially democracy

Theseus That's good to hear
You look smaller than your photograph

Eurydice So do you
Let me walk you round our gardens. Miraculously they survived the war – and they're so cool at this time of the day. Do you have humming birds in Athens?

They exit, followed by the aides, bodyguards.

321

Talthybia gives Harmonia some money.

Talthybia (*to Tiresias*) So what about me? Will you tell me my life?

Tiresias I cannot see you

Talthybia I'm here. What's my destiny, old man?

Tiresias You are a faceless nameless minion. You don't have one

SCENE FOUR

Haemon, Eunomia and Senator Thalia enter. Haemon's eyes have suffered serious injury. They approach Polykleitos, a mechanic.

Thalia My name is Thalia, I'm a senator of your new government. We're here collecting testimony

Polykleitos So I've heard

Thalia Would you like to contribute?
    It's so important that we speak
    That we are heard

Polykleitos You are evangelists, I think

Haemon Evangelists for truth and reconciliation

Thalia These are my trainees

Polykleitos What happened to your eyes?

Haemon Nothing
    They met some flying masonry
    At high velocity
    I was a student doctor
    Now I'm this
    Haemon

Polykleitos Polykleitos
Forgive me if I ask what good will speaking do?

Eunomia Thalia's been taking testimony since the massacre

Thalia Before the war I was a social worker

Eunomia Now she's been elected Minister of Justice

Thalia I care about that word. I want to see it done

Polykleitos Forgive me if I say I've heard it all before

Haemon If this country is to heal, we have to start a dialogue between the victims of the violence and its perpetrators

Thalia We hear you've suffered loss

Polykleitos Truth and reconciliation: pretty words

Thalia We have to give them meaning, make them actions

Polykleitos I've been working for the Athenians
As mechanic
Dismantling these weapons
It feels good.
Turn on your machine

Haemon starts recording.

Before the war I had a garage
My son and me were hiding in the store.
In other countries, children are a precious thing.
In Thebes they have no value.
I can't vomit up the words

Thalia Each child's death should bring this city to a halt
I lost my daughter in this war

Polykleitos I spent my life in service to the gods
Not in service no, in contemplation of the mystery
I thought there was an order to the universe

When I looked up at the sky at night
I'd see a pattern mathematical in its complexity
Now I see random dots
There's nothing
But
An image like a bloodstain
Of the soldiers
Roaring through our streets.
A man broke down our door

Haemon Do you remember when, which faction, which attack on Thebes?

Polykleitos I know exactly who he was
That's why I'm speaking here.
He took my son and –

ELSEWHERE: *Prince Tydeus enters.*

Tydeus OK that's enough, don't look at them; you look at me. I'm more enlightening than anything that's going on there. That is sad old shit. Truth and reconciliation? That is sell-your-neighbour by a different name. That is make up lies about the people you don't like and get them tried for war crimes. I bet I'm being blamed for every murder here in Thebes and none of it is true, no, none of it. I am Prince Tydeus. Not a royal one; my mother brought me up to run her pig farm, actually; it's just that Prince is quite a common name in Thebes – a lot of mothers like to have a little Prince. But I was never going to spend my life with swine. The gods had better plans for me. Now here are three true facts. One: I am a first-class athlete. I have wiped the floor with all the best of Athens and with Sparta. I have won first prize at the Nemean Games. You can see my winning javelin throw on my own website – one of the first in Thebes – designed by the woman I adore, who understands domains

Senator Pargeia enters.

324

Kids have posters of me on their walls draped in the flag
of Thebes – Prince Tydeus: gold. Two: I have had
communication with the gods

Pargeia That's true
  The Prince first saw Dionysus when he was just a little
boy

Tydeus I didn't see
  It's more like I became

Pargeia You hear that?
  He becomes
  Like in that movie where the man puts on the mask

Tydeus Not like that
  I felt him in me when I won that gold;
  Felt him moving in me
  When I led my men through Thebes.
  I feel his light within my heart, my brain
  I hear his holy laugh come out my mouth
  I'll tell you this
  Dionysus is a very complex god.
  He doesn't choose just anyone.
  Three: I fought for justice and for peace

Pargeia That's right. He fought for Polynices

Tydeus He was rightful heir in Thebes and he should be
running it right now. Polynices taught me everything
I know. He was more like a brother than a friend. This is
his wife, Pargeia

Pargeia Hi

Tydeus I was just telling them about your skill with
websites and domains

Pargeia That's nice

Tydeus This woman is a true-life heroine. Not only is she
beautiful –

Pargeia Now now

Tydeus – but she is clever and she's full of heart

Pargeia During the war years, while I worked as loan advisor at the Bank of Thebes, I used my post to raise funds for the orphans

Tydeus Any other information you might hear about her finances is quite unfuckingtrue

Pargeia My husband, Polynices, should be ruling Thebes. But he –
　I'm sorry –

Tydeus He's among the disappeared

Pargeia No he is not 'among'. He is unique. He has uniquely gone. He led his men into the whirlwind of the fight and then –
　Forgive me –

Tydeus He has not been seen

Pargeia Tydeus is my best support
　My truest Prince
　He has sat with me through my hours of grief
　The torment of not knowing –

Tydeus Rumour is that Polynices is residing in the forest, biding time

Pargeia Zeus transported him to safety

Tydeus We like to think his jeep was swallowed by the gods of death and now he is beneath the earth

Pargeia Gathering unworldly power

Tydeus Ready to be spewed back up into the face of Thebes and take, by force, what's his

Pargeia We stood for him in this election
  Prince Tydeus

Tydeus The man with god inside

Pargeia Our policies were strong
  Firm leadership
  Security for all those on our side

Tydeus But then we lost
  It's inconfuckingceivable
  We're merely senators

Pargeia Which only goes to show how pointless an
election is

  Thalia approaches.

Thalia Senator Tydeus

Tydeus That is Prince to you

  She hands him a document.

Thalia The Truth and Reconciliation Commission of
Thebes requests you to appear before it to address
yourself to allegations of war crimes and gross human
rights violations during the course of the Theban civil
war. Failure to attend will result in compulsory subpoena
and criminal prosecution. (*To Pargeia.*) Good morning
to you, Senator Pargeia. I hear they are investigating loan
frauds at the Bank of Thebes. Have a lovely day

  She exits.

Pargeia Hold back
  Resist the rage

Tydeus Oh fuck democracy. I hate the whole idea of it
  We've got enough arms left to take the compound
  And the palace –

Pargeia Do I need to say it twice? Hold back
Sweet Prince
Sometimes you are an innocent.
There are much better ways to fuck those bitches up
One: we need the people on our side
Two: we need the influence of Theseus

Tydeus When I look at you
It's like I feel the god
Rising up in me

He tries to kiss her. Antigone enters.

Pargeia No. Not while my husband Polynices lives
I want to
But I can't

She sees Antigone, who is looking at her strangely.

Pargeia What is it, sister?

Antigone Nothing

Pargeia I don't like the way you look at me
Like I'm not good enough
To be your brother's wife
And I have proved my worth
On my feet and on my back
Please tell me what your problem is

Antigone The dead see everything we do

Pargeia exits.

Tydeus Oedipus' daughters
There are two
The mad one and the cute one.
This one's mad.

He exits.

Act Two

SCENE ONE

Antigone remains. Ismene enters.

Ismene What are you doing? What's the matter?

Antigone They found Polynices. Dead

Ismene I know
Antigone

Antigone I went to look at him.
His eyes were no longer eyes
Open right into the deep

Ismene He's dead and gone
It's over

As they speak, the stage is being prepared for the inauguration.

Antigone I'm going to anoint the corpse with oil
Come with me

Ismene But it's Eurydice's inauguration

Antigone Why should I care for that?

Ismene She wants us with her, by her side

The company are entering and taking up position.

Antigone But he's our brother

Ismene You never lived with him. I did
You were on the road with Oedipus for all those years
And you were spared

Antigone Spared? Out there in the war zone with our dying father?

329

Ismene Polynices was a cunning, red-eyed despot
   And this palace was a prison under him.
   He used to pick up women from the town
   And bring them here to play with and to rape.
   You ask Eurydice. She hated him –

Antigone I don't care what he did

Ismene He let his generals
   High on heroin and gunpowder
   He let dogs like Prince Tydeus –

Antigone I've heard the stories same as you

Ismene Stories?

Antigone I've heard about his necklace made of fingers

Ismene I hated him

Antigone He is our blood

Ismene I won't go back
   The war is over

Antigone Not until we've buried all the dead.
   I've noticed in these days of peace how soon you have
concerned yourself with what to wear, with grooming,
painting of your toes –

Ismene We have survived
   Survived our lives so far.
   Why not start living them?

   Antigone cracks into tears.

Antigone We have to bury him
   He frightens me

   Ismene embraces her.
      *The company enters, Tydeus and Pargeia making a
   flamboyant show.*

Tydeus Senators, good morning

Eris What are you doing here?

Pargeia We are elected representatives of Thebes

Tydeus We're here to offer hospitality to Theseus

Helia There's something here that you don't understand

Euphrosyne Called politics

Thalia We won the votes
We are the government
You lost
You are the opposition

Pargeia So?

Eunomia You're not invited

Aglaea Senators, your place is over there

Pargeia and Tydeus retreat to their positions. A rousing national anthem. The Athenians join in, unsure of tune or words. Eurydice and Theseus enter.

Anthem
In the towns and our plain lands
In the heart of our Thebes
The road to peace and freedom
Is a path for us all
For we will build a new world
Our nation will be reborn
And feel the pride of our plain lands
In the heart of our Thebes

Eurydice stands at a podium, Theseus at her side.
Antigone tries to leave. Ismene holds her back. At last Antigone acquiesces.
The anthem ends. Antigone, an oddity among the dignitaries, keeps her head bowed.

Eurydice Thebans, war is over. We are free
How happy it makes me to say that.
Let me say it again loud and clear:
People of Thebes, we are free.
This is truly a wonderful day.
I stand before you, leader of our new democracy.
My first task is to thank you
Thank you for believing Thebes can rise again
And thank you for believing in
This Theban woman. She believes in you.
I want to talk to the women here
The women in this city turned the tide for peace,
Women put themselves in danger
Walked wearing white in front of guns,
Nagged and pleaded, begged and laboured
Advocated tirelessly, withheld sexual favours
And never gave up. Women gave us peace.
This new administration will reflect their courage.
Women will be given prominence at every level.
Euphrosyne, Minister of Finance
Thalia, Minister of Justice
Aglaea, Foreign Secretary
Bia, Trade and Industry
Helia, Agriculture
Eris, Chief of Police
And men, we love you too:
Xenophanes, Education
We have senators reflecting all opinions here
Some radically different from my own.
We'll learn to listen, compromise and bend
We'll learn the skills of peace
Here, to share our celebration
Theseus, First Citizen of Athens

Theseus There is excitement in the air.
I can hear it, Thebans, feel it.

Like the rhythm of your famous music,
I find it irresistible. As I look down
Upon your city streets and out across
Your towns and fertile plains
I see you all rebuilding homes
Mending roads, reconstructing life.
I'm honoured to be witness at the birth of this
democracy. When I return next time, I hope to see an
open governmental infrastructure, functioning without
corruption. I hope to see the rule of law. I hope to see a
land where business thrives, endeavour is rewarded, and
stability achieved. If peace is maintained, Athens and her
partners could do business here. Imagine this: a vast
economic development zone, bringing investment and
employment; industry that would transform your land.
The quality is there, the opportunity, the will. Your war is
over. Now improve yourselves. Thank you

Eurydice In our hope for the peace, let us not forget the
war.
Thebes has been witness to atrocities
That I can hardly heave into my mouth
We have seen butchery and slaughter
Our girls raped, boys brutalised with guns.
What meaning can we find in that?
The only meaning is to make a lasting peace.
We have lost children, parents, brothers, sisters
I lost my husband Creon, Menoceus my youngest son,
My eldest, Haemon, blinded here

Haemon Not blind

Eurydice I fought with grief through the long night
And in your faces I can see its shadow.
I want to remember those we have lost.
Please join me in two minutes' silence

Tiresias marks the beginning of the silence.

333

All bow their heads. For the first time, Antigone raises hers. About thirty seconds pass. Tydeus falls to his knees. He speaks in a high voice.

Tydeus People – for you I died
A long time I lay in darkness
Then the plates of my skull came apart

Pargeia The dead speak

Tydeus My spirit breathed
Began to rise
It ploughed the night sky
Searching for the hidden side
That keeps Elysium from human eyes
Pargeia: spirit, your name?
But far below where lies the plain of Thebes
There came a roar of souls
Thebes
We mourn for you
The dead are grieving
You have been robbed of strength
Your power is lost in woman's hands
Look to the P—
To the P—

Pargeia Look to the Prince

Tydeus feigns collapse.

Tiresias The dead are all around
You make a mockery of them
You deafen them

Tiresias marks the end of the silence.

Thalia You have insulted the dead

Euphrosyne You shameless fake

Eurydice I know that violent men still lurk

Trying to spin their dark ideas aflame.
But while we breathe we will resist them
/ And we will not let you down

Pargeia Our ancestors are grieving
Thebes, her promises are hollow
/ Eurydice can't keep control

Eurydice I will not let you oppress and silence me

Pargeia / Polynices is true leader
You are standing in our place

Eurydice Your president, people of Thebes
Will not be bullied or harassed

Theseus Listen now
This is a democracy
And everybody gets a chance to speak.
That is what you have a senate for

Pargeia Beloved Theseus, the dead have spoken here

Tydeus Who did they die for?
Not Eurydice, not this

Pargeia They died for Polynices

Tydeus / Don't betray the Theban dead
Revolt against this government of women

Eurydice I did not march into the guns of violent men
To then be cowed by them.
I will speak. I will speak. I will speak.
To reconcile does not mean to forget.
We must never forget,
Lest we make the same mistakes again.
Polynices' body has been found.
It will not be given burial

Antigone steps forward. Pargeia almost collapses.

335

Eurydice This warlord's corpse shall be our monument
  To all the horrors we have witnessed / and survived

Pargeia If you don't bury him his soul will walk / the earth

Eurydice His violent ideology will decompose –
  As peace grows up and / overwhelms it

Pargeia (*to Tydeus*) The voice that spoke through / you –

Eurydice The ground where he / lies

Pargeia He used you as his / vessel

Eurydice It will be a garden of / reflection
  Where we can meditate upon the cost of war

Tydeus People, to the square, come now
  Come in your multitudes
  If you have human feeling then oppose this wrong

Pargeia Polynices

Pargeia's distress is epic. Tydeus escorts her out.

Eurydice I love Thebes
  I see light. I see water
  I see the terror melting like ice
  Let us turn away from shadows.
  If you oppose me, tell me democratically.
  Work hard for peace
  Be part of this great effort
  Join hands, be free

Theseus May I?

Eurydice Thank you.

Theseus leads Eurydice down from the podium.

Antigone Her first act
  As lord, as queen

336

Ismene As democratically / elected –

Antigone As all-powerful ruler is to let our brother rot

Ismene Antigone

Theseus An interesting speech, ma'am

Ismene She is not the monster

Eurydice Thank you

Ismene Don't go

Theseus I should offer you the service of my writing team.
They're very good at rousing with the facts

Eurydice That's very kind

Theseus You know, an expert on language and the
human brain said that women find rhetoric more difficult

Eurydice Thank you very much for telling me

Theseus I mean, next time, before you go up there, you
could run your stuff by my professionals to see if there's
improvements to be made / because

Eurydice I write my own words, thank you. My late
husband Creon said it was statesmanship

Theseus Statesmanship, that's nice. That decomposing
corpse

Eurydice Polynices

Theseus You should have run that by me

Eurydice I didn't know our dead were an Athenian
concern.
    Forgive my inexperience

Theseus (*to Phaeax*) The possessed guy

Phaeax That was Prince Tydeus: electoral opponent

Theseus And she?

Phaeax Senator Pargeia. She's the corpse's wife

Talthybia You'll find detailed profiles of them in my briefing, sir

Phaeax She used to be a dancer

Theseus Fascinating

Phaeax He's the guy who won at the Nemean Games

Theseus Impassioned, isn't he?

Phaeax His record for the javelin still stands

Theseus OK. His name again?

Phaeax Tydeus

Theseus The Prince. (*To Eurydice.*) He is a tough adversary

Eurydice Yes, and so am I.
  This is my son, Haemon

Theseus How do you do?

Haemon I started my medical training in Athens; beautiful city

Theseus Certainly is

Haemon I mean what are your plans?
  Sorry to jump on you like this but
  Healthcare provision
  We need drugs, buildings, trained staff
  / It's critical that –

Phaeax The provision of medical aid is a topic for discussion at conference. It will receive our full attention then

Theseus What happened to your eyes?

Haemon Nothing

338

Eurydice He was / injured

Haemon I've suffered certain functional changes but –

Eurydice He's blind

Haemon Why do you keep –
I'm not blind.
I can see your dress
That thing you're wearing on your head
I can see Antigone

He is pointing at Ismene.

My sight is just impaired

Theseus That happen in the war?

Haemon In the peace
Clearing rubble from our disused university
One of the factions had it booby-trapped with mines

Theseus I'm very sorry

Haemon Yes. They were Athenian made

Eurydice Haemon

Haemon That's the irony, you see. Thebes is not a
weapons-manufacturing state. Most of the arms in our
conflict were / Athenian

Eurydice My nieces: Ismene, Antigone

Theseus Your father was Oedipus, right?

Ismene That's right

Antigone Our father and our brother

He shakes Ismene's hand.

Theseus Yes. I feel I'm shaking hands with someone
destiny has touched. You're Antigone?

Ismene Ismene

Theseus There are some families like that
    Families who get touched by destiny
    Chosen in some way –
    Don't you think so?

Antigone / Yes

Ismene No, I don't

Eurydice My cabinet in waiting; Euphrosyne, Minister of Finance

Phaeax The teacher

Euphrosyne How do you do?

Theseus My pleasure

Euphrosyne I have the honour of holding the purse strings of a bankrupt state. I've explored the lining of this purse in case a coin or two is hiding there but all I've found is fluff and old receipts

Theseus That's too bad

Euphrosyne I also have a cheque for you: the latest instalment of interest on the overwhelming debts we have inherited. Would you like it?

Phaeax Debt relief is down on the agenda but there are various criteria you must fulfil and now is not the time to list them

> *Phaeax doesn't take the cheque.*

Eurydice Eris, Chief of Police

Theseus How do you –

Eris We're going to have the rule of law here
    But we need to retrain, reorganise
    We can make Thebes safe
    But we need your cash

340

Eurydice Xenophanes, Education

Theseus Very nice to –

Xenophanes We have to re-educate our men
A generation now thinks rape and looting is their right.
Education is the road to change
But it's expensive –

Eurydice Thalia, Minister of Justice

Thalia We have so much to talk about. A just society –
how is that achievable?

Theseus Well –

Thalia I hope that Thebes can learn from your mistakes

Euphrosyne He looks like a movie star, doesn't he?

Thalia You have the figure and the bearing of a very
gifted actor

Eurydice Aglaea, Foreign Minister

Theseus How do you do?

Aglaea We met before. I came to Athens just before the
massacre to plead for intervention

Theseus That's right

Aglaea Sadly it was not forthcoming

Eurydice We've arranged a Theban feast. We hope you'll
join us

Phaeax Sir, our caterers have worked alongside theirs to
ensure health and hygiene

Theseus Thank you, Madam President

*Eurydice and Theseus exit with Phaeax and the
senators.*

MOIRA BUFFINI

Talthybia (*to Aglaea*) I have to say it isn't wise. Please tell your people. Don't make Theseus feel that he's at fault. He didn't make this war

They exit. Ismene and Antigone alone.

Antigone I'm going to bury him, Ismene

Ismene Can't you see there's something more important going on?

Antigone His soul can't rest

Ismene If you bury him now you'll be siding with Tydeus and the widow

Antigone / No I won't

Ismene They'll leap on you like a trophy. / They'll use you, Antigone

Antigone This has got nothing to do with Prince Tydeus or anyone else

Ismene It has to do with all of Thebes. We have to be so careful

Antigone Why?

Ismene Because of who we are

Antigone Last remnants of a cursed house

Ismene I want to represent the future, not the past. We must embrace this peace

Antigone Eurydice isn't peace
She's power
Power is never peace
It is barbarity.
Come with me

Ismene Why don't we talk to her?
She's not / unreasonable

342

Antigone What good did talking ever do?
  The only thing to do is act – and you
  Have never done
  Anything

  Haemon enters. They both look at him; Ismene with
  a certain amount of hope.

Haemon Antigone?

  Ismene immediately leaves.

Where are you going? Don't go

Antigone I'm here

Haemon My mother asks if you'll come in and join the
feast

Antigone I'm not hungry

Haemon Antigone

Antigone Don't come too near

Haemon Why not?

Antigone I'm ill

Haemon What with?

Antigone Don't know

Haemon I know what I must seem; how especially
  Disgusting my fading sight must seem

Antigone To me?

Haemon I wish it was an arm or leg
  But it's my eyes. My images of you
  Are stuck now in the past. I doubt I'll see
  Your face again, though I imagine it.
  Are you still there?

Antigone Yes

Haemon It's common to feel
Paranoid like that, they say.
I think that I see people creep away.
They've warned me of hallucinations too.
I might see any nonsense, any lie
And take it for what's real. Don't go

Antigone I'm not

Haemon This is a minor injury in Theban terms –

Antigone You're not especially disgusting
Why did you say that?

Haemon Before I went to Athens I remember you
Leading your blind father
Seeing for him, so small
You were like a bird
Taking him where you found interest
Even if he didn't want to go.
I loved to watch.
You were a proper child
You had a playful spirit
Your smile could penetrate his blindness
Wrap itself around his grief
You were his light, Antigone.
I've always felt it when I looked at you
Some kind of light
Don't know why
You're scrawny, awkward
Not like Ismene, she is radiant I'd say, but you
You're like a flare burning through the night.
Since I've been like this it's you I've seen
Your face, your eyes, those eyes

He reaches out for her.

344

Are you still here?

Antigone I thought it was Ismene that you loved

Haemon It's you

They touch.

Antigone I'm dangerous to touch

Haemon Like fire

Antigone I'm ill

Haemon What with?

Antigone Don't know

Haemon Do you feel anything for me?

Antigone No

Suddenly she is in his arms.

Haemon I knew
I knew you did

Antigone Help me

Haemon Antigone

SCENE TWO

Late at night. Miletus, Scud and Megaera are guarding the body of Polynices. Harmonia is quietly singing.

Megaera More dishonest work for warriors to do

Miletus If we're told to sit here with a stiff, we sit with it. That way we get fed

Scud This kid that I was with
Don't know his name but he was small

A green militia came with faces painted white
After the bullets and the fight,
We found him lying there
His life had gone – but there was not a scratch on him

Megaera Another dead-kid story from the Junior
Lieutenant

Scud He died of fear the big men said
And they pissed on him.
I didn't know that it was possible
To die from fear
He followed us for some time after that
And he was grey.
Once he touched me on the back

Megaera That's nice of him. That's friendly, isn't it? Shut
up

*Eurydice and Theseus lead the company out from
dinner.*

Eurydice When Cadmus founded Thebes
He laid Harmonia, his beloved, in their bed
And drew the seven gates around her
Taking his inspiration from the seven heavens.
Thebes is laid out like a celestial map

Theseus That's poetic. Athens is a grid

Eurydice Our districts have the names of constellations
That's Lyra Town down there
And over here on the hill is the spring where Cadmus
killed the giant serpent

Theseus Wow

Eurydice He threw its teeth on the ground and warriors
sprang up
They helped him build the city

*Eurydice and Theseus move away, followed by
Phaeax, aides, bodyguards and senators. Thalia,
Euphrosyne and Bia remain.*

Thalia She's doing very well

Bia That charm of hers. She makes it look so easy

Thalia Perhaps it is to her

Euphrosyne These Athenians. We speak the same
language, we have the same gods, but they're so hard to
talk to. I felt like an anthropologist in there.

Helia They've got no sense of humour

Euphrosyne I was with that aide

Helia Oh, he's a nightmare

Euphrosyne I couldn't think of anything to say
I started talking about grandchildren
His eyes glazed over straight away
I found myself describing the destruction of my village
The food stayed on his plate
Then I remembered sport –
Thank the gods, he talked for half an hour

Thalia That girl with the stiff hair –

Bia Talthybia

Thalia She asked so many questions
I was actually impressed
I think she's a bit in love with Theseus

Bia So am I

Euphrosyne Well, I'm sorry to inform you that he has a
wife

Bia No match for me

Aglaea enters.

Euphrosyne A beautiful young wife: Phaedra. Their wedding was all over the celebrity sites on the internet. Of course I never look at them. But her dress: so many little precious stones sewn into the organza. You could open several schools for what it cost

Aglaea Can't we rise above the gossip?

Euphrosyne This isn't gossip, this is economics

Aglaea Listen
That's Pargeia and the Prince down in the square
I've told Eris to stand by with her police
What if there's trouble and they can't contain it?

Thalia We have the peacekeepers
It's what they're here for

Bia We'll go and talk to their security

Bia and Helia exit.

Euphrosyne I don't think Tydeus will attempt a coup while Theseus is here

Aglaea Tydeus wants to show him we're unstable and incapable
He wants to show we're overwhelmed / by the task

Euphrosyne Overwhelmed but undaunted. We're planting seeds, her ladies – tiny seeds that will grow and change the land.

Thalia The Athenians are pulling out in ten days' time. We have to have assurances of aid and debt relief. Eurydice has got to sell us hard

Aglaea How I hate the fact that we need Theseus.
That speech of his
It made me livid
Telling us we could improve ourselves

348

As if we're children learning how to spell
And offering the carrot of his economic zone

Euphrosyne He's got to feed the great Athenian god: the
god of profit

Aglaea And Eurydice – I'm sorry but I'm furious.
What was she thinking of – to leave that corpse exposed
without discussion and without advice?

Euphrosyne Your voice is very loud

Aglaea That rabble in the square; she's given them the
gift of self-righteous indignation. What an error – and she
made it like an autocrat

Thalia You see the thing is, I appreciate her gesture.
There is poetry in it. I lost my daughter in this war

Aglaea I know, I know –

Thalia And that unburied monster –
I know it wasn't him that raped and killed her
But the fact that there's just one –
Just one of those ferocious men
Whose soul will never rest

Aglaea You're Minister of Justice

Thalia Yes, I think that it is just
His corpse is made to pay
The dead make reparation
While the living start to heal

Euphrosyne We have to show her loyalty

Aglaea What of her loyalty to us?
We senators must act as a control on her great power

Euphrosyne We need her to have power.
What good is honest, competent committee
In the face of Prince Tydeus?

He genuinely thinks that he's a god.
And he is charismatic, handsome, plausible
Especially with that glossy thief upon his arm.
We're dull, we're ageing, we wear comfy footwear
None of us is sexy any more

Aglaea Tydeus and Pargeia have the crowd
We have to hope that when the food and beer runs out
Their cult of personality will sour

Thalia We must have Theseus

Euphrosyne And to get him we need her, Eurydice
Her confidence, her charm, her gravitas
Her sense of her own right –

Aglaea Her pride

Euphrosyne Your pride

Thalia I feel we're holding floodgates closed
Exhausted with the weight
We have to be united. Please stand firm
Or the approaching rush
Will overwhelm us all

Euphrosyne The greatest threat to Thebes
Is Thebes itself

Phaeax and Enyalius enter with the senators.

Phaeax Excuse me, what is going on down there? I have
concerns for Theseus

Aglaea Keep calm
We should stand by
But not provoke
That way this little fire will burn itself right out

Exit aides and senators.

ELSEWHERE: *the revellers enter, carrying Tydeus on
their shoulders. Polykleitos watches from the shadows.*

Tydeus Breathe frenzy

Pargeia Prince Tydeus

> *A chant starts up: 'Breathe frenzy, Prince Tydeus.'*
> *Polykleitos raises a gun, aims it at Tydeus.*

Fill your stomach, feed your flesh, let your hair voice fly,
breathe frenzy, free your senses, cry joy. Feel the god

Tydeus Breathe frenzy

> *Polykleitos cannot pull the trigger. He lowers the gun.*
> *The revellers exit.*

> ELSEWHERE: *Talthybia is with Ismene.*

Talthybia I've drunk too much

Ismene Me too

Talthybia What is that stuff, that wine?

Ismene Not really wine. It's made out of fermented bread

Talthybia Oh, fermented

> *Theseus enters. He is on his mobile phone.*

Theseus Can you do something for me please?
Call in on your mother? Yes, I know she is;
I mean on Phaedra, she's your mother now

Talthybia Great sky

Ismene You have the same sky over Athens

Theseus I'm only asking you to see if she's OK
She hasn't been returning calls
I don't know what she's doing there

Talthybia Our sky's polluted with a smog of light.
We have an orange glow; couple of white dots
/ But that is just spectacular. That path

351

Theseus I'm worried that –
  Just go
  Find out why she's there. And privately –

Ismene Oh yes, the path of stars

Theseus You keep it in the family. Thanks

Talthybia At first I thought it was a kind of high cloud cover but this Theban guy I met who dismantles guns and weapons said it's actually –

Polykleitos (*elsewhere*) / The Milky Way

Talthybia – the Milky Way

Ismene That's right

Talthybia I didn't know. He said our star, the sun –

Polykleitos Is on an outer spur of a great spiral of the galaxy

Talthybia – and the Milky Way

Polykleitos Or silver river, is our view of the
  Galactic plane going right into the crux
  Full of dust from old, exploded stars
  And ionising new ones – countless
  Suns and moons and planets, and it turns
  Through space at an amazing speed, not just
  A moon around an earth or earth round sun
  But all of it; the galaxy spins round

Talthybia And this mechanic guy said it's just one –

Polykleitos Of billions like it in the universe

Talthybia And at the centre of it all, guess what
  He was looking for?

Ismene A super-massive black hole

Talthybia No, not that. He said he wanted Heaven

Ismene Very nice

Polykleitos / Elysium

Talthybia Elysium; that was the word he used.
    He searches for Elysium

Ismene The centre of the galaxy is actually dark matter

Talthybia Oh. OK

Ismene It's going to eat us up

Theseus She's right. One day you'd better hope
    You're on a space ship out of here

    He laughs. No one else finds it funny. Eurydice enters;
    Aglaea and Eris are briefing her.

I used to do a lot of sailing;
    Love the night sky
    And I'm appreciating what you said about dark matter
    I've read a lot about black holes and stuff, Antigone.
    Dark matter means we've got to make the most of
what's around

    Aglaea and Eris exit. Eurydice approaches.

Eurydice We've had a small disturbance in the central
square
    It's calming down

Theseus Your opposition, right?

Eurydice Just drunken revellers
    Celebrating our democracy

Theseus Making their feelings known about the dead guy

Eurydice That is their democratic right

Theseus (*to Talthybia*) Could we get some music here?
    I hate an evening without music

She exits, with Talthybia.

Eurydice You don't like silence, Theseus?

Theseus You don't like music?

Eurydice Did you make your call?

Theseus Yes, thank you. My wife has left our place in Athens and she's heading for the coast. Why would she do that?

Eurydice I don't know

Theseus Hippolytus my son is stationed there with his battalion. I've asked him to go out and check on her

Eurydice That's very good of him

Theseus He doesn't like her. Not one bit.
I'm not entirely sure that he likes me

Eurydice Families can be very difficult

Theseus You lost a son, is that right?

Eurydice He
Down by the walls
Menoceus, my youngest.
In an ambush
He was –

Pause.

Theseus How did you lose your husband?

Eurydice On his way to Delphi at one of our outlying villages, his convoy was stopped at a roadblock. It was made of human intestines

Theseus No way

Eurydice They were massacred

354

Theseus By this Polynices?

Eurydice By his men. I don't think they knew who Creon was. They were just massacring everyone that day. But when they realised who they'd killed they – let's say they made full use of his remains

Theseus What happens when a whole state
When a place descends into – fuck
It's like you bred some different kind of war out here

Eurydice All war is savage, Theseus, whether it's fought close quarters with machetes or from afar with missiles and computer-guided bombs. Are you more civilised because you can't hear people scream?

Theseus Your war was bestial

Eurydice Our war was very human

Theseus Then I fear a new breed of mankind. Men with no feeling, no idea of order or regard for any tie, men whose only motivation is the basest lust for power

Eurydice That's new?

Theseus The path we've been on for the last millennium or so, the glory of the city state, philosophy and science, freedom, art, enlightenment: the things that Athens stands for. I believe in them and I had thought our progress irreversible. I thought we would continue to evolve towards the gods

Eurydice We're not evolving backwards here

Theseus What happened? How did this exterminating butchery take hold?

Eurydice It could happen anywhere

Theseus You cannot say that

Eurydice Does it frighten you?
    Do you think we brought it on ourselves?
    It could happen anywhere where there is tyranny.
    You should go out and talk to people, talk
    As I have done to those who have endured.
    I'd say they were the finest human beings you could
meet.
    What's happened here is in the past.
    Perhaps you are afraid of us
    Because the chaos here, the great descent
    Just might be in your future

Theseus What the hell makes you say that?

Eurydice An observation, merely

*Ismene and Talthybia enter with a clockwork radio.
Music.*

Talthybia Some music, sir

Eurydice Thank you, Talthybia. Good night

Talthybia and Ismene exit.

Theseus I've made an observation too. You have a way
with people that I envy; got them wrapped around your
finger

Eurydice Have I?

Theseus You appear strong

Eurydice I'm motivated by necessity

Theseus You appear humane, intelligent, compassionate
and wise. But I'm not sure if you are

Eurydice Thebes knows what I stand for and the people
trust me to bring change. It's what I must do – or die
trying

Theseus That's so Theban, bringing death into every sentence

Eurydice Death is everywhere in Thebes

Theseus Like your address; way too dramatic. Some of the things you said

Eurydice I said we must reconcile

Theseus No, you said light and water and men lurking in the dark spinning fire

Eurydice All the most important things were said

Theseus This dead boy that you refuse to bury –

Eurydice The warlord who murdered my son

Theseus Where does he fit in to your reconciliation?

Eurydice I explained that in my speech

Theseus His corpse will be a theme park?

Eurydice Don't misinterpret me. It's vital to the healing of our wounds that he makes reparation. I've no desire to clash with you

Theseus Quite right

Eurydice But this is Theban business. You've no right to interfere

Theseus May I just say how well you argue and defend yourself. For someone new to government, you're good

Eurydice Thank you

Theseus You're also beautiful

Eurydice I – what?

Theseus That is so unusual in politics
Not coming on to you; just stating a bare fact.

357

Beauty is a very powerful thing.
My wife is beautiful
Phaedra: gets mistaken for my daughter.
Don't know why I'm saying this
Relief perhaps
Of being with a woman my own age
A clever, charming, deeply foreign woman

Pause.

Eurydice Thank you but we have no electricity
No schools, no medicine, no roads
No jobs, no drinking water
Children dying in their droves
Our life expectancy is thirty-eight.
I'm old beyond my years

Theseus You don't look old.
I envy you, you know
Envy the adventure, the extremity
Our lives in Athens seem mundane
We have no tragedy. And tragedy
Reminds us how to live

Eurydice I'm glad it serves some purpose

Theseus Eurydice. You'll learn how rare it is to meet an equal

Eurydice Theseus, my hands are tied with monstrous poverty.
For Thebes to thrive where chaos gaped and roared
You can perform that miracle –

Theseus You see this is what I'm saying: metaphors and monsters. Gaped and roared: that's just verbose. It's / not effective

Eurydice What I have said is very clear. We need a future. You can / help us

Theseus You've just been elected.
I can see you're very keen.
You are a natural and I'm most impressed.
But sometimes late at night
When everything official has been said
We leaders of the world like to
Take off the mask
We've done the altruism and diplomacy.
Now let's do something else

Eurydice What would amuse you, Theseus?

Theseus Like look up at the stars
And see what destiny might hold

Eurydice It's worrying that you don't listen. Is it something
that the male brain has inadequate equipment for?

Theseus I do listen and I think you're so naive. There is a
lot that I could do for Thebes

Eurydice Naive?

Theseus But let's remember that essentially you're begging
here, you're on your knees

Eurydice That's what I've said. Thebes is / imprisoned by

Theseus Not Thebes; you. Every thousand that I pledge
keeps you in power. I just offered you equality

Eurydice Did you?

Theseus I had a glimpse of something just back then
Some sort of –
Obviously not destiny, but say
A door swinging open unexpectedly.
This relationship with Thebes
Could be a pleasure, not a chore

359

Eurydice Are you
   Are you suggesting
   That we presidents –

Theseus I'm not a president. I'm just First Citizen

Eurydice That's right, the common man

Theseus Dionysus – he was born here, wasn't he, the god of wine? Don't you women have a dance for him, some sort of rite?

Eurydice Which guidebook have you read?

Theseus I'd like to see it.
   Would you dance for me?

   Pause.

What's up? I'm asking you to dance with me

Eurydice You said for, dance for you

Theseus I said to dance

Eurydice I'm sorry but that isn't / what I heard

Theseus Don't apologise

Eurydice I'm not

Theseus No seriously, don't apologise
   In politics, you can't admit mistakes

Eurydice I haven't made one

Theseus You cannot be wrong

Eurydice I know that

Theseus So then. What are you afraid of? Dance.

   Neither moves.

   First light. Miletus and Megaera sleep. Antigone is

performing burial rites. She picks up a handful of dust.
She lets it fall through her fingers over the corpse. She
repeats the gesture. Junior Lieutenant Scud is watching
her, curiously. Megaera wakes.

Antigone I lead the blind
  I bury the dead
  I follow the path
  I am Antigone

  Megaera raises her gun. She aims it at Antigone.

Megaera Whoosh

Act Three

Tiresias enters with Harmonia. Ismene is making coffee –
a ceremony over charcoal.

Tiresias The ghosts
  Their parched tongues are flickering
  Like unseen negatives upon the day.
  They form another city all round us

Ismene I'm not afraid of you, Tiresias.
  You're like an old pet snake
  Kept more out of pity than from fear

  Harmonia holds out her hand. Ismene gives her a coin.

This child you've stolen from her mother
  Any day now she'll be going to school.
  You're irrelevant in our new Thebes

Tiresias The dead are not irrelevant. They're here

  Theseus enters, with Phaeax and Talthybia. Eurydice
  enters with her ministers.

Eurydice Good morning

Theseus Madam President

Eurydice You must try our Theban coffee

Theseus I did

Eurydice Shall we begin our conference?

Theseus There are people here who eat each other's
brains, people who believe that snakes can change your
gender. There are people who make roadblocks out of

362

human innards, people who leave corpses right outside their gates. Are you ready for a place at the table?

Eurydice How's your wife this morning? Have you managed to get hold of her?

Theseus My wife is not up for discussion here

He exits into the palace with Phaeax, Talthybia and retinue.

Euphrosyne What happened to him?

Eurydice Helia, Xenophanes and Bia
We'll start proceedings with your presentations

Xenophanes I don't think that's Theseus' plan

Helia Look at this agenda they've just given us
They've not scheduled any time for presentations

Bia Our plans are practical, beneficial, cheap
In five years we could be standing on our feet
If only he will listen

Eurydice We'll start as we intended
Agriculture, Education, Trade

Eris His men are armed, you know
Is that appropriate in there?

Eurydice They're bodyguards, not warlords

Eris There should be no weapons

Eurydice To take away their guns would frighten them
We don't want that

Xenophanes No more discussion.
Let's take the floor

They exit. Eurydice holds back Thalia, Euphrosyne and Aglaea. Eunomia also remains

Eurydice I have offended him

Thalia How?

Euphrosyne Child, whatever did you say?

Eurydice It isn't what I said
It isn't anything I did

Aglaea He made a pass at you

Eunomia I don't believe it

Thalia motions for Eunomia to stand further away..

Eurydice He said that he was offering equality

Aglaea The hound

Eurydice He said he envied me
He asked me what I was afraid of

Euphrosyne Oh gods, you turned him down

Thalia You have insulted him

Eurydice Maybe he was trying to make a link
To get beneath the mask
Perhaps I misinterpreted –
He didn't mean it as an insult –
Offered me an intimacy

Aglaea He just can't keep it zipped up in his suit

Thalia Don't be flippant

Aglaea This isn't flippancy

Thalia She has insulted the First Citizen of / Athens

Euphrosyne Gods
What can we do?
We must have his / goodwill

Thalia You can't pretend you didn't see it coming
You were flirting with him
All that stuff about the / seven heavens

364

Aglaea She had assumed equality, respect.
  She didn't realise these were gifts to be bestowed by him

Eurydice He'll mow me down in there
  He'll dance all over me
  The fate of Thebes hangs in the balance

Aglaea Thebes the beggar, yes;
  Not Thebes the whore.
  Well done
  You'll make a leader yet

Thalia Sister
  Words said in haste

  Eurydice reaches for the senators.

Eurydice I think
  Under all the swagger
  He's incredibly alone
  And he can't communicate

Aglaea Are you seriously pitying him?

Euphrosyne If it was me
  I must confess
  I'd have that suit off in a minute
  The things you sacrifice for Thebes

Aglaea You get in there
  Exploit his weaknesses as he would exploit yours
  Now take a big deep breath

  Eurydice and Aglaea are exiting into the palace.

Let's have some coffee in there, child

Thalia Our work is cut out now

  Tydeus enters with Pargeia.

Eunomia What do you want here?

365

Pargeia We're coming to the conference
  So make way

Thalia Let me explain one more time
  You are the opposition

Tydeus So?

Eunomia Go away

  They exit.

Tydeus Opposition, yes
  Let's muster it
  The men want action

Pargeia Will you hold back?
  If we start an insurrection
  The Athenians will crush it.
  We need them on our side
  We have to get to Thesues

  Ismene has finished the coffee. She prepares to take it in.

Tydeus Look at this, Pargeia
  It's a real princess

Pargeia Forget that stuck-up little virgin

Tydeus That's no virgin
  It's an inbred royal

Ismene You're an embarrassment to Thebes

Pargeia Your own brother
  My dead husband lies unburied.
  This is the embarrassment to Thebes
  This is the barbarity
  And you, his sister, you do / nothing

Ismene Nothing, I do nothing, no

Pargeia (*to Tydeus*) Come here
We are getting in this conference
Now

Pargeia exits. Tydeus stares at Ismene.

Tydeus I like the way you keep our special secret.
I hear rape's a designated war crime now
And so I guess if you'd felt raped
You would have told.
Pleases me you treasure it.
You drew my blood
Kicking up against me in the dust.
Your teeth tore through my hand
You see that little scar?
My royal souvenir

Ismene Get back

Tydeus Bet there's no other man
Who makes your heartbeat race like that

Tydeus tries to touch her. Ismene pours the coffee on him.

Bitch
You're lucky all is peaceful now
You're lucky I'm so full of love

Pargeia (*re-entering*) Have I been talking to myself? I said get in

Tydeus Look at my fucking suit

Pargeia What did you do to him, you clumsy little slut? You keep away

Pargeia hits Ismene. Haemon enters.

You and your sister and your motherfucking dad

She spits, then exits with Tydeus.

Ismene tries to compose herself.

Haemon Antigone, where did you go?
  Last night I woke and you were gone

Ismene No

Haemon Why did you run away?

Ismene / It's not –

Haemon Listen, let me say it, marry me
  I love you more than anyone
  You're passionate
  And dazzling
  And good and
  All that grief
  If it is loved
  If you are loved
  It won't hurt so unremittingly.
  Please be my wife

Ismene exits. Tiresias is amused.

Haemon Antigone, Antigone

Tiresias Welcome to the country of the blind

Megaera, Miletus and Scud enter with Antigone, bound.

Miletus (*to Haemon*) We need to see Eurydice

Haemon Who are you?

Megaera Her men

Miletus We have a prisoner for her

Haemon Who?

Megaera You can see for yourself

Haemon exits, without seeing Antigone.

Miletus They might reward us

Scud Who?

Miletus The ones who gave us all a vote

Scud I didn't vote

Miletus You're only old enough to kill, not vote

Antigone It's coming
  My destiny
  Swooping through the air
  Atoms heavy with intention

Megaera Shut your face

Antigone The blow will hit me
  Take me off my feet

Scud What blow?

Antigone I am ready

Scud What are atoms?

Miletus Don't be talking to her, Junior Lieutenant – she
is nuts

Scud She's right. There's something here

Megaera No, Scud

Scud (*raising his gun*) I can feel it: something bad

Megaera What are you, a dog?
  You think you sense things humans can't?
  Resist the madness, friend

Antigone You should have let me bury him

Megaera You shut your face

Scud It's like when those trees bent over us
  The day my sister's spine was shot

369

Miletus Don't think of it, Lieutenant

Scud The trees bent forward / whispering

Miletus You were twisted up with drugs

Scud It was the shadow ones

Talthybia enters followed by Ismene.

Ismene I had the coffee made but then –

Talthybia crosses behind Scud dressed in grey. He spins round, sees her. He instantly has his gun trained on her.

Scud GHOST
GET DOWN
GHOST

Talthybia squirms on the floor. Ismene exits back into the palace.

Ismene EURYDICE

Miletus Don't shoot
/ Don't shoot

Ismene / EURYDICE

Scud DON'T MOVE

Megaera / That is not a shadow

The company enters from the palace.

Tydeus What the fuck / is this?

Miletus Scud, if you shoot her, we will be at war again

Scud / We are at war

Euphrosyne What's happening here?

Miletus At peace, Scud. / This is peace

370

Eris Thebans, put down your guns

Thalia / Oh gods
  Oh gods

  *Eurydice and Theseus enter, Phaeax behind them with
  Enyalius, Plautus and Ichnaea, armed.*

Enyalius Put down the gun or we will take you out

Eris / That is not the way

Megaera You take him out and I will kill this bitch down
dead

Enyalius Plautus – cover her

Eris / No guns
  No guns

Phaeax / Put the gun down, move away

  Megaera has her gun pointed at Antigone.

Plautus (*to Megaera*) One inch and I will kill you

Ismene Antigone
  / Antigone

Megaera I am fury

Antigone NO

Theseus What's happened here?

Enyalius Sir, please step back into the building

Miletus No one move

Enyalius Step back into the building, sir

Ichnaea Talthybia, you're fine

Eurydice What's happened here?

Theseus You need to get back in the building

Miletus We caught her burying the dead

Eurydice / Antigone

Talthybia I haven't buried / anyone

Scud Shut up
/ Shut up

Theseus Her name – quick

Ichnaea Talthybia

Theseus It's OK, Talthybia

Talthybia OK, OK

Scud Shut up you, stay there

Ismene Antigone, what have you done?

Eurydice is approaching Scud like a woman who has walked into gunfire before.

Eurydice No one here will harm you, soldier
Please put down the gun

Theseus Now listen –

Miletus aims his gun at Theseus.

Miletus Don't move
The Junior Lieutenant is my responsibility.
NO ONE MOVE

Theseus is frozen.

Scud, look at me
(*To Scud.*) She's not a ghost
She is Athenian
Touch her

Scud touches Talthybia. Eurydice slowly sits on the ground in front of him.

Scud We came to speak to someone

Eurydice I am someone. Speak to me

Scud Somebody who matters

Talthybia She is the –

Scud Shut your mouth, you bitch, or I will shoot

Eurydice I am Eurydice, your president.
There is no need for violence here
Let's all put down the guns

*Miletus lowers his gun. Theseus' aides do not lower
theirs – neither does Megaera.*

Miletus OK, I'm lowering my gun
The Junior Lieutenant was mistaken, simply.
He means no one any harm

Theseus starts to breathe again.

Theseus I thought this palace was secure

Phaeax / These are palace guards, sir
They're supposed to be security

Eris You brought guns into a conference of peace

Theseus How close are we here to being terrorised and
shot?

Eurydice This is one random action

Theseus So is the death of every president

Ichnaea Talthybia, stay down

Talthybia I'm fine, I'm cool, I'm desperately OK

Ichnaea (*to Miletus*) DON'T MOVE

Miletus Scud, tell them what we came for

Plautus changes position.

Megaera Don't move or I will kill her

Scud We were guarding someone. They were dead

Miletus Polynices

Scud As the dawn came I looked up.
Half the sky was shrouded in black cloud
The other half was blue and clear

Miletus You tell them why we're here

Scud That girl was digging, giving him the rites

Pargeia Antigone

Scud The earth was ready for him. Deep
Below me I could feel it gaping wide

Eurydice What is your name?

The Junior Lieutenant tries to remember it.

Miletus We call him Junior Lieutenant Scud

Eurydice The sky at dawn was trying to speak to you.
I know this because I saw it too.
It was telling us to choose our path.
We can choose the dark
Or chase the coming blue, the night cloud or the day.
Another life awaits you, my young son.
I hope it starts today
May blessings be upon you

Megaera lowers her gun.

(*To Scud.*) Now let your sergeant take the gun

Scud is reluctant.

Enyalius Sir, I need to get you back inside

374

Talthybia (*to Scud*) None of this is your responsibility
I can see that you are just a child

Scud, enraged by this, aims his gun at her again.

Scud I am not a child
I am a soldier

*Phaeax fires. Scud falls against Talthybia, shot. Plautus
is disarming Megaera, Enyalius and Ichnaea; Miletus.
Megaera is thrown to the ground, Plautus' foot on her
back. Talthybia crying out in horror.*

Miletus No, No –

Megaera SCUD

Plautus / On your face

Megaera SCUD

Plautus / I want you on your face

Miletus NO

Eurydice What have you done?

Talthybia cries out.

Ichnaea / It's OK
Talthybia, it's cool

Pargeia Get in there. Pick him up –

Haemon (*to Ismene*) Take me to him

Pargeia I said pick him up

Tydeus does so.

Theseus He was about to kill one of my staff

Thalia Oh gods / Oh gods

Aglaea Disaster /
Disaster

Tydeus I've got you, soldier

Theseus Who is in charge?

Miletus I got him through the war
  Right through the war
  I saw him through it to the end
  And now you cunts –

Phaeax We did our job
  / We did what's right

Enyalius / Shut up

Miletus You've no idea
  No fucking clue

Plautus Don't move

Theseus Who controls this rabble?

Eurydice I'm responsible

Theseus Where is your chief of staff?

Eurydice I haven't yet appointed one

Tydeus It should be me, Prince Tydeus

Aglaea Never

Tydeus You can't have a military force without a leader
  / This is the result

Eurydice I am the leader

Megaera You stand and let them disarm Theban men?
You bitch of Athens

Pargeia That's right, sister, speak your mind

Megaera / I'll shout it from the walls what you have
done

Eurydice Will you call your men away?

*Theseus gestures. His men lower their guns. Scud is
dying.*

Haemon Who has first aid? One of you Athenians must
have first aid

Phaeax I'm trained
I have first aid

Haemon THEN MOVE
How can you watch me and not help?
HE'S DYING

Phaeax and Ichnaea go to assist.

Megaera SCUD
/ SCUD

Thalia The war is over. Why is this boy still in a uniform?

Miletus There's nothing else for him but begging

Megaera SCUD

Miletus They made a killer of him overnight
Do you expect he'll just as easily become a boy again?

Tydeus Weak Theban leadership has almost killed King
Theseus

Euphrosyne You damned hyena
Here to feast upon a dead boy's corpse

Tydeus You almost sent the hope of Athens
Home to his good people in a box
/ This is how incapable these women are

Thalia Theseus, this is a war criminal
/ He means destruction I can promise you

Tydeus Who knows the situation with these armed
militias? Me

Who can control them? Me
Who do you need here?

Pargeia Prince Tydeus

Haemon Get him in
ALL OF YOU GET HIM INSIDE
I need clean water
Bright dazzling lights
Ismene

Ismene Here

Haemon Help me

Thalia Take him in there. Get him on the table

They exit, Miletus, Megaera and Thalia with them.

Aglaea (*to Euphrosyne*) We're going to the barracks, now.
We need the remnants of the army on our side

Euphrosyne / I am with you

They exit.

Pargeia (*to Tydeus*) Go to your men; prepare them.

Tydeus His blood is –

Pargeia Give me some

Tydeus Piglets

Pargeia I'll say I held him by your side

Tydeus Mama would never pay the butcher for the task
We'd hang them up and slit their piggy throats

Pargeia Forget the pigs

Tydeus Catching all the splatter in a pail

Pargeia Tell Theseus you love him. Now

Tydeus I am at your service, Theseus

> *All go except Eurydice, Theseus and Antigone.*
>   *The bodyguards also remain, on high alert.*
>   *Harmonia has watched the death of Scud with horror.*
>   *She is riveted by all that follows.*

Eurydice You sanctioned murder in my house

Theseus I think you'll find that I contained an incident

Eurydice Who rules this land now, Theseus?

Theseus It's ruled by every wild card with a gun who walks in through your gates. My mandate's to / protect my people

Eurydice Your mandate's to provide peacekeepers, not to start another war

Theseus Who was aggressor there?

Eurydice The men who shot that boy

Theseus They kept the peace

Eurydice I had the peace. I had it in my hand. He was about to / give away his gun

Theseus To kill my citizen

Antigone I'm fighting with the gods of death
   They are above ground
   I'm trying to appease
   To do what they require

Theseus She was burying her brother
   Who would not?

Antigone I've fought with them and begged
   And now
   They're feeding on that boy.

This is not
Is not my destiny

Talthybia enters. She is covered in blood.

Talthybia He's dead. Your son tried what he could but –

Eurydice Thank you very much, Talthybia

Talthybia The table
He is lying on the table
Blood
The documents are
All his blood

Tiresias The sun will not race through the day
Before you have surrendered up
One born of your own loins
To feed the gods of death, for what you've done

Theseus What is it with that hag?

Eurydice Tiresias

Theseus Why do you tolerate her here?
How can a modern state have room for this?
(*To Tiresias.*) Who were you speaking to? To her
Or me? Whose loins?
What the fuck are loins supposed to be?
Do men and women both have loins –
Well do they?

Talthybia I don't know, sir

Theseus What do you have, hag?

Tiresias The day comes soon when grief
Will break like waves through halls of power.
A suicide and then a son

Theseus Whose son? What suicide?

Tiresias It's coming. It will come

380

Antigone Many years ago when Oedipus was young
Tiresias saved Thebes. There was an epidemic
And his revelations saved us. He said
My father was the curse upon our land.
Oedipus was murderous incestuous corruption
And his children, all of us so small
He called a crowd of horrors

Eurydice Antigone

Theseus What else has she foreseen?

Eurydice I never listen to a word

Theseus What has it said?

Eurydice Tiresias has only ever spoken once to me. It was just before you came
I took it as a joke. He said

Tiresias 'If you intend to fuck the god of power, don't fall asleep beside him'

Theseus And do you?

Eurydice Do I what?

Theseus Intend to fuck with him?

Eurydice I don't see him anywhere

Theseus Miss

Talthybia My name's / Talthybia

Theseus Could you please organise an imminent departure?

Eurydice DON'T

Theseus Since I stepped on Theban soil I've felt unclean; as if your vile, atavistic war was all my goddam fault. / How dare you –

381

Eurydice Are we not behaving like the pets you hoped to tame?
   Are you discovering instead of women pliable and biddable
   That we're passionate and human; that we're free?
   No one wants a strong and healthy Thebes, not you, not Sparta

Theseus From now on you will be dealing with my people. My sense of international responsibility, my goddam decency prevents me pulling out my men today

Eurydice You're going to run away?

Theseus My personal involvement with you ends right now

Eurydice That is not leadership

Theseus My life was put in danger here. I could have died

Eurydice DON'T GO

Theseus You have / not said a single word

Eurydice Do not abandon us

Theseus There has been no apology

Eurydice I'm begging you
   I'm sorry
   Please don't go

Theseus Pathetic

Theseus exits. Phaeax enters, also covered in blood. He is doing his best to clean his hands with surgical wipes

Phaeax Where's Theseus? We need to know what his instructions are for the disposal of the body

Eurydice THAT IS THEBAN BUSINESS

Talthybia Theseus has just informed us that his diplomatic mission here is over

Phaeax Oh

Talthybia Have you got anything to say?

Phaeax I have some wipes here
   You should use them
   You should really clean yourself
   The blood you know
   It might be –
   Look
   I've only got first aid
   I'm not a surgeon
   And that Theban guy
   He couldn't see
   I saved your life
   You were down there in the dust
   That psycho had a gun right at your head
   I was aiming for his arm, OK? (*He approaches her.*)
   You know I'm not at liberty to take responsibility for this
   If I accept responsibility then our insurance policy won't cover me
   There is a protocol I have to follow here, you know that.
   But off the record, strictly off the record
   Sorry

Talthybia You are going to be my bitch
   You understand that?
   You are now my bitch

   Talthybia exits.

Phaeax Fuck

Phaeax exits. Harmonia inches forward.

Eurydice So this is not your destiny?

Antigone shakes her head.

I can't believe
    That you would side
    With Prince Tydeus and the tyrant's wife
    I thought that your integrity was absolute
    So pure you make the rest of us feel tainted

Antigone For me alone
    I had to bury him

Eurydice Why?

Antigone Because it's right

Eurydice Out of your rightness what will come?
    A boy is dead
    The citizen of Athens turns his back
    I should throw you in a stinking cell for this
    What do you think will happen?

Antigone Send me to the dark

Eurydice So Prince Tydeus can take up your part?
    That widowed spider's spinning up support;
    The forces I have tried so hard to quell
    Are baying once again for power
    This is the entry into chaos

Antigone Let me
    In the dark and squalor of a cell
    Give me the means
    I'll kill myself
    To die is to be free

Eurydice Antigone

Antigone I'm no different from my brother
    I have a violent, prehistoric heart
    I should be dead with Polynices
    Let me be dead

Eurydice I could have smothered him in flesh-dissolving
lime
    And dumped him in the ground
    But
    What he did to Creon, to Menoceus my boy –
    What he did to Thebes
    I hated him
    I hate him
    My heart is violent and it's vengeful too
    And I have dressed it up as reparation
    Shrouded it in reconciliation
    Saying maybe we will learn from staring at his face
    The face of chaos. Maybe we'll choose life,
    Life and order and society
    As the alternative is him. But when
    I stared down at the mottled thing
    I felt euphoria of savage hate
    It made me glad to see him rot.
    It is an act of hatred that I've done
    A desecration
    And I'm guilty
    And it is my fault
    I caused that child soldier's death
    And lost the help of Athens.
    This is the match that lights my own destruction
    Not to do what I've exhorted all my countrymen to do:
    Be reconciled.
    I cannot reconcile
    I hate him, still I hate
    He took my boy and mutilated him
    And if I'm full of vicious, unforgiving hate

The moderate and principled
New president of Thebes
What future is there for us?

Antigone Ismene thinks about the future all the time and
Haemon too.
I've never understood their lack of fear.
My future's always been the desolate track
I walked on with my father
Leading on ahead past rotting crops and bloated dogs
Through burning villages, through war.
Oedipus was saved the sight
But I saw my destiny, my destination
Death

Eurydice Oedipus
The way he fed upon your spirit
Took the youth in you and made it old
Dragged your hand through all his suffering
He was a selfish, blind old man

*Harmonia looks from Antigone to Tiresias. Tiresias
requires a drink. She serves him.*

My son Haemon is in love with you
I wish it was Ismene but it's you
You know that, don't you?

Antigone Yes

Eurydice You see the antidote to suffering
The opposite of great heroic destiny
Is a quiet ordinary life: to love.
You've done enough for death, Antigone
You can retire from service I would say
Tiresias please tell her she is free

Tiresias I only see a suicide
A woman hanging by the neck

386

Her hair like trailing moss

Eurydice You are despicable

Tiresias I wish I could see differently
The shadow of that boy
He's watching you

This deeply unsettles Harmonia.

Antigone What's to be done?

Eurydice There's no such thing as destiny
There's only change

Antigone Please will you bury my brother?

Eurydice You're asking me to admit my mistake

Antigone You already have

Eurydice In politics, I'll die

Antigone I never see the politics
I'm blind to them

Eurydice No, you see too clearly;
You've always seen through me
Right through my careful mask.
If I am weak
If I turn round and put that carcass in the earth
I fear the enemies of freedom
Will run me down like painted wolves.

*The soldiers, Haemon, Ismene and the senators enter.
They are carrying the dead Junior Lieutenant.
Harmonia picks up Tiresias' staff. She sings, high and
free. A funeral song.*

Harmonia
The gods of death
Have feasted here

Lift your soul
Up to Elysium

May you be free
May you be free

*The procession passes. Harmonia, Eurydice and
Antigone become a part of it. Tiresias remains.*

Act Four

Two graves. The senators between them, Antigone,
Haemon, Ismene, Miletus, Megaera; bystanders,
Polykleitos among them. Eurydice stares at both graves,
covered with the mud of digging.

Haemon The crowd, Mumma
 They need to hear you speak

 Eurydice is silent, head bowed.

Talk to the crowd

Eurydice This heavy mask of power.
 It will tear off my face

Haemon When they pulled the shrapnel from my eyes.
 And I was lying, knowing that my useful life was over
 You washed me, dressed me and you said get up.
 I'd have liked it if you'd rained down tears
 But you handed me a stick. Get up

 Haemon helps her up. She turns to the crowd.

Thalia Your strongest words

Eurydice By insulting Polynices
 I've insulted all the dead.
 I have been wrong
 I'm trying to turn back time one hour
 And it keeps buckling against me, flying on
 The death of Junior Lieutenant Scud
 Is my responsibility
 I won't insult him with my sorrow and my shame
 But I must give his death some value

389

Since his life was held so cheap.
Today, we've buried two dead Theban boys;
One, in life a mighty powerful man
One still a child, without a proper name.
General Polynices, son of Oedipus
And Junior Lieutenant Scud.
The way we treat these boys in death
Must illuminate how we intend to live
The Junior Lieutenant will be honoured,
Foremost son of Thebes.
Polynices will lie at his feet,
Marked only with his name.
In death, the general will wait upon the child

Thalia In death, the general will wait upon the child

Polykleitos kneels. Thalia kneels. The rest follow suit.

ELSEWHERE: *Tydeus and Pargeia.*

Tydeus My arteries are coursing with my god
My Dionysus, my amphetamine

Pargeia Where are our men?

Tydeus They're plucked up from the gutters, shacks and bars
Shaken, made alive with guns.
I've been up there on my truck
With Spartan weapons in my hand
Preaching revolution, Theban style.
The coup, swift and irrevocable
Has always favoured men like me –

Pargeia Stop now
Hold back
You keep them on the leash

Tydeus The open tear in time won't last
I feel it closing even now –

Pargeia Eurydice has left the web.
  The big presidential spider
  Should be in the centre
  Feeling every shift upon the threads
  But she's gone, she's scuttled off
  Theseus is all alone up here
  And enmity's between him and Eurydice

Tydeus I have to do some politics

Pargeia Shape up to it, come on, shape up
  Shine up that skilful tongue of yours
  We could have Theseus without the violence.
  If Athens backs us Thebes is ours – elections all be
fucked
  You know it's Athens chooses leaders, props them up.
  All this blah-blah-blah about democracy –
  If they don't like the people's choice, they topple it

Tydeus Why do you always have the fucking plan?

  He tries to kiss her.

Pargeia No time for that
  Not yet, my Prince
  But soon

  She gives him a promise of something more.

Don't go in to Theseus all painted like a wolf.
  That gives the wrong impression straight away

Tydeus I'm going for gold, Pargeia

Pargeia Go for gold

  ELSEWHERE: *by the graves.*

  Euphrosyne and Aglaea speak intimately with Eurydice.

Aglaea Tydeus has coiled up his men
  And they are waiting
  Stationed round the palace set to spring

Euphrosyne We have secured the military with promises of money we don't have. The remnants of the factions – they will fight for you

Eurydice It must not come to that
    Our mission must remain a peaceful one
    Or what have we become?

Euphrosyne Our government's unique in all the world.
It is worth fighting for

Eurydice Our government will be unique if we can maintain power without resort to violence. That is the thing worth fighting for

Aglaea I have imposed a no-fly zone.
    Under the circumstances it seemed pertinent.
    It also means that Theseus can't leave

Eurydice You genius

Aglaea You must get back.
    To spend hours kneeling in the sun
    It is not wise

Eurydice It is essential

    Pargeia enters.

Pargeia Thebes, you do not have a president, you have a coward
    First she desecrates my husband's corpse
    And then, when she perceives the horror of her crime
    She quickly throws my Polynices in the ground

Antigone Did your husband bury those he slew?

Eurydice Antigone

Antigone Their bodies rot there still in fields and streets.
    And now he's dead you've got the next best thing
    Apprentice tyrant Prince Tydeus

392

Pargeia Tydeus is the leader that we need
  He does the work of gods

Antigone I saw his work in villages
  Women, little girls
  All dead and stinking
  Seething with the ants

*Megaera cocks her gun at Antigone – an automatic
gesture of defence.*

Pargeia You have no shred of evidence against the Prince

Ismene I do

Megaera stands with Pargeia. She lowers her gun.

Pargeia Thebans, Theseus is leaving
  Eurydice has driven him away.
  He is packing up
  And with him goes our hope.
  Who wants their children to be fed?
  Who wants a future of prosperity?
  March with me to the palace
  Where your Prince is now with Theseus
  Prince Tydeus, trying to mend
  What these incompetents have broken.
  He is now our hope –
  The Prince
  Come with me for the Prince

Megaera The Prince

Pargeia The Prince

*Pargeia exits. Megaera follows with some of the crowd.
Cries of 'The Prince'.*

Eurydice I wish that Thebes could mend itself without
the rich world's help. I wish that we could find the unity,
the strength. But in the meantime invite the Spartans to
the talks

393

Aglaea Thank you
  I must confess
  I did already
  They arrive tonight
  Say nothing; sack me later

Eurydice You should be our leader

Aglaea Yes, but no one likes me. They elected you

Eurydice Citizens of Thebes
  Theseus is not about to leave
  We will secure his friendship – that I promise you.
  In less than one hour's time
  We will have the hand of Athens in our own
  And all our future hopes secure

  She turns to go.

Aglaea Can we deliver that?

Eurydice Now I've said it, we will have to

  Eurydice exits with her senators.

Thalia You said 'I do'
  Evidence
  Tydeus
  What do you have?

Ismene Nothing
  I have nothing, no

Thalia Please find your courage
  Speak

Ismene No evidence
  I scrubbed it all away

Antigone Ismene

Ismene I'm going to Athens. I'll ask Theseus to let me tag along: a souvenir of Thebes. In Athens I wouldn't

394

have to be a relic from this house. I could wear jeans and smoke

Antigone How can you be flippant?

Ismene I think it's in my nature, buried under years, to be quite shallow and to laugh. I think alone of Oedipus' children I've got a sense of humour. Burying our brother nearly split my sides. And the biggest joke of all is that Haemon has proposed. He has asked you, Antigone, to be his wife.
    It was a nice proposal; very sweet.
    But by mistake
    The stupid, eyeless oaf made it to me.
    (*To Haemon.*) I've been in love with you since I was nine

Ismene exits.

Antigone Ismene
    ISMENE

Antigone runs off after her.

Thalia Polykleitos. You could tell them what Tydeus did

Polykleitos I don't think I could get my mouth to move

Thalia What if he becomes respectable?
    That's what he intends
    Come with me

Polykleitos Who'd believe? The people who can shout with passion always win. There is no point

Haemon They win because the men like you, the best of us, keep quiet

Miletus What happened to your eyes?

Haemon I'm blind
    I couldn't save your friend

Miletus Early in the war
The general I was with
Would kill a child before each fight
And we would drink the blood.
The place I was
Was so far gone
That I could see no harm.
One night I woke to find a bushknife at my neck
A woman holding it
Her hands were stinking with our blood
I was the only soldier she had left alive
'You are our sons,' she said
And somewhere in me
What was human in me woke.
She said she'd spare my life and lift her curse
If I could save as many as I'd killed.
I managed only two
Just one remains.

*Harmonia sings. Miletus leaves his gun on Scud's
grave. He exits.*
    Harmonia gives Haemon Tiresias' staff.
    Antigone enters.

Antigone Ismene said, 'Can you not see?'

Haemon Antigone

Antigone I want to see
What life is like
To live

Act Five

Theseus and Tydeus enter.

Tydeus The women turn him on
They get him all worked up with dancing
Then they run off to the mountains
To perform their rites.
And Pentheus can't find
The thing, you know
The thing that makes us men

Talthybia enters.

Theseus He loses his –

Tydeus Not physically –
All the inside stuff

Theseus Testosterone?

Tydeus Not quite

Talthybia Excuse me
This is Prince Tydeus

Theseus Yes, I know that

Talthybia He's accused of war crimes, Theseus

Theseus I think I left the phone you gave me in my quarters. Would you go and see if there's a message from my son?

Talthybia exits.

So Pentheus is unmanned

397

Tydeus With the help of Dionysus he applies some make-up and he dresses up

Theseus He wants to find out what it's like to be a woman?

Tydeus Have you never wondered, sir?
    The myths are where we risk
    What we would never think in life.
    Pentheus was mad with longing
    He was desperate to join the rites

Theseus To dance

Tydeus He follows them into the wild
    He climbs a tree
    He watches all their secrets
    Feels as isolated as a star
    He cries
    His tears go splash upon the women underneath
    They look up.
    Red alert
    A man in drag

Theseus What do they do?

Tydeus I can't believe you come to Thebes and you don't know this story. That great gang of naked women dragged Pentheus on to the ground and pulled him limb from limb with their bare hands. Those ladies and those little girls dismembered him. They tore his dick off and his head off and his own mother and his aunts were playing with his body parts like they were bits of ram goat ready for the grill

Theseus Shit

The sound of a crowd begins to approach.

Tydeus That's quite a story, isn't it?

Theseus That's fucking elemental

Tydeus It's true
(*Pointing to Tiresias.*) You ask her
She was there

Tiresias The furies
Zeus himself bows down to them
One of them is coming
An avenger to destroy you

Theseus Oh shut up
Shut up
I'm going to build a care home here
For beggarly transgender types
I'm going to take you off the street
Stick you on a rocking chair in front of a TV
And feed you the strongest psychotropic drugs
That medicine can buy

Tiresias Where is my child?
I bought her from her mother
She is mine

Tydeus You can see why we're all wary of the womenfolk
round here

Phaeax enters.

Phaeax Sir, we've just been told that Thebes is in a state
of high alert. Crowds are marching through the streets.
A no-fly zone has been imposed

Theseus Excuse me?

Phaeax Air space has been / prohibited

Theseus I know what a no-fly zone is

Phaeax The Theban senators insist we stay in our
chambers until such time as they can guarantee our safety

399

Theseus Are you a moron?

Phaeax No, sir

Theseus Yes, I think you are

Phaeax This information you may judge to be moronic.
I am merely its deliverer

Theseus You pulled your trigger on that boy. You were
his deliverer. It was moronic

Talthybia enters.

Phaeax We were aiming to disarm, not kill.
We followed your own protocol
I protected you
And then I tried to save his life.
I don't know why I'm getting all this shit

Talthybia (*handing Theseus the mobile*) Theseus, you
have no messages

Theseus hands the mobile to Phaeax.

Theseus Get me my son, Hippolytus. I want to talk to
him right now. He's stationed up at Troezen under
General Pirithous. Young man –

Phaeax Yes, sir?

Theseus Don't cry in front of me

Phaeax exits.

Theseus Tell Eurydice that I have no intention of
resuming talks

Talthybia Sir, if I may –

Theseus Her no-fly zone is a pathetic ruse to keep me
here

Talthybia There's a crowd approaching, some / sort of
protest –

Theseus Get it lifted, crowd or not

  Talthybia exits.

Those women ripping up King Pentheus –
  That's just a myth, that's not your history, right?

Tydeus All violence in Thebes is mythic
  It soon fades into the past
  Loses its immediacy and force.
  You'll find our civil war is mythic too
  Blown into distorted shapes.
  The violence happened
  But it wasn't real

Theseus That's a disturbing answer

Tydeus I can keep order here in Thebes
  I'd see your will was done.
  I'd make sure that Thebes becomes whatever you desire
  Thebes needs a man like you;
  You're strong and clear; you give us hope
  And in this small, material world
  First Citizen of Athens
  You're the nearest thing to Dionysus that I've ever seen

  Phaeax enters. The sound of the crowd is much nearer.

Phaeax Sir, I spoke with General Pirithous. He says your
son Hippolytus is absent without leave. He left the base
last night to see your wife, at your request. Since then,
nothing has been heard of him. The general is offering to
search your coastal residence

Theseus Thank him. Tell him yes

Phaeax There is a crowd sir, gathering down there. The
peacekeepers await your orders. What should I be telling
them?

Theseus To keep the peace

Phaeax And how should they interpret that?

Theseus Could you get out of here?

Phaeax exits.

I'm strangely –
    Since I got here I have –
    My conviction, yes, my certainty has gone.
    My easy access to the gods themselves:
    Suddenly it's all obscured.
    I feel some revelation, some disaster is at hand

Tydeus Theseus

Theseus Said way too much. I'm going to walk away

Tydeus It's Thebes that is off-centre, not yourself.
    You stick an upright man into a gale,
    A cyclone, and the cyclone will prevail.
    Thebes hasn't done with chaos yet.

Pargeia enters. Megaera stays by the door. She watches Prince Tydeus closely.

Eurydice will never hold it back
    The very female nature is chaotic.
    They can't structure or impose
    They won't inspire respect
    The woman
    She should do what she was made for

Pargeia And what's that?

Tydeus Pargeia

Pargeia I've led the people up to greet you, Theseus
    They would so appreciate a glimpse

Theseus For what?

Pargeia News has been leaked that you are going to leave

402

us. Violence is erupting. People feel Eurydice has let them down; they feel betrayed. They've come to beg you not to go. I know you haven't taken well to Thebes but we could find a lot of ways to make your visits here a pleasure

Eurydice enters with Aglaea and Euphrosyne. She is still covered in dirt from digging.

Eurydice Theseus
You are free to leave at any time.
We will ensure safe passage through our air space

Theseus Have you still got authority?

Eurydice Thank you for everything you've done here
It has been a pleasure speaking with you – genuinely.
Now if you'll excuse us, we've a conference to prepare
We expect the Spartans shortly

Theseus What?

Euphrosyne The Spartans are arriving

Eurydice I was hoping beggars could be choosers but it seems we can't

Theseus Let me tell you about Sparta

Euphrosyne We are not ignorant

Theseus The Spartans do not tolerate the weak

Aglaea We are not weak

Theseus They feel no responsibility to improve your lot. They're here to feast upon your natural resources. You can be sure of that

Aglaea And Athens offers us an economic zone

Theseus They'll strip you bare

Eurydice Our people go to bed with hunger craving in

403

their bellies every night. Right now we'll entertain any regime that gives us means to feed them

Theseus If you want an independent, democratic Thebes –

Eurydice I want people to survive
Mine are the politics of dire need.
I am president of famine
First citizen of rubble, plague and debt
And hungry dogs are scavenging the waste.
Athens, Sparta
If you cannot help
May you devour yourselves

Theseus I can't believe you'd speak to me like this.
I came here so compassionate
So full of energy, of admiration;
I was going to pledge myself to your improvement.
You make me feel like I'm a wicked man
And I don't like that, not one bit.
I AM THE HOPE OF ATHENS AND THE WORLD

Eurydice Then come out with me and tell the crowd

Pause.

Tydeus How can I assist you, Theseus?
Because to bring the Spartans into things
That is an insult
I'm insulted here on your behalf

Pargeia After everything you've done for Thebes

Tydeus I would never deal with the Spartans

Euphrosyne Unless you're buying weapons from them

Tydeus You know what I'm reminded of?
With all these ladies situated here
Hyenas trying their weight against the lions

Talthybia enters with Thalia and Polykleitos.

Theseus Tabitha, I asked my aide to make a call for me –

Talthybia My name's Talthybia
  Please have the courtesy to get it right.
  This is Polykleitos, a mechanic
  And you know the Minister of Justice, Thalia

Thalia Please will you witness this man's testimony?

Polykleitos You were my hero
  I taught my son to love you
  We had you on a poster
  Your face
  Tacked up on our garage wall.
  I've meditated on your face
  That tsetse face

Tydeus I don't know you, brother

Polykleitos We were hiding from the massacre
  My son was terrified.
  His name was Opheltes and he was five years old
  You shot the locks
  We saw you kick the door
  The light surrounded you
  That grin.
  My son, he ran to you
  As if you were a hero come to save us.
  And
  You pinned him on a bayonet
  You lifted him
  Laughed at your strength as you held him aloft
  Shaking the gun
  The blood dropped like rain
  My boy
  Bewildered at his death.
  Your twisting laugh;
  It rings in my ears in the night

Tydeus I don't know you

Polykleitos You killed my son
You burned my home
You don't know me
I am the coward who hid
And watched the flames
Even as they
Even as they ate

Tydeus I'm so sorry for your loss
But you're mistaken, friend

Polykleitos I know the moment lies in wait for you
When Opheltes in all his innocence
Will step into your mind and shake your sanity to pieces

Megaera Whoosh

Polykleitos I'd like to go

Polykleitos exits with Thalia. The noise of the restless crowd is louder.

Eurydice Excuse me
The future will not wait

Aglaea Thank you for your interest in Thebes

Eurydice exits with Aglaea and Euphrosyne.

Pargeia Theseus, if you would step outside with Prince Tydeus and myself, I think that we could calm the situation down

Theseus You must be so naive
Political babies, both of you.
You are untouchable;
A tyrant's wife, a warlord

Tydeus But privately, when you and I were speaking –

Theseus I don't recall I ever met you
This private conversation is a myth

Tydeus Our paths will cross again
Much sooner than you think
And when they do
We will remember this

Tydeus and Pargeia leave. Megaera follows them.

Theseus I'm cold
I felt a sudden fear go down my back
My hairs are standing up

Talthybia Thebes has a very strong effect.
I'd like to stay here
The Theban attitude would seem to be
That in the face of our destruction
The only thing humanity can do
Is to create

Phaeax enters.

Phaeax Sir, I've General Pirithous on the phone

Theseus What is it?

Phaeax He
Is at your home

Theseus What is it?

ELSEWHERE: *Pargeia, Tydeus, Megaera enter.*

Pargeia You fucked it up
You fucked it up

Tydeus You fat degenerate obscene salacious slut

Pargeia I am not fat

Tydeus You fucking threw yourself at him

Pargeia You were in love with him
  I saw it in your eyes
  Big Theseus
  You dumb cocksucker

Tydeus I had him so he almost called me brother

Pargeia You would have given him your naked butt
  If I had not arrived.
  You're all the same, you men
  You go round raping women to disguise the fact
  You like it from each other best

Tydeus You're filth

Pargeia I'm debris, I am waste, I'm dereliction, I am frenzy

Tydeus You could survive in hell itself

Pargeia I have.
  Give your men the word

Tydeus It's time

Pargeia Unleash the god of uproar on this town

Tydeus Uproar

Pargeia Cry fury

Tydeus / Fury

Megaera Fury

Megaera stabs Tydeus. He falls against Pargeia.

Pargeia What have you done?

Megaera I have seen that mouth before
  Against the sun, above me, twisting, hurting
  In a village by a river where I used to be a girl

Pargeia Prince –

Megaera Let me go now, furies

408

Let me go

Megaera exits.

ELSEWHERE: *Eurydice is washing. Ismene waiting.*

Eurydice I can go out without him
Go out before the people quite alone.
I'll tell them Thebes must find a way
To be a nation that regenerates itself
That without the crumbs of help
From monstrous foreign powers
We can begin to grow

Ismene That is a fantasy
I'm sorry but your optimism's ludicrous
It sickens me

Eurydice Ismene –

Ismene What special quality allows you to believe
That you can challenge or change anything?

Eurydice What's happened?
My sweet girl

Ismene Not sweet
Not girl
Forgive me
I have not survived this war

Theseus enters.

Theseus You refuse to see me

Eurydice This is my private room

Theseus That is childish
And it is a great mistake

Eurydice I have not refused to see you – I am washing

Theseus I offered you equality

Eurydice No you did not

Theseus It's not equality you want
You think yourself superior in every way
Behaving like a prehistoric queen

Eurydice Theseus, I am a beggar not a queen
I beg you to keep faith with me
And with my government.
Come before the people with me please
Or everything I'm fighting for is lost.
I have no desire to sell myself to Sparta
If it comes to that then I would rather dance for you

Pause.

Theseus Two snakes, slithering mistrust
That's what your prophet said.
Do you think in essence
That it's like that with a woman and a man?

Eurydice If they're politicians.
I would love to trust you, Theseus

Theseus I got a call
From General Pirithous
He is in my house
He said –

Eurydice What is it?

Theseus Phaedra
She is dead

Theseus is suddenly exhausted, as if a great shock has hit him.

Eurydice Ismene

Ismene gets a stool.

Theseus Phaedra
She is hanging
Hanging from the beam
Above our bed.

Theseus half collapses. She helps him on to the stool.

The scale of chaos here:
    To mend it is beyond me.
    The haemorrhage of cash
    The manpower it would need
    To bring Thebes to prosperity –

Eurydice Theseus

Theseus I knew
    That something in my life was going to break
    Phaedra
    My son

Eurydice Where is he?

Theseus They don't know
    What did he do to her?
    He hated her

Eurydice You cannot know that it was him

Theseus Curse him

Eurydice Please don't say that

Theseus CURSE HIM

Eurydice You are speaking in your grief

Theseus I know your government is brave
    And you deserve success.
    Forgive me but –
    I haven't got the –
    Cannot deal with Sparta
    But
    I'll come outside with you
    Give you my hand

Eurydice I married Creon at sixteen
    He was forty-five.
    The young feel such despair

411

Phaedra
There was a time –
To die like that
It could have been my end

Theseus I'm sorry that I asked you for a dance

Eurydice These fists of yours
One force, one gentleness
Open them

Theseus Athens
Come to Athens
We will reconvene
You have my word

Eurydice Next time we meet
I hope that when our battle's done
We'll see each other
Masks off, as ourselves

Theseus Eurydice
Perhaps we'll risk our trust

They exit, out to the crowd.

ELSEWHERE: *Antigone enters with Haemon. She sees Tiresias, alone. She helps him up.*

Antigone What do you see, Tiresias?

Tiresias My child has gone

Antigone Where is my destiny?

Tiresias In darkness

Antigone You see nothing?

Tiresias Nothing, no

Antigone Then the future's mine to make

Haemon The future is the country of the blind. It must belong to me

Antigone In Athens, they have great machines that see inside your head. In Athens, they have doctors who could mend your eyes

Haemon Not just mend; they can transplant. They take the eyes from fresh cadavers and with surgery as skilful and as delicate as art, they can insert them in a blind man's skull. In Athens we could see through reawakened eyes. What do you say to that, Tiresias?

Antigone I say it is a land of miracles

Tiresias Numberless indignant birds
Are making storm clouds in Athenian skies.
One day men of Thebes, as conquerors
Will walk into that devastated town
And sweep away the ruins of its power.
Greed that eats, will eat itself.
Athens' time will come

Aides prepare for a departure, taking all the paraphernalia of a diplomatic visit.

Polykleitos continues his work.

The senators enter, preparing for the arrival of the Spartans.

Through the politics, Antigone, leading the blind men.

Ismene, dressed in Athenian clothes, pleads with Phaeax to be let on the helicopter. He is unforthcoming. She exits after him, still pleading.

Talthybia enters. Harmonia is holding papers for her. They crouch together in the blast. Talthybia loses her hair-do. They exit, as the noise of the helicopter begins to fade.

Epilogue

Dust and emptiness – but for the figure of Miletus.
  Megaera enters.

Megaera Miletus, where are you going?

Miletus Athens

Megaera Why?

Miletus Because I want

Megaera Want what?

Miletus That stuff they got

Megaera And what's that?

Miletus Everything

Megaera But Athens
  They won't let us in

Miletus You coming too?

Megaera I'll keep you company
  As long as you don't give me all your shit

Miletus Be fair

Megaera That sergeant shit
  Don't try and pull that
  You are not my sergeant now

Miletus I'm just the man that's standing here
  His pockets full of breeze.
  There's nothing more to me than this

Megaera That's man enough for me

Miletus Glad to hear it
  Glad you finally have eyes

Megaera So how you going to get to Athens, in your limousine?

Miletus The Theban way

Megaera How's that?

Miletus On my big Theban feet

Megaera It's far away

Miletus So far away they got a different sky

Megaera They don't like Thebans there

Miletus I heard that too

Megaera We're likely to get shut outside their gates

Miletus That's right. At best, they'll give us shitty jobs like sweeping up their streets

Megaera Their streets are clean already. And those dingy places no one wants to live, I hear they've all got flushing toilets and TVs

Miletus Athens has a lot of crime

Megaera That's right. It's quite a violent place

Miletus You think you'll handle it?

Megaera I cannot wait. You think they'll stop us at the gates?

Miletus Megaera, woman, what do you suggest?

Megaera Miletus, man,
  They give us any shit
  They stand there in their marble palaces and try to keep us out
  We'll soak our rags in petrol
  And we'll burn their city down

HANDBAGGED

For Susan Buffini
Bigger than both of them

*This play would not have been written
without the help and encouragement
of Indhu Rubasingham*

Handbagged is a fictional account which has
been inspired by true events. Incidents, characters
and timelines have been changed for dramatic purposes.
Often, the words are those imagined by the author.
The play should not be understood as biography
or any other kind of factual account.

Handbagged was first performed at the Tricycle Theatre, London, on 26 September 2013. The cast, in alphabetical order, was as follows:

Q Marion Bailey
T Stella Gonet
Liz Clare Holman
Actor 1 Neet Mohan
Actor 2 Jeff Rawle
Mags Fenella Woolgar

Director Indhu Rubasingham
Designer Richard Kent
Lighting Designer Oliver Fenwick
Sound Designer Carolyn Downing

Characters

T
an older Margaret Thatcher

Q
an older Queen Elizabeth II

Mags
a younger Margaret Thatcher

Liz
a younger Queen Elizabeth II

Actor 1
playing
A Palace Footman
Kenneth Kaunda
Nancy Reagan
Enoch Powell
Michael Shea
Neil Kinnock
Kenneth Clarke
A Protestor

Actor 2
playing
Denis Thatcher
Peter Carrington
Gerry Adams
Ronald Reagan
Michael Heseltine
Arthur Scargill
Rupert Murdoch
Geoffrey Howe
Prince Philip

ONE:
THOSE ARE PEARLS THAT WERE HER EYES

Mrs Thatcher, elderly. She prepares to address us.

T   Freedom
Freedom and democracy
They are things worth dying for.
We must never
Never stop resisting those who would take them
from us
And when they have been taken
We will fight until we get them back.

The act of resistance is our defining act as
human beings.
To say 'No, I will not stand for that,'
I will not collude, collaborate, negotiate
I will not compromise'
To say to the enemies of freedom 'You are
wrong'
To resist, whatever the cost

To say No

This is courage
This is integrity.
I would be proud if this word defined me:

NO

I'd like a chair
I don't need one but I'd like one
I will not ask for one
If I wait, they will notice

They will bring me one

One of the men

Dancing around me in their suits
Ties flapping in the wind.
Holding their documents like babies
The men
I could pin them wriggling with my gaze
And then release them with a smile
I liked to do it
Girlish
I was girlish

Queen Elizabeth II enters dragging a chair. She is elderly.

Q   You look as if you need a chair

T   I'm quite capable of standing, thank you

Q   I'm bringing you a chair

T   There really isn't any need

The Queen places it.

Q   Here

T   No thank you

Q   I've gone and brought it now, sit down

T   Thank you, no

Pause.

Q   We conceive parliamentary institutions, with their free speech and respect for the rights of minorities, to be a precious part of our way of life and outlook. They inspire a broad tolerance in thought and expression.
During recent centuries, this message has been

sustained and invigorated by the immense
contribution, in language, literature, and action,
of the nations of our Commonwealth overseas.
Our Commonwealth gives expression, as I pray
it always will, to living principles as sacred to
the Crown and Monarchy as to its many
Parliaments and Peoples. I ask you now to
cherish them - and practise them too; then we
can go forward together in peace, seeking justice
and freedom for all men

T   Why don't you sit down?

Q   No thank you

Pause.

What can one say here?

Q   How far can one go?

T   Oh, don't hold back
It's all beyond our control

Q   Indeed

T   All artifice and sham

Q   I've never been fond of the theatre

T   No

Q   We saw *War Horse* recently
We liked the horses

T   One would like to speak frankly

Q   One doesn't want to blab

T   Oh no, there's nothing worse than a blabber
We have never blabbed

Q   Whatever we say must stay between these three
walls

T   Nothing uncontrolled
             No outpouring

Q   Then we'd better have some tea.
             When one needs to control the pouring
             Tea can be most reassuring

TWO: MAY THE FOURTH BE WITH YOU

*A younger Queen (Liz) and a younger Thatcher
(Mags) enter.*

Mags   We knew we had won by the early hours of
             May the fourth. Finchley roared with jubilation
             Maggie
             Maggie
             Hours later it was still thundering in my ears

Liz   Philip and I had put money on the result

Q   No we had not

Liz   He was sure the lady would carry the day. I
             thought the nation might baulk at a female PM

T   I can remember an odd sense of loneliness when
             I received the call, which summoned me to the
             palace

Mags   The audience, at which one receives the Queen's
             authority to form a government, comes only
             once in a lifetime. When one is re-elected, one
             doesn't go. So that first meeting is unique

Liz   She was my eighth

Q   Winston, Sir Anthony,

Liz   Harold M, Sir Alec

Q   Dear Harold W

Liz Heath –

Q And Jim Callaghan. He bade me farewell that morning

Liz It is affecting when they go
One doesn't have time to turn around
Out goes the last and in comes the next with barely a pause
And one has often built up a relationship

Mags My feelings on the way to the palace –

T I wasn't thinking about feelings
I was thinking there is so much to do.
I wanted to get behind that desk in Number Ten and get doing

Mags My teeth ached from smiling
And as we drove through the palace gates
I felt almost lifted off the ground
As if the hands of fate –

T I wasn't sentimental

Mags – were holding me
And words were coming to me from my childhood, from our chapel.
I wanted to

T I didn't

Mags I wanted to give thanks

Liz It wasn't the first time I'd met Mrs Thatcher, but this was different. Meeting one's PM is like
Like meeting the other side of the coin
We are both Britain

T I never said 'there is no such thing as society'

Q Yes you did. It was in *Woman's Own*

T I said there is a living tapestry of men and women

Q   You said 'Who is society? There is no such thing' and then you repeated it

T   I said the beauty of that tapestry will depend upon how much each of us is prepared to take responsibility for ourselves

Q   Society is the people

T   Society is a framework for freedom
Freedom that gives a man room to breathe
To make his own decisions and to chart his own course
There is the individual
And there is family.
There is no such thing as –

Q   No such thing as Britain
That's how you sounded

T   It's the idea that the state is society that I reject
People in this country feel entitled to state help
I reject this entitlement
'I'm homeless, the government must house me – why?'

Q   Because one doesn't want homeless people everywhere I would have thought

T   Your Majesty –

Q   This is a big discussion
And we're not going to have it now

Mags   I found the monarch's attitude

Liz   I found the Prime Minister's attitude

Mags   Towards the working of government

Liz   Towards the working of monarchy

Mags *and* **Liz**
       Absolutely correct

Footman I am a Palace Footman and I'll be leading the
Prime Minister silently and respectfully to her
Majesty the Queen

Mags One enters a different world at the Palace

T Everything is hushed

Footman I am a functionary whose purpose is to serve
To do my job well is to be unnoticed
You may be interested to know that I have a
City and Guilds Diploma in Butlering, and that
the Royal Household is committed to equality
of opportunity

Q Thank you for mentioning that
We're quite modern you see

Footman Prime Minister, the formal kissing of hands –

Mags I know all the protocol. You don't need to tell
me a thing

T Denis was with me

Mags I need Denis

T I want Denis

Mags Where's Denis?

Denis (*entering*) Denis Thatcher
I'm an honest-to-God right-winger and I don't
care who knows it

Mags Denis

Denis Always been a fan of Prince Philip
Big, big admirer
Leader of the pack in this male consort lark;
Absolute model – thought I'd ask him for some
tips

	I reckoned after years and years of PM's wives, He might be grateful for a chap like me
T	Denis came to the door with me
Mags	Why do I suddenly feel like I'm back at school?
Denis	Come on, Boss You'll get on like a house on fire – bound to Just be yourself
Mags	I always am, dear. What a silly thing to say

Mags curtsies, deeply. She holds it, frozen.

Liz	With my previous Prime Ministers There was a gallantry A mutual letting down of hair
Q	Goodness gracious, what a curtsy
Liz	They were all older than me and each in his own way quite charming. One always hopes for a confidant

Mags finishes her curtsy.

Liz	Congratulations on your victory, Prime Minister
Mags	Thank you, Your Majesty
T	She's ever so small
Q	She colours her hair
T	We're the same age
Q	Of the same era Formed in the war
T	In every way, we are peers

Mags kisses Liz's hand.

Liz	Britain's first female leader You must be feeling very pleased

430

T Of course I don't notice I'm a woman
I regard myself as Prime Minister

Mags I always say if you want something said, ask a man
But if you want something done, ask a woman

Liz Couldn't agree more

Q My father never let Prime Ministers sit down

Liz Please take a seat

They sit.

Q We met every week for all the years she was in power

T Our meetings were private

Liz We never took notes

Mags We are the only two who know what was said

Q Of course stories about clashes

T Nonsense

Liz There was never any question

Mags Stories about clashes

Q We have got on very well with all of our Prime Ministers

Liz I was very taken with your prayer on the steps of Number Ten

Mags Oh yes, St Francis

T I said

T *and* **Mags**
Where there is discord, may we bring harmony
Where there is error, may we bring truth
Where there is doubt, may we bring faith

Liz	Are you hoping the Conservatives will bring harmony? Because truth and faith are tricky things to supply
Q	I didn't say that. I said –
Liz	What a crush there was on the steps of Number Ten
Mags	Yes
Liz	Journalists and policemen are always so big One finds them enormous They rather crowded you I thought
Mags	Yes, they rather did
Liz	Yet you kept your self-possession
Mags	I am used to the hustle and the bustle
Liz	It'll only get hustlier And bustlier I'm sure
Mags	I shall relish it. I've lived the life of politics since I was twenty-five
Liz	You were a scientist before that?
Mags	First scientist to be PM
Liz	You really are a pioneer
Mags	I was a research chemist for Lyons Developing methods to preserve ice cream And make it fluffier I worked on Mr Whippy Which led the way with hydrogenated fats. Have you heard of it?
Liz	No

Mags   I am of course a barrister as well
             I qualified four months after my twins were born

Liz   Good gracious

Mags   So between the Party, law, twins and cooking
             Denis breakfast I have always been very busy

Liz   I am genuinely in awe. I never even went to
             school

Mags   No

Liz   Your voice changed
             On the television
             When they asked about your father

Mags   Well I owe him everything
             I really do

Liz   One's father shapes one, doesn't he?

Q   I was interested in her family's shop

Mags   It was a very modest home
             Of course everyone knew deprivation in the war

Liz   Oh yes

Q   I'd done some discreet asking around
             And her mother, Beatrice –
             Methodist, terribly devout –
             Was the daughter of a cloakroom attendant.
             I thought that was an interesting fact

Mags   My father was very careful with money
             He abhorred debt – and I have that too

Liz   Your mother must have worked very hard

Mags   Oh yes but of course she was far more domestic.
             And after I turned fifteen, I had nothing to say
             to her

Q   Goodness

Liz   I still can't get my mother off the phone

Mags My father took me out to council meetings and debates
He was passionate about politics and about education

Q   Where did she get that accent?

Mags When I got to Oxford and saw what was being taught –
Somerville was very Left and I knew I wouldn't fit in –
Something in me thought
No, this is wrong, this is wrong
No, these consensus economics cap profit
You see what we have now is a failed socialist experiment

Q   Everything she said slipped into lecturing mode
It was a feature of her conversation

Mags Socialism

T   Socialism

Mags Socialism is inimical to freedom. The left-wing slide we have been on leads inexorably to poverty and human bondage

Liz   I'm not a proponent, Prime Minister, but isn't the purpose of socialism to bring people out of poverty?

T   How wonderful; to enter into discourse with her

Mags Have you read Friedrich Hayek's *The Road to Serfdom*, Ma'am?

Liz   No

Mags   He talks about the trend towards socialism as being a break with the whole evolution of western civilisation

Liz   Really

Mags   You see, our civilisation has grown from foundations of liberty and individuality laid down by the Christians and the Greeks. This individuality is our inheritance. Socialist centralised planning / is a negative to human development. The only way to build a decent world is to improve the level of wealth via the activities of free markets. My father knew this

Q   I'm afraid I 'tuned out' – as Charles would say – And when I tuned back in she was talking about her father again

Mags   He taught me that you've got to sell your goods every day
It's a constant battle that's never won
It's those who sell who will lift us out of poverty

Liz   Yes

T   I wasn't sure Her Majesty had understood

Liz   I wonder if Number Ten will be like that

Mags   How do you mean?

Liz   Like living above the shop

Mags   Oh yes. I'm sure I shall feel very much at home

Pause.

Liz   Prime Minister
One likes to know what's going on
One likes to feel that one's a sort of sponge

You can come and tell me things
And some things stay
And some go out the other ear
One might occasionally do some good
And one can put one's point of view

Mags   This is such an honour

Liz   One is unelected, yes
But one is experienced

T   Disraeli stood in this very room and gave Suez
to Victoria

Liz   And perhaps because one cannot publicly
express opinion
One can be a trusted tool
Especially abroad

T   Winston stood here with her father as the war
raged around them

Liz   One's perhaps like an emollient
One sometimes smoothes the way.

T   And now me

Liz   One cherishes one's service

Mags   Yes, the weight of the cup in the hand
The shape of the handle, just so – is it Spode?

Q   My God, she hadn't listened

Liz   It's rather an everyday service I think

T   You have no idea what it meant for me
Meeting you on such an equal footing

Liz   Will you be bringing any pets to Number Ten?

Q   I thought, if she's got a dog we've got a subject

Mags   I believe there is a cat

Q   There was no intimacy with her
         No letting down of hair

T   You are my Queen
         I am your subject
         The first move towards a close relationship
         Could not have come from me

Mags   You never made it

Q   You didn't hear it

Liz   You hadn't listened

Denis   Margaret had always adored the Queen,
         absolutely revered her. We stood in the crowd
         cheering at her Coronation. Seemed sad to me
         she came out so deflated

T   On my way back to Number Ten
         A thought stayed there insistently
         Despite my every effort to dispel it

Denis   Felt a bit like the grocer's daughter did you, love?

Mags   Not at all
         I felt as soon as I had left the room
         Her Majesty would shake me off – with a laugh

Liz   You're quite wrong

Q   There was nothing remotely funny about you

T   I had worked so hard for my achievements
         Her Majesty's were birthrights

Q   I have to accept that here I am
         And this is my fate

T   Fate has nothing to do with me
         It is all discipline and enterprise

THREE: SPANKING

Liz   I notice the Prime Minister didn't eat the biscuits. Let's try her with a sponge next time

Footman Very good, Ma'am. May I ask you a question?

Q and Liz allow it.

Is it different because this Prime Minister is a woman?

Liz   It is different because this Prime Minister is Mrs Thatcher

Footman (*to T and Mags*) Prime Minister. May I ask you a question?

T   Of course you may

Footman When you said that socialism was inimical to freedom, what did you mean?

T   I meant that –

Mags Socialism is the philosophy of failure, the creed of ignorance, and the gospel of envy. Its inherent virtue is the equal sharing of misery

T   Winston Churchill said that and I agree with every word

Mags One cannot have liberty without economic liberty and we shall attain it with our monetarist policies and our strong stance against the trade unions. May I offer you our manifesto?

Footman Thank you.
Don't you think you should have something about the other side?

Mags They lost

438

T	They are utterly discredited and that is thanks to me
Footman	Only there's a generation that don't know what they were about
T	Yes, aren't you lucky?
Footman	But the Labour Party –
Mags	May we push on?
Denis	Prince Philip and I House on fire But Margaret was struggling
Mags	Your Majesty, I have a query A slightly awkward one About our wardrobe It has occurred to me that when we attend the same event, our outfits may present complications For example, one wouldn't want to wear a similar colour or a clashing one
Liz	I never notice what anyone else wears
Mags	One wouldn't like to upstage
Liz	I shouldn't worry about that
	Pause.
Mags	Do you have a lady, Your Majesty One of your ladies That perhaps my lady could speak to?
Q	The way she said 'Your Majesty' grated. Why couldn't she just call me Ma'am?
Liz	I have Bobo Bobo organises all my clothes
Mags	I have Crawfie Crawfie does everything for me

She turns me out every morning looking
spanking.
Would it be acceptable if Crawfie were to ask
Bobo? . . .

Footman The butler who trained me has worked in the
Palace for thirty-five years. He said you
overheard all sorts of things and that your job is
to forget them. Then he told me some of the
things he'd forgotten. The Queen used to call
Mrs Thatcher 'that bloody woman'

Q No one from the Palace ever said that

T Yes they did
You and your sister did
You think things didn't get back to Number Ten
But I heard everything
I knew exactly what you thought of me

The Queen ignores her, shaking invisible hands.

Q One has so many people to meet
So much to do

T I never held an unkind thought about you
I am your most loyal subject

Q How do you do?
Yes, community service is so important

T Don't ignore me please

Q Two mayors? How lovely

Mags The Queen is a continuum
A line drawn through time
From the dawn of England to the present day
Her family symbolises all that is perfect and
proper in British life
She is

Liz   Completely useless
          That's the impression one got
          She thought we were fit for nothing more than
          shaking hands

Q   Oh, Barbados? Terribly nice place

T   I felt a tremendous desire to protect the Queen

Liz   One had been patronised before, of course
          But it was worse being patronised by Mrs
          Thatcher

Q   A hairdresser, really?

FOUR: DANCING AT LUSAKA

Liz   I soon gave her proof of my usefulness.
          Rhodesia –

Q   Now Zimbabwe –

Liz   – had been a thorn in our side for fifteen years

Footman Shall I fill them in on the history, Ma'am?

Liz   Do you have to? I don't want this to get dull
          and there's a lot to get through before the
          interval

T   We don't need an interval

Q   What?

T   I'd like to go right through

Q   But I enjoy the interval
          Sometimes it's the best part of the play

Liz   In my opinion, the people of Rhodesia deserve a
          fair election

Mags In my opinion, the existing government of
Rhodesia, whatever its flaws, is the only one
that won't ruin the country

T It was our first real disagreement

Q Of course it wasn't. We never disagreed

Footman The young people might need the background,
Ma'am. I can cover it in a sentence or two

Q Oh very well

Footman Rhodesia – now Zimbabwe – was ruled by a
white minority led by Ian Smith. It refused to
hold fair elections and there had been an
escalating guerrilla war for several years as a
result. The Zimbabwean Patriotic Front was led
by the hugely popular Robert Mugabe, who was
currently harboured by Zambia

Q Thank you. Very concise

Liz The people deserve democracy

Mags The Zimbabwean Patriotic Front is Marxist.
Marxists do not respect democracy

Denis I knew Rhodesia very well from my days
at Burmah Oil. And if the blackies got in the
whole place would go down the bloody plughole.
And with it, a great hairball of British interests
and British trade

Liz The Heads of Commonwealth conference is in
Lusaka this year

Footman Lusaka is the capital of Zambia

Liz I think it's an ideal opportunity for us to get all
the parties round the table

T   *Us?* Is the Queen suddenly a member of Her
        Majesty's government?

Mags   Your Majesty, your government has grave
        concerns for your safety in Lusaka. We strongly
        advise you not to go

Liz   You advise me not to go?

Mags   It has been bombed. It is unsafe

Liz   I have only ever missed one Heads of
        Commonwealth meeting and that's because I
        was having Andrew

Mags   Your Majesty, Kenneth Kaunda of Zambia is
        thick as thieves with Mugabe and the guerrillas. /
        It is dangerous

Liz   We've known Kenneth Kaunda for years – he
        wouldn't let anything happen to me

Mags   Your government is responsible for your safety;
        you must let your government decide

Liz   So you are *telling* the monarch not to go?

Mags   I am merely trying to protect you, Your Majesty

Q   We were jolly well going

Liz   And if anyone tries to stop us there'll be a whole
        song and dance about it I can tell you

T   Of course, if the Queen wanted to go then the
        Queen had to go and all the security had to be
        provided

Q   You were the one who needed protecting
        You were too green to see it
        I knew I could be useful
        To you and to Britain
        So obviously I was going

443

Footman Would it be helpful if I changed parts now,
Ma'am?
I could stop being Palace Footman
And play Kenneth Kaunda, President of Zambia

Q Can you do that?

Footman Yes, I'll just go and prepare
And when I come back, I will be him

Actor 2 smoothly changes his glasses.

Carrington
Prepare? I'm Peter Carrington, Foreign Secretary

Actor 2 exits.

T You're not Peter Carrington

Carrington
Yes, for the moment I am

T You're Denis

Carrington
Yes I was, but now I'm Peter Carrington

T How can you be Peter Carrington when you're
Denis?

Carrington
I'm representing Peter Carrington
Just for a moment or two

T Why?

Carrington
Because I'm responsible for the Lancaster House
Agreement. It gave Zimbabwe peace and
democracy

T Are you Denis or not?

Actor 2 No, I'm not

444

T   How dare you
         How dare you attempt to impersonate him

         T exits.

Actor 2 Look I'm playing several roles here – I mean,
         some of them have only got one line and others
         are horrible, thin caricatures, but times are hard
         and it's a job. I don't want to offend anyone. All
         right?
         I am currently Foreign Secretary and Minister
         for Overseas Development; Peter Carrington

Q   He goes on to be Secretary General of NATO

Liz   Quite a gentleman, Peter

Mags   Yes, you hail from the days when the
         Conservative Party was run by men from Eton

Carrington
         Of course you change all that – for a while

Mags   What if I want you to be Denis again?

Actor 2 I am employed to be anyone you need

Mags   Thank you. I shall go and make that clear

         She exits.

Q   I have always loved Africa.

Liz   My first trip abroad was to South Africa

Q   I can honestly say it was one of the happiest
         times of my life

Liz   It was just after the war and there was such a
         feeling of hope and renewal in the air

Q   There were picnics and big game hunts

Liz   And coloured balls

Q   On my twenty-first birthday I made a speech

Carrington
            Ma'am, no one who heard it will ever forget

Q   I felt the whole Empire was listening

Mags   (*entering, with T*) Come on, Peter. We're going
            to Lusaka

Liz   'I declare before you all, that my whole life,
            whether it be long or short, shall be devoted
            to your service and the service of our great
            Imperial family, to which we all belong . . .'

Carrington
            It was most affecting
            To hear the young princess
            Take on that great burden
            With such a sweet pure voice

T   There's a whole generation of men, Peter among
            them, who went through the war and are quite
            batty about the Queen

Carrington
            We would have lain down our lives for her –

Mags   Are you coming, Peter?

Carrington
            And still would

Mags   Peter – I'm already on the plane

Kaunda   (*entering*) I'm Kenneth Kaunda, Father of Zambia

Q   That's very good

Kaunda   I'm about halfway through my twenty-seven
            years of rule, during which time I abuse
            democracy and amass a huge personal fortune.
            But that's another story.

When we Commonwealth heads of government
meet, we are all equal under the Queen. In other
words, the British government is just one of
many

T   Purgatory

Kaunda The Queen is like a mother confessor to us all
A very down-to-earth person
Always asking her incisive questions
Really, she is an icon

Q   I arrived in Lusaka before Mrs Thatcher. I was
determined to smooth her way

Liz   Kenneth, I want to know all about the
Zimbabwean Patriotic Front. You let them train
here; you give them arms – what are they like?

Kaunda Her Majesty never wastes time

Liz   What about this Mugabe chap? I'm hearing
such conflicting things

Kaunda You know you can trust my opinion, Ma'am

Mags   On the plane, I was sick with dread

Carrington
Margaret, the Americans support free elections.
The UN supports free elections. Frankly, our
position is becoming untenable

Mags   But I cannot back down. This is my first outing
on the international stage and –

Carrington
And you can be seen to be listening

Mags   Peter, when one knows one is right, that is very
hard

Carrington

The thing that people forget is how cautious
Margaret was
She was very careful
And she was persuadable
In the early years at least

T   By the end of the flight my address was written

Mags   I should like to make it clear that the British
government is wholly committed to genuine
black majority rule in Rhodesia

Carrington

Zimbabwe

Mags   Zimbabwe

Q   Thanks to Peter, the lady had turned

Carrington

Margaret put on a large pair of dark glasses
I said what on earth are those for?

Mags   I am absolutely certain that when I land at
Lusaka they are going to throw acid in my face

Kaunda   Welcome to Lusaka, Prime Minister
I'm sure you will find it a very convivial place

Liz   I had taken Kenneth aside
I told him you'd be nervous
Pointed out that you were new

Kaunda   I have great love and respect for Britain's
Queen. So I made her Prime Minister welcome.
And in spite of everything I'd heard, I found the
Iron Lady quite conversable

Mags   It turned out that Kenneth Kaunda was not as
black as he'd been painted

Q   Did you really say that?

T   Yes, what of it?

Carrington
Margaret's speech was very well received. With British support, a free Zimbabwe was on the agenda

Kaunda The atmosphere at the final reception was quite extraordinary

Liz   My work behind the scenes paid off
Mrs Thatcher was accepted by the African leaders
And I swear she began to enjoy herself

Mags Crawfie had packed something special and I thought well by golly, I'm going to make a splash

T   No I didn't

Kaunda Mrs Thatcher's dress was a dramatic shade of lime with a pineapple motif. Her blond hair shone through the crowd
Margaret, may I have this dance?

They dance.

Q   Denis was overheard asking the New Zealand High Commissioner

Denis What do you think those fuzzy-wuzzies are up to?

Liz   I made it known I was available for a dance

Denis and Liz are dancing.

Denis The Queen certainly kept her cool in the tropical heat. In fact she was quite chilly

Liz   Not quite the Gay Gordons, is it?

449

Mags   And so Rhodesia expired and Zimbabwe was born

T   Has Carrington gone?

Denis   He took the rap for the Falklands, old girl. Resigned when the Argies barged in

Mags   He was very good over Rhodesia. He brought it off

Denis   Yes but he didn't dance with Kaunda

Mags   I should hope not

Denis   You did – and that's what turned the trick

Kaunda   I'm being forgotten here. My diplomacy brought all the parties to the table

Mags   I doubt if that's what history will say

T   The atmosphere was very special at Lusaka And that was due to the Queen

Q   Twenty-three years later she publicly expressed her gratitude

Mags   I've always loved to dance. We had American servicemen in Grantham during the war. They were so glamorous

Liz   Oh yes

Mags   And I begged and begged to go dancing. My father wouldn't hear of it

Liz   We crept out on VE Day, my sister and I, with some officers we were friendly with; went into the crowd incognito – dancing on the street

Mags   Did you really?

Liz   Of course they recognised us. But the crowd was lovely

T I was deeply gratified when she shared things
   with me

Mags I cried when they brought down the Union Jack
   in Rhodesia

Liz Did you?

Mags I thought 'the poor Queen . . .'

Liz Why?

Mags Doesn't it grieve you? The demise of the Empire?

Liz The Commonwealth has more value to me.
   Every nation is there by choice

T I felt pain for Britain's decline
   To see how low we'd sunk in the world's esteem

Q Not everything was in decline
   I for one thought it was wonderful
   How many schools and hospitals I'd opened in
   my reign

T We were an economic snail
   An international nonentity

Q Society had never been more equal

Mags Someone had to stop the rot
   Someone had to change it all

FIVE: BOMBS I

T If I had my way, Irish citizens in the UK would
   lose their right to vote and they'd be subject to
   the same immigration laws as everybody else

Mags I never said that

T But crikey I thought it

Q   Mrs Thatcher had lost her friend and mentor
           Airey Neave in an IRA bomb blast just before
           she was elected

Mags   He was one of freedom's warriors.
           No one knew how great a man he was except
           those nearest to him
           We must not let the people who got him triumph

Liz   Her voice cracked as she spoke of him

T   We had barely been back from Lusaka a week
           when the IRA murdered eighteen of Our Boys at
           Warrenpoint in a hideous ambush

Mags   At the security briefing one of the officers
           presented me with a torn epaulette. I said what
           is this? It was all that remained of his friend

T   Carnage

Liz   On the same day, at his home in Sligo, our
           cousin Louis Mountbatten –

Q   Dickie to those who knew him –

Liz   – set off with his family in his boat, the *Shadow
           Five*

Adams   Gerry Adams, Sinn Fein. What the IRA did to
           Mountbatten is what Mountbatten had been
           doing all his life to other people; and with his
           war record I don't think he could have objected
           to dying in what was clearly a war situation. He
           knew what he was doing, coming to our
           country. In my opinion, the IRA achieved its
           objective: people started paying attention to
           what was happening in Ireland

Q   The explosion was violent in the extreme.
           It was heard across the bay over two miles away

Nothing but flotsam remained of the *Shadow Five*

Liz   It was terrible for Philip in particular
Dickie was his uncle
Had been like a father to him

Q   Two children died in that blast
Boys aged fourteen and fifteen

Liz   You didn't phone me

Q   She didn't phone

Mags   Because I was new you see and I didn't know
whether one telephoned the Queen or not
Normally, you go through the system

Q   Members of my family had died

Liz   And I had to phone you

T   Of course I went to Ulster straight away
And I got doing

Mags   We put a thousand more men in the RUC

T   I never ever compromised with terror
I told them compromise? That is out

Mags   That is out

T   That is out
I wanted troops on every street

Mags   I would root out

T   I would vanquish

Mags   Crush

T   Pulverise the IRA

Mags   And if they protest

T   If they protest

Ron   The ten most dangerous words in the English language are, 'Hi, I'm from the Government and I'm here to help'

Mags *and* **T**
Ron

Q   One has seen many Presidents come and go
And from this peculiar position
One can see that power rests in the office

Liz   Not in the individual

SIX: THE REAGANS ARE COMING

Ron   There were two guys in Moscow waiting in line for vodka and one them says, 'This line is too long; I've had enough. I'm going into the Kremlin and I'm going to kill Brezhnev.' So off he goes and after about an hour he comes back. And the other guy says, 'So did you kill him?' and he says, 'No that line was even longer.'

T   Ron was even funnier than Denis

Mags   The first time I set eyes on Ronald Reagan –

T   Apart from on the screen of course

Mags   – was in the Royal Albert Hall in 1969.
There was the Governor of California
Speaking as if it were just to me

Ron   We're at war with the most dangerous enemy that has ever faced mankind in his long climb from the swamp to the stars: Communism

Mags   I knew in an instant that here was a visionary
Not only that –

454

T	He was gorgeous I'm sorry but why not say it?
Mags	Never said it, never thought it
T	Who can deny it? Not even Denis
Ron	Someone once said to me, 'How can an actor be president?' I said, 'How can a president not be an actor?'
Q	Have we seen any of his films?
Liz	*The Cattle Queen of Montana*, that was one of his
Q	Oh yes, we liked that
Liz	We liked the horses
Q	Didn't he have a bit part in *Dark Victory*?
T	I've no idea
Liz	He did. He flirts with Bette Davis before she gets the brain tumour
Mags	Long before he was elected, I used to cherish copies of his speeches in my bag –
Ron	Ladies and gentlemen, this is my wife
Nancy	Hello, how do you do? I'm Nancy Reagan
Mags	The First Lady
Nancy	We first met Maggie and Denis back when Ron was fighting for his nomination And those two? They hit it off straight away
Ron	She had a lot of spunk
Mags	We'd talk half the night about the dangers of big government

Nancy	They even had a conversation that went something like Wouldn't it be great if we two ruled the world? And then lo and behold –
T	I was the first foreign leader to visit him in Washington after his inauguration
Liz	No you weren't. The Koreans were
Mags	We in Britain stand with you
T	America's successes will be our successes
Mags	Your problems will be our problems
T	And when you look for friends we will be there
Ron	In a dangerous world, one element goes without question: Britain and America stand side by side
Mags	We must be free or die who speak the tongue that Shakespeare spake
Ron	Margaret, I believe a real friendship exits between us
Mags *and* T	So do I, Ron
Nancy	Dinner at the British Embassy was a warm and beautiful occasion Bob Hope was there; all sorts of wonderful people
Liz	I hear she's notoriously brittle
Mags	Who?
Liz	The First Lady
Mags	She's very slim, yes
Liz	Apparently it's her hustling that's propelled him into the White House – and now that she's

there, I've heard she's knocking down walls and
throwing out all the china

Q   I love gossip

Mags   She is undertaking some refurbishments

Q   Why wouldn't you gossip?
You knew I wasn't going to tell anyone

Liz   Well, I would have told Philip

Q   And my sister

Liz   And probably Mummy and Anne

Mags   The First Lady adores the President
She's always at his side
I'm sure he relies on her

Liz   I heard she sees an astrologer about absolutely
everything. One of these people who won't get
their hair cut unless the moon's in the right
place

Mags   We haven't discussed astrology, Your Majesty

Q   Oh, it was such hard work

Liz   Do you not feel it's a bit of a performance with
them?
They are both actors, you know

Ron   When I got shot in March '81, Margaret's letter
of concern was top of the pile

Nancy   I cannot describe what I went through on that
day

Ron   You don't have to, Nancy

Nancy   Yes I do, Ronnie. Because people need to know.
A crazy man called John Hinkley, was obsessed
with a teenaged actress called Jodie Foster – I'm
not kidding – and he thought he would please

her somehow if he shot my husband.
He let off six bullets

Ron He was a lousy shot. Only one of them got me

Nancy It stopped in his lung, an inch away from his
heart

Ron I was a lucky man. The surgeons who operated
on me were all Republicans

Mags His wit, even in such adversity. That showed
real mettle

Nancy You can be one of the premier people in the
world, protected round the clock by servicemen
and bang –
All it takes is one lunatic with a gun

Mags It was sobering

Liz Very sobering

Q Because of the shooting, The President was
unable to attend Charles and Diana's wedding
that summer

Nancy I wasn't going to let him travel

Q But luckily the First Lady came

Nancy It was a fairytale event. Diana was so beautiful
And no one does a Royal occasion like the
British
I missed Ronnie terribly

T Yes, we all did

Nancy I was in London five days and I had eighteen
different engagements

Q One of them was a polo match
She came to meet Charles and Diana

Nancy   He was such a delightful, earnest young man
And I could see even then that Diana had a
stunning personality
This was the romance of all times

Liz   I'd driven there in my jeep
Headscarf on
Mrs Reagan arrived in a cavalcade – of how
many cars?

T   Six

Mags   One just for her hats I think

Liz   Really, Mrs Thatcher, was that a joke?

Mags   No

Liz   It was – you were being funny

Mags   It just slipped out

Q   She actually made a joke. It was a first. I thought
she had no sense of humour whatsoever

Mags   I didn't mean anything. I admire the First Lady

Liz   But you've got to admit that the sixth car was a
bit much

Mags   Thank goodness for such a lovely wedding,
Your Majesty
It's transformed a horrible summer

SEVEN: THE GUNS OF BRIXTON

Ron   Nancy must have hit it off with Queen Elizabeth
because that winter we received an official
invitation to Windsor Castle. No US president
had ever stayed there before

Actor 1   I'm sorry but is that it about the summer of '81?

T   I beg your pardon?

Actor 1   Are we moving on from the summer of '81?

Mags   Yes

Actor 1   You don't want to mention the riots?

T   No

Actor 1   The race riots that flared up all over the country?

Q   Oh one found them very distressing and one
            said so in one's Christmas message

T   You're Nancy Reagan

Mags   Nancy Reagan was never concerned with
            unlawful rioting in British cities I can assure you
            of that

Q   May I refer you to my Christmas message?
            My feelings are made very clear

Actor 1   I just feel there's some massive omissions here –
            The huge job losses; unemployment leapt by a
            million in one year
            The unrest in Northern Ireland
            The hunger strikes –

Actor 2   Look – it's not our gig, OK?

Actor 1   I'm just saying that if you miss out the riots and
            all the unrest, people – you know, like younger
            people – might think nothing else happened in
            1981 apart from the royal wedding and – Bucks
            Fizz winning the Eurovision

Actor 2   How did you know about Bucks Fizz?

Actor 1   My research. I Wiki'd the eighties

Actor 2   You Wiki'd the eighties?

Q   One's Christmas message is the only major
        speech of the year that is written without
        government intervention

Liz   This Christmas, we should remember especially
        the people of Northern Ireland who are
        attempting to live ordinary lives in times of
        strain and conflict; the unemployed who are
        trying to maintain their self-respect without
        work and to care for their families; and those
        from other parts of the Commonwealth who
        have come to Britain to make new lives but have
        not yet found themselves fully accepted

Actor 1 That must have really shaken things up

Q   Listen

Liz   Governments now regard it as their duty to try
        to protect their people, through social services,
        from the worst effects of illness, bereavement,
        joblessness and disability

Q   How much clearer could I have made things?

Actor 2 Look, I don't think you should be disrespectful
        Constitutionally she's not allowed to state her
        opinions

Actor 1 I'm not being disrespectful
        I'm just saying that in the midst of all that royal
        carriage big dress Diana wedding stuff
        The whole country was boiling with rage

Mags   The whole country?
        The whole country?

Actor 1 Well, people on the street

Mags   Which people on the street? How many?

Actor 1 Crowds, you know

Mags	How many in each crowd?
Actor 1	Well, in Brixton there was about five thousand
Mags	Five thousand yobs? – The whole country?
T	(*to the actors*) I'd like to remind you what you're here for and whose company you're in. Her Majesty was shot at during the trooping of the colour, two weeks before the Prince of Wales' wedding and did she go on about it? No she did not She passed it by without a word Such is her dignity Such is her courage
Q	One doesn't want to be standing here all night
Mags	We choose what is spoken about here and if you don't like it you can get on your bike *Pause.*
Actor 1	I'm just saying. But in a stroke of casting genius I've been asked to play Nancy Reagan – so I'll play Nancy Reagan
Mags	I fell over myself to be useful to Ron I would give him my careful advice at any hour of the day or night
Ron	Margaret certainly never held back with her advice
T	I would have guided his finger as it hovered over NATO's button I'd have made sure he held firm
Mags	But the first time I really needed him He let me down
Q	Can we skip this bit?

T   Pardon?

Q   We've been here aeons and we're not even
       though your first term

T   Your Majesty, how can you even suggest it?

EIGHT: ISLANDS IN THE STREAM

Ron   When Al Haig told me that Argentina had
       invaded the Falkland Islands, I said where in the
       name of ding-dong are they?

Nancy No he didn't

Ron   A little ice-cold bunch of land down in the
       South Atlantic, of no strategic value to anyone

Mags   On the 2nd of April 1982
       Argentina, led by General Galtieri and his
       Junta –

Q   We're not going through the whole thing, are
       we?

Liz   We don't need a blow-by-blow account

T   I'm sorry?

Q   It's been gone over again and again in all sorts
       of other places and I don't want to trudge
       through it here

Mags   Three days later,
       With UN approval
       A task force set sail from Portsmouth

Q   She's ignoring me

Mags   There would be no negotiation till these bullies
       had got off

Q   Did you see that?

T	That's when Ron should have stepped up
Q	Totally ignoring me
Mags	He should have said I support you one hundred per cent We are side by side This invasion is an outrage against democracy
Q	She's just going to carry on, isn't she? I might as well not be here
T	Ron sat on the fence When I needed him most
Mags	He sent a jet-lagged proposal Suggesting we negotiate
Nancy	I think you Brits forget how close we are to Latin America
Ron	There was a lot of Soviet-funded trouble going on down there – and Galtieri was no Communist
T	Negotiate? I said no
Mags	No, Ron
T	Absolutely not
Mags	You're asking me to lie down And let naked aggression walk all over me I am a not a doormat And you may not wipe your feet
Liz	May I interrupt you for a moment?
T	Of course
Liz	I was directly involved in the South Atlantic war Firstly, as head of the armed forces
T	Oh yes

Liz	Then, as sovereign of the country that was being invaded
T	Yes, of course, but that's all titular isn't it
Liz	And I was mother of a combatant
Q	My son Andrew was out there
Liz	Your Cabinet tried to give him a desk job But I insisted, insisted that he went Countless other mothers were waving off their sons Why should I be spared?
T	We were very grateful for your sacrifice It was a battle of good over evil
Ron	Margaret, you've got to try the diplomatic initiative
Mags	I had an absolute clarity of purpose I knew I had to hold my nerve
T	And I was put, by Ron, on an equal footing with the Junta
Ron	We decided in the end on a pro-UK tilt
Mags	A tilt
T	Ron came through with a tilt
Mags	I felt personally let down
Q	You'd think Wouldn't you That she did the whole thing by herself That there was no one else involved
Liz	Well, Andrew was on the HMS *Invincible* And I can tell you there were a lot of people involved

Mags	I was stricken at our losses They caused me acute distress I wrote personally to the families of all the men who died
Liz	There it is again – I, me, I
T	This is all about taking the salute, isn't it?
Q	Nonsense
T	This is because when it was over I took the salute and not you
Q	I have kept silent on that subject, always
Ron	We could see that a certain amount of damage had been done to our special relationship
Q	So thank heavens for me
Liz	When the Reagans visited Windsor, the conflict was still at its height
Nancy	The Queen was so thoughtful She showed us up to our room herself And you should have seen the little things she'd put out for us There were letters from Abraham Lincoln There was a note from George the Third saying 'America is lost to us!'
Ron	I found that very poignant
Nancy	And there was the sweetest letter from Her Majesty's parents, written when they were visiting President Roosevelt. It described a picnic they'd been on, where the King had eaten a hot dog for the first time in his life
Liz	For the only time in his life
Nancy	I was knocked out by Windsor Castle

Liz	Yes that's rather the idea
Mags	The battle for Goose Green was raging
Ron	The Queen had suggested we have a ride. Now, I was worried I can tell you; At home in Santa Barbara I'd just pull on some jeans And leap on, you know, John Wayne style –
Mags	There was vicious hand-to-hand fighting on Mount Tumbledown –
Ron	But the last thing I wanted to come over as, was a cowboy –
T	They sank the *Atlantic Conveyor* –
Q	And who was first on the scene to lift off the survivors? Andrew, in his Sea King
Mags	I was existing on one or two hours sleep
T	I felt intensely, intensely alive
Nancy	We wrote to the palace and asked what the President should wear
Liz	Boots, breeches and a sweater No need to be formal
Nancy	In the end we decided on something Old Hollywood Beautiful sports jacket over an open-necked shirt
Liz	We rode Burmese, our favourite
Nancy	Ron looked so elegant So did the Queen, in a charming head scarf
Ron	You know, she was in charge of that animal
Liz	Those images were beamed around the world From Moscow to Buenos Aires

Q   Britain and America side by side in in perfect
           harmony

Liz   It's marvellous, the benefits of a good ride

Mags   Of course the important thing about Ron's visit
           was his speech to Parliament, when he talked
           about putting Marxism on the ash-heap of
           history

Q   No one remembers that

T   Four days later
           The Union Jack was flying over Port Stanley
           Right had prevailed
           Victory was ours

Mags   Enoch Powell stood up in the house and he said:
           Pause.

Actor 2   That's you

Actor 1   No it's not

Actor 2   Yes it is

Actor 1   I made sure at the audition; I don't have to do it

Actor 2   Well, it's you. I'm still Reagan

Actor 1   I'm not Enoch Powell

Q   Shall we move on?

Mags   Enoch Powell stood up in the house and he said:

Actor 1   I'm not doing it

Mags   I beg your pardon?

Actor 1   I'm just not

T   Then you're very poor value for money

Mags   You yourself pointed out current levels of
           unemployment. If you don't want this job –

Actor 1 I do

Mags Then I suggest you get on with it

T Enoch said:

Powell Her substance is ferrous metal of the highest
quality
Of exceptional tensile strength
Resistant to wear and tear
Usable for all national purposes

Mags I agree with everything the gentleman has said

Q Gloriana, the papers called her
Boadicea in pearls

Liz I'd spent those weeks
Along with countless other mothers
Agonising for the safety of my favourite son –

Q I have no favourites

T All right, I took the salute
It felt right at the time and Our Boys wanted it
They wanted me
I had brought them safely home
Restoring Britain's honour and your flag

Pause.

Mags It's done
If I'd known you'd be this upset
I'd have –

Liz You'd have what, Prime Minister?

Mags I know my son wasn't out there but the
following year when Mark got lost in the desert
and I didn't know where he was for four whole
days, I got an inkling of what you must have felt

Pause.

Are you freezing me out?

Liz is silent.

T   She froze me out for weeks over that salute

Q   Nonsense

Liz   The following year we visited the Reagans in California

NINE: CALIFORNIA DREAMING

T   I won the next election with a landslide

Q   California please

Ron   We invited Queen Elizabeth to our home, Rancho del Cielo

Nancy We threw them a Hollywood dinner. We invited movie stars; Julie Andrews was there, Rod Stewart sang

Ron   I figured she'd like a ride, American style
And where better to provide it?

Mags If Ronald Reagan knew
If he knew what I really thought of him
His lazy intellect,
His mawkish sentiment
His fumbling with briefs
It would damage our interests irrevocably

T   On one thing, Ron was clear

Mags The evil of socialism

T   I held on to that one thing

Mags I brought him Gorbachev
I gave Ron the Soviet empire in a golf cart

T   To anyone who says that my diplomacy was
        poor I give them this: we ended communism.
        We brought down that wall

Mags   The first time I met Mikhail Gorbachev, I knew
        this was a man we could do business with

Actor 1 Hold on, what year are we in?

T   1985

Actor 1 Are you going to miss out the government's
        decision to allow America to site its Cruise
        missiles on British soil?

Mags   Yes

Actor 1 What about the women protesting at Greenham
        Common?

Mags   Eurgh

Actor 1 Or the huge CND marches?

T   They weren't huge

Actor 1 What about the miners' strike? Are you going to
        miss that out too?

T   I'd be glad to talk about the miners' strike. Let's
        talk about the miners' strike

Mags   Where's Michael Heseltine?
        He was useful

Hesel   I'm Michael Heseltine
        Most handsome member of the cabinet

Mags   Hezza

Hesel   We knew there was a confrontation coming.
        The most meticulous planning had been put in
        place. We'd been stockpiling coal for years

Mags   There'd be no power cuts on my watch

Hesel   Arthur Scargill was teased on to the worst battle
plan at the worst possible time for him – and
the rest is history

T   We planned it like a military campaign

Mags   We had to fight the enemy without in the
Falklands.
But the enemy within is more difficult
And more dangerous to liberty

Liz   Have you ever been down a mine, Mrs Thatcher?
I have
I thought it was a dark and dangerous place to
work
I was deeply impressed by the men who
laboured there.
I've spoken with a lot of miners and their wives

Mags   Then you are very knowledgeable –

Liz   And never, at any time
Have I found them to be
The enemy within

T   We had to win. Anything else was unthinkable

Q   (*to Actor 1*) Perhaps you'd like to be a miner?

Actor 1   (*still dressed as Nancy*) Can I go and get
changed?

T   We're not hanging around whilst you cover
yourself in coal dust

Mags   They are behaving as a mob
And we have no choice but to treat them as a
mob

Liz   I don't like the way you're pitting my police
force against them. They fought side by side

during the war and it upsets me how you have divided them

Mags I have not divided them. Arthur Scargill has divided them

Actor 2 Shall I be Scargill?

Mags *and* T
No

T The only helpful thing that Arthur Scargill ever did was neglect to hold a strike ballot. That was very helpful. Very helpful indeed

Mags It revealed his undemocratic soul

Scargill We've had riot shields, we've had riot gear, we've had police on horseback charging into our people; we've had people hit with truncheons and people kicked to the ground

Mags You are stepping over the mark

Scargill The intimidation and the brutality that has been displayed are something of a Latin American state

Mags (*to Scargill*) He is the dictator
He is the general

T His real aim is the breakdown of law and order and the destruction of democratic parliamentary government

Liz Neither would back down an inch

Q When one thinks about it, they were very similar

Liz I felt particularly sorry for the miners' wives, as the strike dragged through the winter

Mags It is up to the miners' wives to tell the miners to be sensible

Actor 1 Did you really say that?

Mags No husband of mine would have gone around shaming the country in that lawless way; picketing here, rioting there

Actor 1 But you were going to close all the mines

Mags All the *unproductive* mines

Q It was a whole year of strife

Mags I welcome strife
I welcome it
In the cause of making Britain great again

Q And in the end, the miners were beaten

Liz Some of the wives handed them carnations at the pit gates as they returned to work; a flower which symbolises the hero. I thought that rather affecting

Actor 2 In 1983, Britain had one hundred and seventy deep coalmines; now there is one

Mags It is simply bad housekeeping to keep unprofitable pits open

Actor 2 Whole communities lost their work. It was a tragedy; it was heartbreaking

T Who said that?

Actor 2 No one important

T Is that your own private opinion?

Mags It is. It's his own opinion.
Would you tell me whose opinion these people have paid good money to hear?

Actor 2 Her Majesty's opinion

T	And?
Actor 2	And your opinion
T	What does your opinion count for here?
Mags	What does your opinion count for?
Actor 2	It destroyed more than people's livelihoods. It destroyed the whole idea of the dignity of labour
Mags	Have these people paid to hear that?
Actor 2	No
T	Then what does it count for? I'm sorry, I didn't hear that
Actor 2	Nothing
Q	I'd like an interval now, please
T	We don't need an interval Whoever ordered an interval they can cancel it
Mags	There's too much to do
Q	Don't you want an interval Prime Minister?

T *and* **Mags**
          No

          Pause.

Q	There will now be a fifteen minute interval

10. THE GAP

Actor 1 Why don't you tell them what you were telling me, back in the dressing room?

Actor 2 No

Actor 1 Why not?

Actor 2 I don't want to

Actor 1 What are you scared of?

Actor 2 I'm not scared

Actor 1 You're being a chicken

Actor 2 I'm not a chicken.
What's history for you is life lived for me
I can't heave it into my mouth like you can
It is not easy to talk about those years. Not in public anyway

Actor 1 Go on, before they come back

Actor 2 OK. My parents loved the Tories, I loathed them

Actor 1 Why in particular

Actor 2 You've seen Act One.
It was their hypocrisy I hated most. They allowed homophobia to thrive. They passed legislation that was blatantly prejudiced – Section 28 for example

Actor 1 What was that?

Actor 2 If I was to tell you publicly, I'd be in breach of Section 28

476

Actor 1 Seriously?

Actor 2 Who are you playing in this half?

Actor 1 Michael Shea – he's the Queen's press secretary

Actor 2 I'm Murdoch – got a line of Prince Philip; look out for that one, folks –

Actor 1 And I'm Kinnock

Actor 2 Are you?

Actor 1 Yes

Actor 2 I wanted to be Kinnock

Actor 1 Did you?

Actor 2 I can do a good Kinnock

Actor 1 Yes, but he's in my contract

Actor 2 Have you got his 'I warn you' speech?

Actor 1 No

Actor Oh what a shame, you should have the 'I warn you' speech. It's bloody good

Actor 1 I know but he said it in '83
We've already gone past it

Actor 2 I warn you that you will have pain – when healing and relief depend upon payment

Actor 1 I'm Kinnock

Actor 2 I warn you that you will have ignorance – when learning is a privilege and not a right

Actor 1 You can't just take my part

Actor 2 I warn you that you will have poverty –

Actor 1 Do you want a Kinnock-off?

Actor 2   When pensions slip –

Actor 1   Cos I'll give you one

Actor 2   And benefits are whittled away –

Actor 1   By a government that won't pay in an economy that can't pay

Actor 2   I warn you that you will be cold

Actor 1   When fuel charges are used as a tax system that the rich don't notice and the poor can't afford

Actor 2   I warn you that you must not expect work

Actor 1   I warn you not to go into the streets alone after dark

Actor 2   Or into the streets in large crowds of protest in the light

Actor 1   I warn you that you will be quiet

Both   When the curfew of fear and the gibbet of unemployment make you obedient

Actor 1   I warn you that you will borrow less – when credit, loans and mortgages are refused to people on your melting income

          Mags and T have entered.

Actor 2   If Margaret Thatcher wins on Thursday, I warn you not to be ordinary

Actor 1   I warn you not to be young

Actor 2   I warn you not to fall ill

Actor 1   I warn you not to grow old

          The Actors notice Thatcher. Pause. Actor 2 puts Denis's glasses on

T	Denis
Denis	Hello love
T	Come away from him. Have you had some refreshments?
Denis	Yes, fully tanked up; ready for anything
Mags	Let us never forget this fundamental truth: the state has no source of money other than money which people earn themselves. If the state wishes to spend, it can do so only by borrowing your savings or by taxing you more. It is no good thinking that someone else will pay – that 'someone else' is you. There is no such thing as public money; there is only taxpayers' money
Denis	Well, there's the North Sea oil and gas money And the money from all the public industries you're selling off That's flooding the old coffers isn't it, Boss?
T	Pardon?
Mags	Don't try to pull the wool over my eyes Denis Never Said any of that
Footman	Ladies and gentlemen Pray be upstanding for Her Majesty the Queen

Q and Liz enter through the audience, shaking people's hands. Asking questions such as: 'Did you enjoy the interval?' 'Are you a regular theatregoer?' 'Do you live far away?' 'Very friendly staff here, don't you think?'

| Q | That was most enjoyable
We met everyone, all the stage management |

	They went to such trouble (*To Footman.*) Thank you
Liz	I thought the canapés were rather dry.
Q	Where are we?
T	My second term, Your Majesty
Q	(*wearily*) Oh yes
Mags	We were unleashing new forces in the land
T	Old orders everywhere were being questioned The unions, the NHS, the BBC and yes the Palace
Liz	It felt as if the Palace and I had been shifted – Bottom priority in your Number Ten
Q	We had to provide value for money
Liz	I ask you – the Royal Family
Q	She started cancelling our meetings
T	They were always a distraction
Mags	One was pulled away from whatever one was doing And one was doing an awful lot
Liz	One wouldn't have minded if it was for matters of state
Q	But one week she put us off to entertain some Swedes
	Mags curtsies.
Liz	I thought we might walk out in the grounds today, Prime Minister It's such a pleasant evening and the dogs could come
Mags	Of course, Your Majesty

480

T   A whole hour wasted in the chill
And those dogs . . .

Liz   I was in Kenya when my father died. I remember
sitting perfectly calmly feeling the future gaping
before me

T   Why's she talking about this?

Liz   The local people were terribly kind. They simply
lined the road as we drove back to Nairobi,
heads bowed in respect

Mags   The whole Empire grieved for him

Liz   The press were wonderful too
Not one camera was raised
Not one photograph was taken; not one.
Their hats were off, to the last man

Mags   Really?

Liz   Hard to believe now, isn't it?

Q   Michael, would you mind filling the young
people in?

Shea   Not at all, Ma'am
I'm Michael Shea, the Queen's press secretary
I'm a Scot and I'll have a go at the accent.
I have a background in diplomacy
And I also write thrillers under a pseudonym
Pretty good ones in fact –

Q   You can skip that

Shea   The tone of the press had changed towards the
Palace. In previous times it had been universally
reverential

Murd   The press had basically printed whatever
fawning flummery the Palace had given them.
But I wasn't going to have that in my papers.

I'm Rupert Murdoch, obviously.
When I bought *The Sun* in 1968 it was a soggy
broadsheet. And I said to the editor – you're
now part of a tabloid revolution. I want a
tearaway paper with lots of tits in it. I bought
The Times and the *Sunday Times* in 1981. I was
doing the same thing there

Liz   Prime Minister, I am worried about the pressure
being put on my children – especially the Prince
and Princess of Wales

Murd   Princess of Sales

Shea   Diana was hounded by the press wherever she
went

Murd   Complained all the time – but she loved it too

Shea   I organised an informal lunch for the editors of
the papers to meet the Queen, so that she might
voice her concerns

Q   It is hard on a girl if she can't even go to the
local sweet shop without being cornered by
photographers

Murd   One of my editors replied: 'Why couldn't she
send a footman for the sweets?'

Q   I think that is the most pompous remark I have
ever heard in my life

Liz   Prime Minister, you have a better relationship
with Mr Murdoch than I

Mags   Your Majesty, freedom of the press is one of the
things upon which true democracy is founded

Liz   I quite agree
But I must lay my family's predicament before
you

Q   This conversation never happened
           We never walked in the garden
           It would have been too hard on Mrs Thatcher's
           heels

Mags   Mr Murdoch may not be a monarchist
           But he's a very good thing for a free press
           The print unions have had their way too long
           And Murdoch will take on the closed shop

Actor 1 What's a closed shop?

Actor 2 The reason actors used to earn proper money
           Bar. After

Murd   If corporations ran things we'd all be better off
           I believe in as little government as possible
           As few rules as possible
           I'm not saying it should be taken to the absolute
           limit
           But I'll spend my whole career pushing it

Mags   We have to trust business and industry to
           regulate itself

Liz   Then may one ask about the economy?
           Because it strikes one that the caps and the
           controls you have removed from our financial
           institutions –

Mags   The greater freedoms we have given

Liz   – are widening the gap

T   What gap?

Liz   Between the rich and poor

Mags   The country is getting richer. For the first time
           we have working-class people buying shares and
           owning homes

Liz   But what about those who are not working?
         There are more children living in poverty than
         ever

Mags   How can one relieve their poverty, unless it is by
         creating wealth? I know that socialists regard
         the pursuit of wealth as an evil, but right-
         minded people must surely see it as a good

Liz   But the culture that seems to be prevalent,
         This insatiable materialism –

T   Has she forgotten she's the world's wealthiest
         woman?

Liz   One sees these young men in the city really
         revelling in greed – lording it over the
         unemployed

T   And there we have it. The true rise of the
         working class. My barrow boys in the city –
         that's what she can't brook

Mags   I believe in the working class; not the shirking
         class

Q   How can she reel off these ludicrous slogans to
         me?

T   I didn't

Mags   People remain poor because they know they will
         get state handouts
         We want to encourage them to get up, to seek
         work, to make money

Liz   Prime Minister, we've travelled a great deal this
         year
         As we do every year
         And the problem is not just in Britain.
         The poor are getting poorer

	And we have seen first hand
	The growing gap
T	It would be impolite to mention the fact that Her Majesty,
	Even as she championed the poor,
	Paid no tax until 1993 –
Liz	I had some very interesting talks with Mrs Gandhi on my visit to India recently and her view is that the uncontrolled free market is widening the gap –
Mags	With respect, Indira Gandhi was a radical communist in her youth
T	The wealth created by a free economy will trickle down
Liz	Thank you for listening, Prime Minister
Denis	We had some smashing people down at Chequers for Christmas that year. Jeffrey and Mary Archer came
	We had the Murdochs
	The Hamiltons; lovely couple
	The Krays – just joking
	Dear old Crawfie
	Carol
	And after the turkey we turned on the gogglebox for Her Maj
Liz	The greatest problem in the world today remains the gap between rich and poor countries
Mags	What?
Q	My Christmas broadcast
	Jolly good one that year
Liz	We can ignore the messages we don't like to hear but –

485

Mags	What's she talking about?
Liz	– we shall not begin to close this poverty gap until we hear less about nationalism and more about interdependence
Mags	That is quite wrong
Liz	One of the main aims of the Commonwealth is to make an effective contribution towards redressing the economic balance between nations
T	Denis
Mags	Denis, she's flouting our policies The entire British effort is to distance ourselves –
Liz	We in the Commonwealth are fortunate enough To belong to a world wide comradeship

Mags, T *and* **Denis**
Comradeship?

Liz	Let us make the most of it Only then can we make the message of the angels come true: 'Peace on earth, goodwill towards men'
Mags	Good God
Liz	God bless you all
T	Is Her Majesty a socialist?
Denis	I don't think she's an actual Trot, old love
Mags	Then why, in her Christmas speech, is she expressing dubiously socialistic principles?
Q	They are in fact Christian principles And as Head of the Church One must freely express them
T	We were being undermined

Mags	Your Majesty, I'm sorry to tell you that your Christmas message has been interpreted, by some, as divergent to government policy
Liz	Really?
Mags	It is your government's aim to reduce Commonwealth claims on the British taxpayer. Whatever your personal sentiments are, constitutionally you must ally yourself with your government
Liz	I have a duty to the Commonwealth as well as to my government
T	None of this was said This is all crass surmise
Liz	I vowed that duty before God. It is not something I can bend to / your convenience
Mags	If I may continue
Liz	You are asking me to / tear myself in two
Mags	If I may, your first duty –
Liz	I have pledged a duty / as Head of the Commonwealth
Mags	Your first duty is to the British people Not to a collection of nations Run by communists and mendicants
T	I never said that
Liz	She cut me off She actually cut me off
Q	Attila the hen I think that was Denis Healey
Liz	Who called her The Maggietollah?

Q   One had to laugh

T   The Palace found our fervour for improvement
         funny. It was hurtful

Liz   You held the Commonwealth in contempt
         And that attitude trickled down

Q   The new free market wealth did not

ELEVEN: BOMBS II

Liz   I was in the United States on a private visit to
         inspect some American studs
         When the news came that a bomb had exploded
         at the Conservative Party conference in Brighton

Q   When any great disaster happens where there is
         loss of life
         One feels a physical sense of dread

Liz   It was hard to get accurate news at first
         No one knew how many casualties there were –
         or whom

Mags   It was three a.m. I was putting the finishing
         touches to the next day's speech, when –

         An explosion is heard.

T   The second it happened I thought
         I'm amazed this hasn't happened before

Mags   The noise
         Windows blown to smithereens
         I thought Denis –

T   It was like an earthquake

Denis   Margaret –

Mags But the lights stayed on

T In the corridor, people were thrown against
walls
The bathroom gone in a cloud of dust

Mags One always imagines that one will be plunged
into darkness at a moment like that
But the lights stayed on

T I was still in my evening gown from the night
before. Had I been in that bathroom I would
not have . . .

Mags I would have . . .

T We were very lucky

Denis Put your speech in the bag
If it's in your handbag it won't get lost

Q There were five dead,
Others with terrible injuries
Four floors of the hotel had collapsed

T It was an attempt to destroy, to cripple, to wipe
out Her Majesty's democratically elected
government. That is the scale of the outrage

Liz When I was eventually put through
Before I could even speak
Mrs Thatcher said

Mags Are you having a wonderful time?

Q Wasn't that strange? Wasn't that a peculiar
response?
Such bizarre forced jollity
At a moment like that

Liz Margaret, are you all right?

Mags Yes, thank you. We are fine

Liz   You must be experiencing very deep shock

Mags   Of course one isn't thinking of oneself
           One is thinking of the injured
           And the victims

Liz   Of course
           Have they given you lots of tea?
           Tea is terribly good for shock

Q   I didn't know what else to say

Mags   I am perfectly, perfectly fine and untouched

Liz   Philip and I are watching images as they come
           through on the news
           It is dreadful

Mags   Thank you so much for your kind concern.
           There's a Marks and Spencer's

Liz   Pardon?

Mags   We're sending out to Marks and Spencer's
           We need clothes
           They're helping us with all the delegates who
           came out in pyjamas
           And we're going on –

Liz   Are you?

Mags   – with the conference. We're going on

Q   We watched her speech the next day
           Not a hair out place

Liz   She made reference to the atrocity and then she
           just carried on

Mags   The fact that we are gathered here now, shocked
           but composed and determined, is a sign that not
           only has this attack failed but that all attempts
           to destroy democracy through terrorism will fail

Q	Profoundly impressive But at what cost?
Denis	After Brighton, I started thinking she should look to an end You know, towards getting out
Q	Two weeks later, Indira Gandhi was assassinated outside her own home
Liz	Mrs Thatcher brought me the news
Mags	It wasn't terrorists or strangers. It was two of her own personal guards
Liz	Good God
Mags	One of them discharged three rounds into her abdomen. And then his accomplice opened fire on her as she lay on the ground
Q	They removed thirty bullets from her body
Liz	She feared that something like this might happen
Mags	One does fear it, doesn't one
T	No, no, it wasn't fear that I felt; it wasn't fear
Q	It's not fear exactly. One just knows it could be over – that quickly
Liz	If I die a violent death – the violence will be in the thought of my assassin, not in my dying
Mags	Who said that?
Liz	Indira She knew. One cannot make so many enemies And not know
T	It was her own trusted men that did it. That's what I could not brook

Liz Are you all right?

Mags After Brighton the IRA said
Today we were unlucky
But remember, we only have to be lucky once.
You will have to be lucky always

Q Yes; it was chilling

Mags The hatred in it
And the number of people
The number of people in this country who
Who wish they had got me

Liz I'm sure that can't be true

Mags Well, they didn't get me
I am not that easy to dispose of
And as long as there is breath in my body I will –

Liz Would you like a scone, Prime Minister?

Mags Thank you

T Denis bought me a watch
Unusual gesture of affection
Engraved on it is 'Every minute counts'
I won't waste one of them

Liz The jam is home-made
There's damson and that one's bilberry

Q I didn't say that
We never have bilberry jam

Liz One likes to support the village fetes around Sandringham
One's always buying little jars at local sales of work

Mags I think one's always looking for the jam that tastes like home. No one made jam like my

mother could. She was very much a woman of
the home and I can remember the smell of her
gooseberry like it was yesterday

Liz   I don't think there's a woman of our whole
generation who can't make jam

Q   And marmalade

Mags   We all learnt from the homily of housekeeping
And I still believe it would save many a financier
from failure

Liz   You see sometimes it could almost be nice

TWELVE: WET WET WET

T   Wets

Mags   Do you know what a 'wet' is?

T   My backbench was full of them
I knew the enemy across the floor in the House
The Left

T *and* **Mags**
Kinnochio

T   I had that enemy in my sights
Where I could squeeze and pulverise it
But another enemy began to appear

Q   She changed after Brighton

T *and* **Mags**
Wets

Q   One spoke with people in her own party and the
feeling was that she was rather cutting herself

T	These were often the old grandees Dripping with titles, land and wealth Not like Norman Tebbit and me
Mags	Wets and ultra wets
T	Spineless
Q	One sees it again and again The longer a leader serves The less open they become
Mags	Our monarch I'm sorry to tell you Is wet
T	We never said that
Liz	For a Methodist, she's remarkably unchristian
Q	We never said that
Liz	One wondered if she was a religious person
Q	No one didn't
Liz	Yes one did One talked about it with the Archbishop
Q	Oh yes
Liz	He felt sure she had faith but he wasn't sure that the doctrine of grace meant much to her
Howe	Geoffrey Howe, Foreign Secretary. I wasn't a wet
Mags	Yes you were
Howe	No I wasn't, Margaret. I was one of your own I sat by your side with Willie Whitelaw And I must say I heard one question more and more often
T	Where's Willie?

Howe   No. Is he one of us?
Whose side is he on?
About people in our own party

Mags   Sometimes I think you're dripping, Geoffrey
A big wet sheep

Q   She bullied poor Geoffrey terribly

Howe   I think one of the things that you never fully
absorbed, Margaret, is that it's bad management
as well as bad manners to reproach as it were
officers in front of other ranks

Mags *and* **T**
Oh dear

Howe   If you want to tick people off or have arguments
with them then you should, as a matter of
courtesy, do it in private

Mags   You are Foreign Secretary. Foreign affairs are
interesting, Geoffrey – they are interesting! And
your endless drone has the whole Cabinet
comatose

Howe   You are becoming increasingly reckless, if you
like, of the way in which you conduct your
personal relationships

Mags   Go and tell Crawfie I'm ready for my comb-out

T   To be wet is to be like a soggy August
The whole concept reminded me of Balmoral

Q   I'm sorry to tell you that Mrs Thatcher didn't
care for Balmoral

T   Bagpipes
Wellingtons
Torment

495

Q   She came for three days every year like all
        my PM's

Liz   Harold Wilson brought his dogs
        We always had a jolly time

Mags   I said, Crawfie, pack something warm
        For heaven's sake pack thermals

Liz   We love throwing on a head scarf and striding
        over the moors
        And we especially love our picnics

T   It's an unnerving experience
        Prince Philip cooking drumsticks under damp
        tarpaulins
        Eating with Tupperware on the side of a wind-
        blown hill

Liz   Would you like the gherkins, Mrs Thatcher?

Mags   I'll get them
        Let me serve them
        Let me pass them round
        Your Royal Highness, would you like a gherkin?

Liz   She kept on jumping up to help
        But we enjoy serving people at our picnics

Mags   It completely dismayed me

T   The Queen, rolling up her sleeves to rinse the
        mugs

Mags   Let me do that Your Majesty, I'm a dab hand
        with the washing up – Let me

Q   Philip said

Philip Someone tell that bloody woman to sit down

T   It was more stressful than a NATO summit

Q   I know our life up there does not appeal to
         everyone
         But it is home
         And when one opens it to guests –

Liz   She used to leave at six in the morning
         Really as soon as she could
         One found it rude

Shea   Michael Shea again
         Mrs Thatcher's style became ever more regal
         She began to use the royal 'we'

Mags   I am not an 'I did this' 'I did that' person. I have
         never been an 'I' person. I prefer to talk about
         'we' – the government . . . It is not I who do
         things, it is we, the government

T   We have become a grandmother

Q   Have you come to talk about 1986?

Shea   Yes I have

Q   I expect a lot of you were not yet born
         Or still at school
         Or listening to all those dreadful bands Diana
         used to like

Shea   In 1986

T   Prince Andrew got married to Sarah Ferguson.
         A lovely wedding

Shea   I wasn't going to talk about that

Liz   The press called her an unbrushed red setter
         trying to get out of a potato sack. I thought that
         was a bridge too far

T   The Queen's trooping horse Burmese retired
         after seventeen years

Shea   I wasn't going to talk about that either

T   Well, what else are you qualified to talk about?

Shea   I was going to talk about your decision to allow
          America to bomb Libya, using Britain as its base

T   The Queen has no wish to discuss that

Q   Yes I do
          She let Reagan send his planes from our air bases
          None of the other NATO countries would

Liz   And I was the last to know

Actor 2   There was an all-time hullaballoo in the House.
          I would like to remind the Right Honourable
          Lady –

Actor 1   Who are you being?

Actor 2   Kinnock

Actor 1   I'm Kinnock

Actor 2   You're Michael Shea

Actor 1   I can be Kinnock and Shea

Actor 2   Then don't miss your chance

Actor 1   (*as Kinnock*) I would like to remind the Right
          Honourable Lady that the hullaballoo came not
          just from the Labour Party but from her own
          back benches, from her own cabinet

T   You're not Kinnock

Kinnock   Would the Right Honourable Lady agree that
          there is only one reason why President Reagan
          sought her co-operation?

T   You're not anybody

Kinnock   The President knew that when he said jump, she
          would reply, 'How high?'

Q   (*to Actor 1*) Would you be Michael Shea again, please?
I think you were about to mention South Africa

Shea   I was about to mention South Africa

Q   Thank you

Shea   The international community was putting pressure on Great Britain to impose sanctions on the apartheid regime

Mags   Britain will not be imposing sanctions on South Africa

Liz   But the Commonwealth has made a pledge to eradicate apartheid

Mags   Ma'am, the ANC is a Marxist Leninist organisation –

Liz   Apartheid, Prime Minister
Now we fought against the Nazis
And I can see no difference

Mags   Were the ANC to take power, South Africa would be plunged into socialist chaos / and the economy –

Liz   The Commonwealth's position is clear
Apartheid is out

Mags   Firstly, anyone who thinks the ANC can form a government is living in cloud cuckoo land –

Liz   / That's up to the people. Don't forget what you learnt in Zimbabwe

Mags   Secondly, to impose sanctions
Would not only plunge the poor into further poverty
It would be inimical to British trade

Ron   And American trade
Margaret and I, yet again we shared a vision . . .
You know, I attempted to veto US sanctions
But can you believe it?
I was overridden by Congress

T   I had Ron's personal support if not his government's

Ron   It was the first time this century that any president was overruled on foreign policy

T   Why did they not see that we were right?

Ron   Margaret, we were just too far ahead sometimes

T   Oh, Ron

Q   She wouldn't listen. She stuck with her opinion

Liz   Alone in the UN, alone in the Commonwealth, in the Commons

Q   Alone in her own Cabinet

Howe   Geoffrey Howe again. The resignations had begun. Michael Heseltine went

T   Jolly good riddance I say

Howe   I think, Margaret, that he felt his views weren't being listened to. I wish I had some Heseltine lines to convey his indignation but I haven't

T   He threw quite a tantrum – stormed out of Cabinet with a flick of his hair

Howe   Then Leon Brittan went. And when Willie Whitelaw retired Margaret lost her best restraining influence

T   Every Prime Minister needs a Willie

Howe   She became more and more reliant on her unelected advisers –

Mags You are interrupting a scene. The Queen is about to speak

Howe Beg pardon, Your Majesty

Mags You haven't even got the correct year. Willie retired in '87 and we are still in '86

Howe Oh

Mags Why don't you go away until you have your facts right?

Liz One sees black South Africans seeking basic human rights
Being violently oppressed –
Surely this is this very thing
That you abhor in communist countries?
The utter lack of freedom
And the brutal state control?

Mags The political science here
Is quite different

Q So patronising

Liz There comes a time
When morally
One must say no

Mags I welcome your point of view
I value your advice.
Thank you for the tea-cake, Your Majesty

THIRTEEN: BREAKFAST AT HOLYROOD

Q One suspects she is racist

T I am not a racist I am *not*
What I feel about the black South Africans

501

> Is exactly the same as I feel about the Germans
> The Italians, the Greeks
> Or anyone else not blessed to be British

Mags   I never said that

Q   But your attitude trickled down

Shea   Michael Shea again
The Commonwealth Games were held in
Edinburgh that year
The opening ceremony was spectacular
Five thousand children in a human mosaic

Liz   But Michael, thirty-two nations have boycotted
in protest
Hardly an African country there – because of
her intransigence on sanctions

Shea   The Games were indeed looking very white

Liz   It cannot be borne. It simply cannot

Shea   Something had to be done
Of course I didn't do it
I didn't do anything at all

Mags and Liz open newspapers.

On July the twentieth, the *Sunday Times*
Announced Her Majesty's dismay
At the policies of the government

T   It was a huge, huge spread

Q *and* **T** Pages

Shea   The journalists
Michael Jones, political editor
And Simon Freeman (backstabbing bastard)
Claimed irrefutable evidence
That the Queen found her Prime Minister

T	Uncaring, confrontational and socially divisive
Shea	It was very precise
T	The journalists said the Queen was fully aware it would be published
Shea	Here are the bullet points. One:
Liz	One feared that the suppression of the miners' strike had done long-term damage to the fabric of the state
Shea	Two:
Liz	One objected to America's bombing raids on Libya departing from British airbases
Shea	Three:
Liz	One supported sanctions in South Africa and abhorred apartheid
Shea	Four:
Liz	One had deep concerns about our own disintegrating race relations and inner-city decay
Shea	And that overall
Liz	One felt the whole direction of government policy was –
T	What a betrayal
Q	Never said it Never wrote it Nothing to do with me
T	For an unelected monarch To oppose the government – Unconstitutional and dangerous
Shea	Ironically we were together when the news broke One of the rare occasions I was with them both

> The Queen
> The Prime Minister and myself
> At Holyrood in Edinburgh
> It was breakfast time

Mags and Liz are both reading the revelations.

Shea Well, I couldn't eat a thing
   The silence was so sickening

T   I didn't trust myself to speak
   I wasn't angry; it's not that.
   I was surprised

Q   It was her friend Mr Murdoch's paper
   I felt like leaping up and saying there
   There you are
   This is what it's like when the papers turn on you
   No one is safe from a ruthless press

Shea The Prime Minister's face was quite unmoving

Liz Well
   One wonders how this happened, Michael

Shea I'd like to apologise
   Profusely to you both
   Your Majesty
   Prime Minister
   Yes, it's true I did meet Simon Freeman
   And we were talking off the record
   Quite informally
   And he asked about the Commonwealth
   I replied that as Head of the Commonwealth
   The Queen . . .
   Is naturally very keen on it
   And so forth
   The rest is all his supposition
   Prime Minister, I can assure you that

I had no briefing with Her Majesty

The Queen had no prior knowledge of this article
And indeed
I have never, ever heard her
Speaking critically of you
Or any of her previous Prime Ministers

Shea   Mrs Thatcher said only three words to me:

Mags   Never mind, dear

Shea   That was it

T   Never mind, dear

Shea   It was the most excruciating breakfast I was
            ever at

            Pause.

T   I was knocked sideways
            I was very, very down

Liz   Margaret
            I'm sorry this has happened

Mags   Thank you, Ma'am
            Really I am so respectful

Liz   That is mutual, you know

FOURTEEN: THE WORLD WON'T LISTEN

Q   The President of the United States
            May only serve for two terms

Liz   No matter how powerful one's allies are, they
            are passing.
            There is no permanence in politics

Q   I've spent a lifetime in the ebb and flow of power
            It brings its gifts

But then it's an intoxicant
One must beware lest one consumes too much

T   We tried to advise and assist George Bush as we had Ron, but he didn't seem so –

Mags   He didn't have Ron's friendly personality
And sadly we disagreed over Germany

T   No one but me could see the threat of reunification

Mags   We've beaten the Germans twice and we don't want them back

Howe   Her attitude to Europe confounded me

T   Are you back, Geoffrey? You'd better have something worthwhile to say

Mags   We have not rolled back the frontiers of the state in Britain only to see them reimposed at a European level

Howe   She could undo the careful work of a whole conference with a single utterance

Mags   No No NO

Clarke   Kenneth Clarke, Education Secretary
Margaret began to believe her own propaganda; she began to fly by the seat of her pants. She began to get more scratchy. And the poll tax – what a disaster. Geoffrey, explain what it was, would you? I have to be Kinnock

Howe   Margaret felt the rating system put too much pressure on home-owners, so the poll tax, or community charge –

T   If Geoffrey explains we'll still be here at breakfast time tomorrow

Kinnock The community charge is the most flagrantly unjust taxation we have seen since the Peasants' Revolt in 1381

T The community charge is the flagship of the Thatcher fleet.
I can defend it clearly, explicitly, at any time, in any place and to any person

Liz So how does it work then?

Mags It is designed to prevent overspending left-wing councils from squeezing home-owners any further. Everyone pays the same

Liz A bus driver in his council flat pays the same as the Duke of Westminster in his mansion – have I got that correct?

Mags Yes. And you, Ma'am, pay nothing at all

Kinnock It is fundamentally unfair, costly and crushing to families

Howe Margaret thought her will alone could push it through – but she got the mood of the people wrong

Q The people didn't think her tax was fair
They refused to pay it – and they rioted

Protestor No, they demonstrated

Mags They were anarchists and scum

Protestor Two hundred thousand citizens marched peacefully up Whitehall

Mags The rabble set Trafalgar Square on fire. The looting and rampaging, violence and destruction went on for hours

T I was brought up to respect law and order

Protestor   The police blocked both ends of Whitehall, so the crowd couldn't disperse. Then, with no warning, they sent in the riot squad

Mags   We are moving on

Protestor   No we're not.
I am protesting.
By three o'clock, the police had corralled us into Trafalgar Square. How to turn citizens into a mob? Charge at them on horses. Drive through them in riot vans at high speed. Fear makes you defend yourself; it is incendiary. Demonstrators became rioters and on that day the act of protest was made criminal

Howe   I feared her flagship was sinking

T   I was brought up by a Victorian grandmother

Mags   You were taught to respect law and order, to work jolly hard, to improve yourself, you were taught self-reliance, you lived within your income

T   You were patriotic, you had self-respect, you were a good member of your community

Mags   These things are Victorian Values

Howe   She was losing her touch. Opinion polls were very low. By-elections disastrous

T   In the Cabinet I could almost hear knives being sharpened

Q   It's rare for a leader to know when to go

Mags   I will go on to win a fourth term and a fifth – as long as the people want me and Britain needs me

Howe   I knew when to go
This is my resignation speech

Q   Not all of it Geoffrey, please

Howe   I'll cut the references to cricket, Ma'am
The conflict of loyalty, of loyalty to my Right
Honourable Friend the Prime Minister and of
loyalty to what I perceive to be the true interests
of the nation, has become all too great

Mags   His was a slow poison

Howe   I no longer believe it possible to resolve that
conflict from within this Government. That is
why I have resigned

Mags   That quiet voice of his

Howe   The time has come for others to consider their
own response to the tragic conflict of loyalties
with which I have myself wrestled for perhaps
too long

T   He gave them permission to revolt

Liz   Philip showed me a cartoon from *The Times* the
next day. It was of Geoffrey Howe as a huge
sheep, swallowing Mrs Thatcher whole – just
her heels sticking out. A caption read 'Howe's
That?'

Mags   I will call their bluff

T   Flush the traitors out

Mags   If they want a leadership challenge
By golly I'll give them one

T   I'm a world stateswoman

Mags   On the verge of committing our troops to Kuwait

T   I'm a proven election-winner

Mags	And I can count on my party to back me to the hilt
T	When someone says you have a contest, you do not run away, you fight it
Mags	Come on, boys Let's have a leadership challenge Who's up to it? Who thinks that they can take me on?
Hesel	I've been waiting years for this
T	The mighty Heseltine
Hesel	I've sat long enough on the back benches
Mags	Festering
Hesel	Watching as you've estranged the brightest and the best in your Cabinet. You never appreciated my contribution and you took credit for all my triumphs
T	It's all about you isn't it, Michael?
Hesel	This party would have got on just as well and achieved just as much without you, Margaret
Mags	That is preposterous
Hesel	When I was at Oxford, I plotted my future on an envelope
Mags	I bet you did
Hesel	Millionaire twenty-five – and I was MP thirty – and I was Cabinet member – yes
Mags	And Prime Minister? I don't think so, Hezza
Hesel	They say a man should be judged by his enemies. I am very proud of mine

T	Tarzan stood against me
Hesel	I am the man to lead Britain into the 1990s

FIFTEEN: DIAMONDS ARE FOREVER

Mags	I was in Paris for the first vote Bush, Mitterrand, Gorbachev, Kohl They were all there
T	I was advised to stay at home and canvass people in the Commons tea room. I ask you. I was Prime Minister
Mags	The vote was counted as I was signing one of the treaties that ended the Cold War. Denis phoned me through the news
Denis	You did very well, old love. But not well enough. You're four votes short. I'm afraid there's got to be a second round
T	Ever so slightly, the ground shifted under my feet
Denis	It's the rules, sweetie pie
Mags	I'm going forward, Denis The party will rally now In my hour of need they'll come back to me
Denis	I knew then she was done for
T	That night, Crawfie and I stayed up. We talked
Mags	Grantham
T	School
Mags	The horrible headmistress who attempted to thwart my ambition
T	Oxford

Mags	How they tried to look down on me
T	Denis
Mags	My twins
T	The way I would often forget to wave up at the nursery window on my way to work
Mags	As dawn came we were still talking. We didn't go to bed at all
Liz	At our audience on her return, the Prime Minister told me she'd contest the second ballot –
Mags	I shall carry on batting for Britain, with all the vigour and energy I have
Q	What could one say?
Liz	As a human being, one always has hope – and the gambling instinct
Q	We did not put money on it
Clarke	Kenneth Clarke. Margaret said she wanted to see us, one by one. I was first in
Mags	Kenneth, can I count on your support?
Clarke	Look, Margaret, this whole process is farcical. It's time to go. Do you really want to see Michael Heseltine Prime Minister? It's time to clear the field for Douglas Hurd or Major; someone who can win
T	At least Kenneth Clarke stabbed me in the front
Mags	A dismal procession followed
T	Old school ties and sweating brows. One of them even cried

Tory 2   I will vote for you, Margaret

Tory 1   I am on your side

Tory 2   You know you have my loyalty

Tory 1   I'd walk on broken glass for you

Tory 2   Stick hot pins

Tory 1   But honestly?

Tory 2   I don't think any of the others

Tory 1   Nobody will vote your way

Tory 2   The support just isn't there

T   The message was clear

Tory 1 *and* **2**
   You will never win

Mags   I considered you my friends and allies and it
disgusts me that with your weasel words you
have transmuted your betrayal into frank
advice. It sickens me that you pretend concern
for my fate. Because this is treachery. It is
treachery with a smile on its face
I've have won three elections and I could go on
without you. By God I have deserved it. I've
done everything for years. Not one of you could
have achieved one-tenth

Denis   Margaret
Give it up
Give it up, old girl
Come on

Mags   I am not a quitter
I am not a quitter

Denis   Let it go

Pause.

T   And so
The following morning I went once more to
my Cabinet

Mags   And I stood down
As their leader
As Prime Minister

T   I then telephoned world leaders

Mags   There was utter disbelief

T   Bush said some very gracious things
And then he asked about my successor

Mags   I was already history
I was exhausted. Found it very difficult to –

T   Crawfie called a doctor. Got a vitamin shot
And when I was back on my feet again, I went
to the Palace

Q   Mrs Thatcher sat where she had sat every week
for the last eleven years. She told me she was
going to stand down

Liz   That must have been a very difficult decision

Mags   You don't take a decision like that without it
being difficult
Without there being heartbreak
Yes, there is heartbreak
But it is the right thing

Liz   Mrs Thatcher's emotion was not perceptible in
anything she said. Her effort to contain it was
remarkable

Q   It was the same for me when our Royal Yacht
Britannia was decommissioned. I was resolutely
determined that no tears would be seen to fall

Liz	The last few days must have been traumatic for you
Mags	Yes But we got through them And tonight we will leave Number Ten for the –
T	For the last time
Liz	Would you like a whisky?
Mags	Thank you, Ma'am
Liz	I shall have my Gin and It One tries to keep everything together One does one's very best But sometimes the harder one holds on, the more things fall apart. I fear there are some tricky times ahead
Mags	For you, Ma'am?
Liz	My children are all unhappy If they had privacy they might have found a private solace but There is a crisis brewing, Margaret. Charles and Diana cannot reconcile And I won't have divorce I will not, cannot have it
Liz	Here's to certainty
All	To certainty
	They drink.
Mags	I hope that in my years at Number Ten I have done what I set out to do
Liz	You have achieved a great deal; that, no one can deny
Mags	I set out to change the soul of this country

Q	How very disturbing
Liz	And now, where will you go?
Mags	To the back benches I won't shirk it I'll confound them all
Q	You always have
Liz	Where will you live?
Mags	We've a house in Dulwich Denis chose it Spanking new Right next to his golf course On the South Circular
Liz	I'm sure it will be an exciting new chapter
Mags	It will never happen to you, Your Majesty
Liz	I'm sorry?
Mags	You will never relinquish your power
Liz	But Prime Minister In our democracy I have none
Q	How do you do? How do you do?
T	We regard the Royal Family as the greatest asset Britain has. They are a focus of patriotism, loyalty, affection and esteem.
Liz	When one sees you in the House And hears them baying at you One can't imagine how you keep your poise They really are so dreadful Like an awful pack of schoolboys
Mags	Yes, they can be odious

But I thrive on it, you see
I stand out in my blue and blond
And I thrive

Liz   Quite so

Mags   Without it I'm not sure what I will do

Q   That afternoon, she took Prime Minister's Questions in the House. We watched her on the television

Liz   Her performance was pure Iron Lady

Mags   The Berlin Wall has been torn down and the Cold War is at an end. These immense changes didn't come about by chance. They have been achieved by resolution in defence – and by a refusal ever to be intimidated. And all these things were done in teeth of the opposition of the Right Honourable Gentlemen opposite – and their ladies
Should we be censured for our strength?
It is because we on this side have never flinched from difficult decisions
That this House
And this country
Can have confidence in this government today

Mags exits.

Footman 1
The atmosphere on the street is amazing, Ma'am. There are people dancing out there, shouting 'She's gone, she's gone'

Liz   Really

Footman 2
Absolute jubilation

Actor 1 Do you remember it?

Actor 2 It was amazing. A tremendous feeling that
anything could happen
That . . .

Actor 1 That what?

Actor 2 That things could only get better

Actors 1 and 2 exit.

Liz It is affecting when they go
One doesn't have time to turn around
Out goes the last and in comes the next with
barely a pause
And one has often built up a relationship

Liz exits.

Q Of course stories about clashes

T Nonsense

Q There was never any question

T Stories about clashes

Q There was never a rift

T We have always loved the Queen

Q The Baroness read out the eulogy when Ronald
Regan died
It was impeccable

T We here still move in twilight
But we have a beacon to guide us
We have his example
Let us give thanks for a life that achieved so
much for all of God's children

Q I would have put it slightly differently
The fortieth President

Like Michael Shea our dear Press Secretary
Died of dementia

T   One doesn't die of dementia, Ma'am,
It is not a fatal condition
One dies of something else.
One lives with dementia

They are both standing.

Q   Won't you sit down?

Pause.

T   No.

The End.